The Value Net

The Value Net

A Tool for Competitive Strategy

Cinzia Parolini
SDA Bocconi, School of Management, Milan, Italy

JOHN WILEY BOOKS
Chichester · New York · Weinheim · Brisbane · Singapore · Toronto

Other Wiley Editorial Offices

John Wiley & Sons, Inc., 605 Third Avenue,
New York, NY 10158-0012, USA

Wiley-VCH Verlag GmbH, Pappelallee 3,
D-69469 Weinheim, Germany

Jacaranda Wiley Ltd, 33 Park Road, Milton,
Queensland 4064, Australia

John Wiley & Sons (Asia) Pte Ltd, Clementi Loop #02-01,
Jin Xing Distripark, Singapore 129809

John Wiley & Sons (Canada) Ltd, 22 Worcester Road,
Rexdale, Ontario M9W 1L1, Canada

Library of Congress Cataloging-in-Publication Data

Parolini, Cinzia.
    [Rete del valore e strategie aziendali. English]
    The value net : a tool for competitive strategy / Cinzia Parolini.
        p.   cm.
    Includes bibliographical references and index.
    ISBN 0-471-98719-0
    1. Strategic planning.   2. Value.   I. Title.
HD 30.28.P31713   1999   99-25241
658.4'012 – dc21   CIP

British Library Cataloguing in Publication Data

A catalogue record for this book is available from the British Library

ISBN 0 471 98719 0

Typeset in 11.25/13pt Sabon by Acorn Bookwork, Salisbury, Wilts
Printed and bound in Great Britain by Biddles Ltd, Guildford and Kings Lynn
This book is printed on acid-free paper responsibly manufactured from sustainable
forestation, for which at least two trees are planted for each one used

To Arturo

Contents

Preface

Research into the Value Net started at the SDA Bocconi School of Management at the beginning of 1996. Begun as an individual research study, it soon involved other researchers and finally became the principal area of investment for the Strategic Management Department of SDA Bocconi in the triennium 1997–1999.

Looking back on the first presentations made by the research group, I have to admit that the supporters of the Value Net were initially considered with a certain scepticism. It seemed at the time that Porter's studies had provided a solid framework for the structural analysis of industries and value systems, which would be difficult to improve in a significant manner. In terms of the search for innovative fronts in the field of strategic management, the majority of us felt that the most promising lines were those relating to the resource-based view and cooperative strategies: the former had contributed towards switching attention from the way in which activities are configured at a given moment to the resources underlying their future configuration, thus finally offering a dynamic perspective of the process of strategic analysis; and the studies of cooperative strategies were revealing the importance for companies of a strategic perspective extending beyond company boundaries towards networks of companies, thus delineating new strategic and organisational contexts.

It therefore gives me great pleasure to see, some years later, that the work done on the Value Net has identified the existence of significant room for innovation also in the field of structural analysis. By concentrating on value-creating activities and resources associated with them, and considering company and industrial boundaries as a dependent variable, the Value Net has made it possible to re-examine structural analysis in a dynamic perspective. The Value Net offers a sound theoretical framework in which structural analysis can be associated with attention to resources and the broadened perspective of cooperative strategies. Furthermore, by suggesting that the view of final customers offers important clues for entrepreneurial innovation, the Value Net makes a significant contribution to entrepreneurship studies, an area in which our School has a long experience in terms of research and executive education.

The strength of an instrument is also measured on the basis of the welcome it receives from company managers, and our researchers have the fortune of being able to test their ideas with reference to the thousands of managers who every year attend the executive courses of SDA Bocconi. Over the last two years, the Value Net has been incorporated in the programme of many of the courses offered by the Strategic Management Department: not only has it stood up well in front of a non-academic public, it has also generated numerous requests for further information and its application to specific situations. This is a clear demonstration that its theoretical rigour and the linearity of its underlying concepts are much appreciated by company managers who are urgently looking for new means of reading the competitive environment.

I therefore hope that the publication of this book represents only an intermediate stage in the work of its author and all of the members of the research group involved in the project, and that the international communication of the concepts elaborated so far will provide new opportunities for their further development.

Vittorio Coda
Professor of Strategic Management
Bocconi University, Milan
April 1999

Foreword

The world-wide web site of the Global Business Network shows a map made by Herman Moll, a cartographer. The text which accompanies it reads as follows:

'If you were an explorer in the early 1700s this map might well have guided your explorations of North America. It is, for the most part, recognizable to modern eyes, except for one thing – it shows California as an island.

This error was the result of good Cartesian reasoning: Spanish explorers coming from the south had encountered the tip of the Baja Peninsula; voyaging further north they sailed into the Straits of Juan de Fuca. When they connected the first point to the second they created the Gulf of California.

This would be merely a historical curiosity were it not for the missionaries sent from Spain to convert the heathens in New Mexico. After landing in California, they prepared to cross the Gulf as their maps instructed: they packed up their boats and carried them up over the Sierra Nevada and down the other side, and found ... not sea, but the longest, driest beach they'd ever seen (a desert).

When they wrote back, protesting that there was no Gulf of California, the mapmakers replied: "Well, the map is right, so you must be in the wrong place". This misunderstanding persisted for 50 years until one of the missionaries rose high enough in the Church to be able to persuade the King of Spain to issue a decree to change the maps.

Once you come to believe in a map, it's very difficult to change it, and, if your facts are wrong, then you'll be relying on a map that's wrong too. At Global Business Network (GBN) we challenge "mental maps", that is, perceptions about the world that shape how individuals and corporations think about the future. Too often these mental maps act like blinkers rather than guides – preventing us from acting effectively.'

Cinzia Parolini worries that the maps strategists are using today to navigate value creation do not correspond with how value is actually created. Her book convincingly conveys this warning, and this alone makes it commendable. Furthermore, this book does this through a refreshing combination of reader-friendly writing and good scholarship. It digs diligently into the way researchers, strategic planners, and managers have been slicing out the every day reality of business to make maps. These maps are supposed to help analyses to be made, decisions to be taken, work to be organized, and managerial actions to be undertaken. Just as the Global Business Network claims to do, Parolini questions too whether the slicing we have grown up with makes sense for emerging, and ever more widespread forms of value creation – those which are information- and/or knowledge-intensive; those which are interconnected across time zones and oceans.

The answer which Parolini gives to this question is unambiguous. We can not chart the territory of interconnected, knowledge-intensive business using yesterday's map-making technologies. Doing so distorts reality, is unhelpful to researchers, and makes it dangerous for practitioners whose competitors have abandoned the outdated technologies.

It is this argument: do not use yesterday's tools in territories for which the tools were not designed which is the core strength of the book. The book conveys this argument – this criticism, this warning – successfully, and illustrates it with an impressive amount of evidence. The examples span continents, industries, and other limitations – and often concern items with which readers are readily familiar: books, shoes, music recordings, coffee. The book has the merit of being very specific in the use of its key terms. For example, a full chapter is dedicated to examining what value means, which is rare in the literature.

Beyond its outlining the limitations of existing, established map-making technology, the book has a second purpose. This is to offer the outlines of an alternative. Here the book is more tentative, and more exploratory. The arguments it advances are intriguing and thought provoking.

In meeting this second objective, Cinzia Parolini avoids being overly prescriptive. With her we are not in a packaged tour where off-the-shelf items are to be deployed to guarantee results. Instead, we are in a vessel which carefully surveys the outlines of a new continent, whose topology, flora, and fauna are different from those of home base. The differences are noted, and call for another way of seeing, of slicing out. The book invites us to follow the author's reasoning upon facing this uncharted territory.

Cinzia Parolini explicitly situates her work in relation to many mainstream, established schools of strategic management. This helps to link this second, exploratory purpose to established thought patterns. The link helps the reader to make bridges between past and emerging maps. Academically-oriented readers, for example, will find it helpful that she explicitly operates a sort of figure-ground reversal in relating to the transaction cost school initiated by Coase and developed by Williamson. Whereas in transaction cost-based analyses, separability and distinction involves technical considerations; in Parolini's proposed alternative it is economic separability that defines units of analysis, the most basic of which she terms nodes.

Parolini's nodes form value nets, which are located within value-creating systems. Consistent with her careful approach, these are not radically new units of analysis. Instead, they are re-interpretations and refinements of existing and proven units of analysis. Nodes are thus bundles of the acknowledged atom of many strategic studies, notably popularized by Porter: an activity.

These re-interpretations and refinements make the book evolutionary rather than revolutionary. The evolutionary approach provides well argued, grounded, analyses of established, mainstream conceptual maps; critically delineating the extent of their applicability to information- and knowledge-intensive, interconnected businesses. Well researched examples include the music business and book publishing.

With her analysis of book publishing, the relation readers have with Professor Parolini takes on an interesting twist. The book critically examines whether the book is the author–reader relation we readers would like. As one reads this part of the book, questions arise:

Did I really want to buy the whole of this book?
Would I have bought it if an unbundled (on-line, self-service intensive) alternative had been available?

Which chapters would I have acquired? Which paragraphs?
If alternatives were available, how would my relationship with
the author develop over time?
How would my relationship with other readers be?
Does the book-as-node help value to be created? How? What
value creating does this node prevent?

Cinzia Parolini analyzes book publishing mainly from the reader's
point of view. In the same way, she analyzes the music business
mostly from the point of view of the listener. Explicit, examined,
subjectivity is at the core of her proposed alternative: according to
Parolini, one can no longer map emerging actual business independent of each actor's singular perspective. The subjectivity of the
actor, much like Simon's bounded rationality, thus contingently
determines the level of aggregation which node and value net will
entail. The CEO of Volkswagen Group will deal with different
nodes and value nets than will the head of a Volkswagen factory in
Brazil, even if both are in what for an outside observer is the same
value-creating system. And the CEO will aggregate activities differently if he is talking to a Californian pension fund representative
than if he is considering changes in supply-chain logistics.

One actor which Parolini considers to have a particularly helpful
point of view in determining strategy is the customer. She provides
many examples of companies catalogued as belonging to different
industries according to outmoded frames of reference; but which
compete with each other for the customer's money, time, or attention. The book will thus be of great interest to researchers and
practitioners seeking to link marketing and strategic issues.

Parolini embraces what strategy researchers such as Bente
Løwendhal and Øvind Revang have recently (1998) proposed: that
new concepts, taking into account the breakdown of old distinctions
(such as internal/external, or industry), be explored and offered. It is
in conveying the necessity of doing this that the book is at its strong-
est. Combined with its being a delight to read, it will certainly meet
with considerable success.

Rafael Ramírez,
H.E.C., Jouy-en-Josas,
France, March 1999

Acknowledgements

The concepts presented in this book are based on a research study financed by the 'Strategic Management Department' of SDA Bocconi School of Management, Milan.

I would therefore like to thank all of my colleagues who have participated in this study by offering original comments, by helping me to 'photograph' the various problems that came to light during the development of the model, by highlighting the inconsistencies emerging from the first draft, and by significantly contributing towards the collection of company case data and information that could be used to test the model. In this sense, I would like to thank Carlo Alberto Carnevale, Mikkel Draebye, Paola Dubini, Umberto Lago and Gabriella Lojacono, with particular thanks to those who helped me develop the cases in the fields of coffee (Carlo Alberto Carnevale), publishing and cosmetics (Paola Dubini) and electronic publishing (Mikkel Draebye).

I am also extremely grateful to Giuseppe Airoldi, Giorgio Brunetti and Vittorio Coda, who offered me stimuli and suggestions during the preparation of the final version, and Donatella Depperu and Paola Varacca, who had the patience to read the earliest versions of some parts of the book and helped me identify the points that were weak or required more detailed work.

Finally, special thanks go to Kevin Smart, who did much more than simply translate the book by helping me to identify the parts that were unclear and making many of the passages more effective.

The publishers would like to thank Global Business Network for permission to reproduce the extract taken from the GBN web site. This extract was used by Rafael Ramírez in the foreword and also features on the back cover.

Introduction

It is difficult to find any recent book on strategic management that does not deal with the technological and economic changes that are affecting businesses, as well as our own private and working lives. Thousands of pages have already been written to describe 'paradigm shifts', 'the digital economy', 'hypercompetition' and 'boundaryless corporations'. The aim of this book is to explore the consequences that such changes are having and will increasingly have on the configurations of industries, and the economics and behaviours of companies. What will become the new key success factors? What are the economic rules governing a networked economy? How can we define competitors and other competitive forces in industries with blurred boundaries?

In order to answer questions like these, it would be useful to have models and tools of strategic analysis that could help us to understand how to compete and create value in this new economic context. However, despite the interest aroused by the epochal changes currently taking place, it is difficult to find any publications aimed at developing original means of analysing the new competitive environment. Terms such as 'borderless', 'virtual', 'extended', 'connected' or 'integrated' companies, 'the convergence of competitive systems', and the 'blurring of industrial boundaries' are effective means of describing the different facets of this new environment, but there is still a lack of practical means capable of helping us to handle these realities. Consequently, strategic analysts find that their 'working tool kit' still contains models and instruments (such as portfolio matrices, the five competitive forces, and the value chain) that were essentially conceived as a response to the very different world of the 1970s or 1980s.

This is particularly surprising because, if we are really facing a fundamental change in the economic paradigm, it has to be expected that this will lead to profound reconfigurations in the structural characteristics of industries and the strategic management of companies, and that this will require an equally profound revision of the traditional concepts and tools of strategic analysis.

The difficulty in developing analytical models that really reflect the new environmental context is fundamentally due to a reluctance to reconsider deeply-rooted logical categories that are simply taken for granted. This is particularly true in the case of two of the keystones of economic studies: the concepts of 'industries' and 'enterprises'.

The techniques for analysing competition and competitive systems are still generally based on the definition of industries as homogeneous sets of interdependent companies producing similar goods, and the concept of an enterprise has led to the development of instruments such as the business idea model, the value chain, business definition tools, and portfolio matrices.

Current environmental changes are redefining the characteristics of these two cardinal points of reference. The increasing importance of products incorporating different technologies, and the growing weight of the technologies and know-hows that cross the boundaries between one industry and another, have in many cases made it more difficult (if not impossible) to define the borders of the competitive environment and identify direct and indirect competitors. This raises a series of questions to which it is difficult to find appropriate answers. If it is true that there is a tendency towards the blurring of industrial sectors, what can we do to define competitors and competitive systems? What can we do to monitor the evolution of such broad, varied and continuously changing environmental contexts? If it is not possible to identify clearly what an industry is, what else can be used as a basis upon which to develop a competitive strategy?

The changes in competitive systems inevitably form the backdrop for evolutions concerning individual enterprises. In the past, it was relatively easy to establish the boundaries between a company and its external environment, but this has recently become increasingly difficult as a result of outsourcing and deverticalization, production decentralization, the growing importance of strategic alliances, the creation of strong and stable supply lines, the increase in information flows and interactions between different economic players, etc. Although the legal boundaries of companies remain clear, a growing number of them are finding that these are considerably different from their *strategic boundaries*: i.e. the boundaries enclosing the activities that form part of a single strategic design and between which there is a sustained information flow. The new business model seems to be characterized by an emphasis on well-defined distinctive skills, the ability to exploit these in different markets by interacting with various systems of economic players, the capacity to participate in stable alliance networks and take advantage of external resources, a high degree of internal integration, and highly dynamic internal configuration, boundaries and external connections. Dynamic boundaries and the creation of close external connections have led to the development of sets of economic players which, while remaining legally and strategically distinguishable, operate jointly as elements of a single integrated organism.

What is said above is, of course, not intended to imply that the concepts of an industry and enterprise no longer have any use, but simply to underline the fact that it is now time to begin looking for additional elements that provide a better description of the complex phenomena underlying the new economic paradigm.

The development of tools of strategic analysis that are consistent with the changed environment can only start by identifying objects of analysis that are more representative of the new reality. The first step in this direction is to change our view from that of an enterprise-focused perspective to one that is extended to include value-creating systems (VCSs).

The concept of 'value-creating systems' is not new in the field of strategic management studies. According to Normann and Ramírez (1993): 'Increasingly, successful companies do not just add value, they reinvent it. Their focus of strategic analysis is not the company or even the industry but the value-creating system itself, within which different economic actors – suppliers, business partners, allies, customers – work together to co-produce value'. Although adopting a slightly different point of view, Porter (1985) underlined the fact that 'a firm's value chain is embedded in a larger stream of activities that I term the value system ... Suppliers have value chains (upstream value) that create and deliver the purchased inputs used in a firm's chain... In addition, many products pass through the value chain of the channels (channel value) on their way to the buyer.' It is true that Normann and Ramírez suggest overcoming the prevalently sequential view characterizing Porter's model but, in their different ways, both approaches highlight the fact that the value received by consumers represents the fruit of the activities carried out by a set of economic players. One important difference between the perspective of Porter and that of Normann and Ramírez is that the former takes the company value chain as his starting point, whereas the latter underline the greater importance of the value-creating system.

This book is intended to offer a further development of the work already done by Normann and Ramírez by assuming that, rather than being considered simply as sets of economic players, value-creating systems should be seen as sets of activities that are jointly involved in the creation of value. The choice of activities as the elementary unit of strategic analysis lays the basis for a flexible and wide-ranging approach because it allows us to begin by identifying the activities leading to the creation of customer value and describing their structural characteristics, before moving on to explore how these activities are divided among the various economic players involved in carrying them out. In a period characterized by continuous changes in the configurations of economic players, and the presence of companies with increasingly permeable and dynamic boundaries, an approach of this type has the advantage of concentrating on the process of value creation without considering (at least initially) the make, buy or connect choices made by individual companies. Furthermore, in a reality characterized by companies with profoundly different configurations that nevertheless operate in the same competitive environment, it also permits a more profound analysis of competition, and thus makes it possible to distinguish the differences concerning the boundaries of the various competitors from the differences relating to the configuration of the VCSs.

There is a considerable affinity between this and the transaction costs approach, which has long proposed transactions (i.e. the transfer of goods through a technologically separable interface) as the elementary unit of analysis. The origins of this line of research can be traced back to Institutional Economics and the pioneering studies of Commons (1934) and Coase (1937), and more recently of Williamson (1975). Transaction management may take place in the market under various contractual forms, or in the ambit of organisations in which the transactions themselves are regulated by hierarchical relationships. Analysis of the characteristics of the transactions to be carried out makes it possible to understand whether it is more appropriate for a given transaction to use the market, the hierarchy or other intermediate forms of transaction governance. Some more recent studies (e.g. Demsetz, 1991) have underlined the fact that an analysis of the characteristics of trans-actions is not sufficient to identify the most appropriate form of governing a given transaction; it is also necessary to analyse the characteristics of the technologically inseparable activities between them.

Especially in this last form, the transaction costs approach is close to the one presented in this book. The adoption of such elementary units of analysis as transactions or activities enables a perspective that is powerful in terms of its ability to interpret economic phenomena. By removing previously crystallized schemas, these approaches make it possible to see the continuity between the internal and external aspects of an organization, and remind us that an enterprise is not a universal concept but simply an economic structure aimed at managing activities and transactions. Furthermore, it is a highly unstable structure that is subject to different definitions in time and space: for example there is a big difference between the enterprises of the 18th and 20th centuries, as well as between the enterprises currently operating in Europe and those currently operating in China. On the other hand, activities and transactions represent fundamental elements of economic activity that are present at all times, in every place and within the ambit of every socio-political regime. Although it is true that the usefulness of working directly on elementary economic phenomena is relatively limited in periods of marginal changes (i.e. within the framework of the same paradigm), they can provide highly interesting starting points in times of structural evolutions by favouring a broader and more detached analytical perspective.

The concept of value-creating systems will be explored in depth in the second chapter of this book, but it is perhaps worth summarizing here their main characteristics:

- a VCS can be defined as a set of activities that creates value for its customers;

- these activities are carried out using sets of human, tangible and intangible resources;

- they are linked by flows of material, information, financial resources and influence relationships;

- VCSs also include consumption activities, insofar as the value that final customers enjoy also depends on the way they use and 'consume' the potential value received;

- final customers not only receive and consume the created value, but can also participate in value-creating activities;

- value-creating activities may be controlled by the market, a hierarchy or intermediate forms of co-ordination (company networks);

- various economic players may participate in a VCS (companies, families, public bodies, non-profit making institutions) by taking responsibility for one or more activities;

- an economic player may participate in more than one VCS.

Starting from the hypothesis that value-creating systems provide a valid perspective of investigation, this book will review the traditional instruments of strategic analysis and, where necessary, propose an alternative methodology.

Given that any such change in perspective can only be fully understood within the framework of an in-depth analysis of the changes taking place in the overall economic context, the first chapter is dedicated to analysing the new economics of value-creating systems. The second chapter explores such systems in depth and introduces the value net as a means of analysing them, whereas the third chapter concentrates on the concept of customer value, the various ways in which it can be interpreted, and the different elements that come together to create it. Finally, the fourth chapter describes the activities involved in the creation of value and identifies the typical configurations of value-creating systems and the way in which they work. It also illustrates the usefulness of this approach in terms of the acquisition of competitive advantage at company level.

1

The new economics of value-creating systems

The last few years of the twentieth century have seen a series of technological, economic, political and social changes that have been so profound as to cause structural changes in economic systems, the configuration of enterprises and their relationships with each other and with the environment, our individual private and working lives, and the way in which groups of individuals interact and work together.

The developments taking place in the environment are in some cases so radical that they can no longer be adequately interpreted using the models developed in the past. The mass of information arriving through the increasing number of media appears fragmentary and it is often difficult to understand the phenomena they express as a whole. There is therefore a widely felt need for broad and flexible logical frameworks in which changes can be inserted in such a way as to make it easier to understand the causal links between different types of evolution. Such frameworks are becoming all the more necessary as the experiences and models of the past increasingly lose their interpretative capacity.

The first chapter of this book will be dedicated to describing the principal developments taking place in the economic environment, as well as their causal inter-relationships. The reason for this is the conviction that models of strategic analysis need to be judged above all on the basis of their capacity to provide a perspective that accurately reflects the characteristics of the economic environment at a given historical moment. However well-conceived they were, the models and perspectives developed in the 1970s and 1980s can no longer take into due consideration all of the characteristics of an economic environment that is structurally different from that of the past. In other words, the changes in our reality also require changes in the way in which we conceptualize it.

1.1 A Schema For Interpreting Current Changes

Figure 1.1 summarizes the relationships between the changes currently taking place in economic systems and the developments affecting the other major poles of civil life: politics, technology and social relationships. These changes are interdependent and, to different extents and degrees, affect not only the Western economy (as we would have called it up to just a few years ago), but the economy of the entire world.

The changes in economic systems can be classified into two broad categories: those that are prevalently contextual (the geopolitical order, socio-demographic and cultural evolution, technological

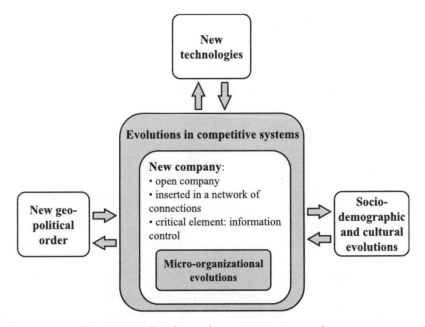

Figure 1.1   The advent of a new economic paradigm

progress) and those that are mainly economic in nature, such as changes in competitive systems, company configurations and internal organisation.

As far as the contextual factors are concerned, the geopolitical changes that have taken place over the last ten years have radically modified the order established after the Second World War. The dissolution of the Soviet empire, the process of European unification, the tensions and tumults of Islamic populations, the reawakening of China, the continuing difficulties being faced by the UN, the re-affirmation of the United States' leadership role in the area of foreign policy, and the dynamic and frequently oscillating development of many of the emerging countries in the Far East, are just some of the factors that make the political panorama of the end of the second millennium very different and more volatile than the situation 'frozen' by the presence of two contrasting blocs that characterized the decades of the 'cold war'.

Significant socio-demographic changes are also taking place, such as zero population growth in economically advanced countries, the increasing gap in the incomes of the richest and poorest classes, growing demographic pressure in some of the least economically developed areas of the world, the consequent reinforcement of migratory flows and the tensions generated by the cohabitation of populations that are ethnically and culturally very different from each other.

Striking though these political and social developments may be, the technological changes that have taken place during the last few years of the century are even more surprising. Radical innovations in the fields of telecommunications, information technologies and biotechnologies, combined with the introduction of new industrial materials, engineering technologies and design techniques, are making available products and services that could not even be imagined just a few years ago, revolutionizing production processes, affecting company cost structures and redefining the borders of a large number of economic sectors.

However, the main element supporting the hypothesis that we are experiencing a qualitative leap in our economic and social life is not that the speed of technological innovation continues to increase (which is after all not as new as it might seem), nor that the spread of technology itself is also increasing at an ever-growing rate. What is different about the most recent technological developments is their profound impact on the way organizations work and the pervasive influence that some of them (particularly those associated with information) have on our lives not only at an economic level, but also in psychological, cultural and sociological terms.

The anticipated effect of the progress being made in the fields of information technology and telecommunications is evident to all of us, particularly when we consider that every development in communication has always led to profound changes in individual behaviour and national socio-economic structures. The invention of the printing press by Gutenberg made available a formidable instrument for the spread of culture and certainly played a major role in setting the industrial revolution on its way (it is no accident that this started in the most culturally advanced countries). The arrival of the railways and the telegraph between the end of the eighteenth and the beginning of the nineteenth century made obsolete the way in which business was conducted one hundred years ago: the initiative of single individuals and small groups of people was replaced by new methods of economic management. Similarly, the introduction of the telephone, radio and television radically changed our society, driving us towards new models of individual and organizational behaviour.

In the same way, the current developments in information technology and telecommunications are destined to have an equally profound effect on the socio-economic structure of advanced countries, the way value is created, and our own individual and organizational behaviour. As Schendel (1995) pointed out, the new information technologies are not only making available new products and more entertaining ways of spending our free time, but they also have a significant impact on the way in which we use our hands and minds to create products and services, on how working groups interact and how companies need to be managed. The advances made in the chemical and engineering fields over the last thirty or forty years have undoubtedly improved our quality of life but, when we come to think about it, have 'only' given us new or better tangible products. The innovations in information technology are important not so much because of the new products and services they have made it possible to create, but above all because of their social and organizational consequences.

The changes that have taken place in this field have been such as to prompt many observers (Tapscott and Caston, 1993) to speak about a change in the technological paradigm and the advent of a second computer age. During the first decades of their development, information technologies mainly allowed enterprises to contain their administrative costs by limiting the number of 'white collar' personnel necessary to run increasingly complex organizations. It was not until the 1980s that they began to take on strategic value. Technological evolution, combined with a large increase in volumes and the consolidation of non-proprietary open systems, led to a dramatic reduction in costs, and a simultaneous improvement in performance that drove the all-pervasive spread of information technologies. An increasing number of companies began to exploit not only their processing capacity but, above all, their connectivity potential as a means of acquiring competitive advantage, reducing design and production times, offering new services and improving those already in existence, changing their distribution channels, and maintaining closer ties with their customers. In terms of connectivity, the 1990s have seen a qualitative leap. The coming of the Internet and its offshoots (intranets and extranets), as well as the consolidation of standard communication protocols, have laid the basis for radical changes in communication and integration possibilities, not only between companies themselves, but also between them and their final customers. Universal connectivity is bringing with it a new economic and technological paradigm that requires a profound transformation of companies and individuals, and imposes what we can call a 'cultural leap forward'.

With reference to the economic factors, the developments taking place in the environmental context have triggered a process of change at all levels of economic life, involving the fundamental characteristics of the economic environment (the competitive systems level), the configuration of companies (company level), and the way in which individuals and groups work (the micro-organisational level).

At all of these levels we can see an increase in the number and intensity of the inter-relationships existing between systems, whether these are competitive systems, companies or sub-systems within a particular organization. Previously inter-related but clearly distinct systems are now finding that the boundaries separating them are becoming increasingly narrow as the existing communication barriers between them begin to fall, and the advantages asso-ciated with the exploitation and maximization of inter-relationships are becoming increasingly evident.

The following sections will be dedicated to the in-depth explora-tion of some of the elements summarised in Figure 1.1, in particular the changes taking place within competitive systems (1.2) and at company level (1.3). Although of great interest, we shall not consider micro-organizational changes because they are not strictly pertinent to the value net model described in Chapter 2. We shall end this chapter with an analysis of some of the published literature that is useful for interpreting current changes and, finally, outline the main characteristics that a model of strategic analysis must have in order to describe the new economic context.

1.2 DEVELOPMENTS AT THE LEVEL OF COMPETITIVE SYSTEMS

Over the last few years many competitive systems have been increasingly involved in change processes which have led to the moving and blurring of industrial boundaries, the entry of new competitors coming from different competitive systems, the contin-uous modification of relative competitive positions, the globaliza-tion of markets and the shortening of product life cycles. Richer and more rapid information and communication systems have led to faster feed-back mechanisms that allow companies to become aware of environmental events occurring far away (information relating to markets, competitors, and the way companies work in other sectors), trigger learning and/or imitation processes, and therefore lead to change. In the same way, richer and more efficient inter- and intra-company communications have accelerated the process of change, and created previously unimaginable opportu-nities for connection and sharing. As a result, the degree of risk and uncertainty in economic activities has increased, and it has become more difficult to make forecasts. Finally, it has to be remembered that all of this has taken place in a context in which the invest-ments required to launch a new product have become more expen-sive.

No company can consider itself immune from a situation of increasingly dynamic and pressing competition. Even world giants such as IBM, General Motors, Volkswagen and AT&T, whose competitive advantages were considered impregnable until only a few years ago, have had to come to terms with an increasingly aggressive and difficult competitive environment. The result of these changes is such as to have induced some authors to adopt the term 'hypercompetition' (D'Aveni, 1994) in an attempt to describe the shifting and uncertain economic environment that by now characterizes not only high-technology industries and those subject to major regulatory changes on the part of governments (such as air transport and telecommunications), but also those that were until recently considered mature and stable, such as the food, domestic appliances and watchmaking sectors.

However, we shall not consider here the questions relating to globalization, shorter product life cycles or hyper-competition because they have been widely dealt with elsewhere, but shall concentrate on trying to identify some of the macro-causes underlying the changes described above, describe their profound consequences, outline some mini-theories that are useful for the structural analysis of value-creating systems, and place the current trends within a single overall framework. The main macro-causes underlying competitive changes can be summarized as follows:

- a movement away from realization to support activities;

- connectivity and unbundling;

- the growing importance of systemic products and the spread of sector standards.

1.2.1 From Realization to Support Activities

Economic progress can be measured by means of the reduction in activities directly aimed at producing consumer goods. Evolved economies use relatively few resources for the realization of goods and services insofar as these activities are carried out in a highly effective and efficient manner. This is possible to the extent that many resources are used to develop the context in which realization activities are carried out. This type of change is particularly important because, as we shall see, it has an impact on the economic

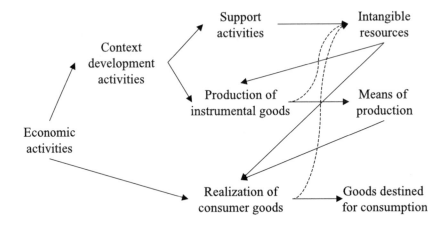

Figure 1.2   Types of economic activity

structure of value-creating systems, the competitive strategies that enterprises can pursue, and the way in which consumers are involved in the creation of value.

In order to understand the profound implications of this change from realization to support activities, it is worth making some terminological clarifications. Figure 1.2 shows the different types of economic activity.

The activities relating to the realization of consumer goods (e.g. the cultivation of a piece of land, the assembly of a domestic appliance, the transport of a batch of goods) are directly aimed at producing and distributing goods intended to satisfy human needs. Their output is a consumer product or service that is available at a given time and in a given place. On the contrary, activities of context development are aimed at producing the resources that make the realization of consumer goods more efficient and more effective. It is here that we find the production of instrumental goods (such as plants, machinery, computer networks) and support activities aimed at developing intangible resources. Examples of intangible resources are administrative procedures, skills and know-how, and brand image. We can also classify as intangible those resources which, although directly satisfying a need, are not 'consumed' by the act of consumption. Examples of these are data banks, editorial contents, pieces of music, etc.

The aspect that most differentiates support and realization activities is that the latter must be repeated every time an additional unit of the good is produced and distributed, or every time an additional unit of service is provided, whereas the former are carried out upstream of the realization activities and are not directly related to the volumes produced.

Intangible resources can be increased directly by carrying out intangible support activities (e.g. research and development, marketing, the establishment of data banks, personnel training), but can also be increased as result of activities relating to the production of instrumental or consumer goods. When a cabinet maker produces a piece of furniture to sell, for example, he also acquires knowledge about the characteristics of the wood and improves his skills in terms of cutting techniques, gluing methods, and so on. However, the knowledge acquired as a by-product of the production of instrumental or consumer goods is incremental by its very nature, and is unlikely to change significantly the way in which the realization activities themselves are carried out. By the same token, the reputation that a craftsman acquires by doing good work is unlikely to reach a large number of consumers. Only support activities can therefore lead to significant changes in the stock of intangible resources, and consequently in the efficiency and effectiveness of other economic activities.

Given that it has been taking place since the beginning of human history, the decrease in the weight of activities directly aimed at producing consumer goods is hardly a new phenomenon; however, it has accelerated exponentially over the last two centuries. The industrial revolution and the subsequent process of industrialization caused the first major shift in this direction. During this phase, the most evident phenomenon was the transformation of acquired knowledge into instrumental goods, which enormously increased realization efficiency. The information revolution and the explosion of connectivity have further enhanced the productivity of realization activities. Increasingly sophisticated intangible resources have, also made realization activities more efficient by increasing the dematerialization of many consumer and instrumental goods. The most obvious example is the computer: the laptop on which I am writing weighs just a few kilograms but has more processing capacity than the first-generation computers that occupied an entire room. Other examples can be found in all economic sectors. Heavy and difficult-to-carry telephone directories can be replaced by light CD ROMs or an online consultation service. Machine tools with complex mechanical controls have been replaced by lighter and more flexible numerically controlled machines. The production orders that were once made on paper can now be transmitted by computers on information networks that are directly connected to flexible production systems. The enormous transistor radios of the beginning of the century have been replaced by small portables. The weight and number of car components have been considerably reduced.

The relevance of the dematerialization process depends on the type of product. Catering services, for example, still have a preponderance of production activities; in refrigerator production, the possibilities for dematerialization are extremely limited and the weight of instrumental production activities is particularly great. On the other hand, support activities represent the lion's share of all of the activities involved in managing an online financial information service. There are some goods (such as software packages, drugs, data banks, discographical products and banking services) for which the process of dematerialization can reach extreme limits, and realization activities can in some cases be virtually eliminated; but there are others (such as air transport, buildings and cars) for which realization activities play a much more significant role and can never be totally done away with. What is it that determines the incidence of realization activities? For what goods can we expect a more accentuated shift towards the activities of context development and, in the end, the complete dematerialization of the product itself and the elimination of realization activities?

It may be useful to take the example of music industry products, a sector that has always been characterized by the remarkable weight of its support activities. The most important activities in the making of a record (and which have the greatest impact on its final price) are the production of the pieces of music, the selection of the composers and the pieces to be reproduced, the adaptation of the music to current market trends, the recording of the music in a recording studio, the production of promotional videoclips, the activities aimed at supporting the image of the artists, and the advertising launch of the new products. All of these are support activities that have to be carried out regardless of the number of copies sold. The realization activities involve the reproduction of the music on different physical supports (CDs and cassettes), the production of packaging materials, physical distribution and pre-sale shelf displays. These are activities that could account for no more than 5% of the overall costs if it were not for the fact that a certain number of discs and cassettes remain unsold and it is therefore necessary to sustain the production and distribution costs of products that will never be bought by end-users. As has happened in many other sectors, the last few years have seen a reduction in the weight of the realization activities (due to the greater efficiency of recording equipment and transport systems), and an increase in the weight of support (particularly marketing) activities. This is simultaneously the cause and effect of other phenomena, such as the increasing concentration of record companies and the progressive globalization of the market, which are redefining the competitive rules of the sector.

However, the changes that the music industry has undergone over the last few years pale into insignificance when we consider the revolution that technological evolution is likely to lead to. As a result of the spread of the Internet, MPEG technology (which allows the compression of musical and video files) and the availability of low-cost CD writers, it is now technically and economically possible for users to produce their own CDs. As things stand at the moment, it is possible to download an entire album from the Internet in little more than half an hour, home record a CD whose quality is directly comparable with that of traditional CDs, and store hundreds of songs in compressed format on a CD-R. Furthermore, if we are prepared to sacrifice the advantages of compression, we can use the Wav format to record the files on a CD-R that can also be read by a normal audio CD reader. Technological progress has thus created the conditions for a radical change in the way that music is produced and sold: it is now theoretically possible to eliminate activities (such as the physical distribution of pre-recorded CDs, their shop display and the production of CDs that will remain unsold) which, although necessary in the traditional context, do not give any added value to the final customer. The new technologies make it possible to conjure up a scenario in which all of the realization activities are carried out by the final user, while the other players limit themselves to intangible support activities or, at most, the production of instrumental goods.

This is not to say that the home production of CDs will become normal in the near future, nor that it will completely replace industrial production. However, it is clear that the premises for a different way of working in the music sector already exist and that traditional operators must seriously consider the effects of what is happening. What will be the role of record companies in this new scenario? Will they become superfluous? It is interesting to note that some musical groups have already started to offer their music directly via the Internet, thus by-passing the record companies. This direct contact between artists and final consumers means the absence of the support activities (essentially selection and cataloguing) traditionally carried out by producers and record companies. The absence of selection and cataloguing activities means that users would have to spend hours searching the Internet in order to find the pieces of music that they like among the thousands that are unacceptable. Consequently, it will still be necessary to undertake activities such as the selection, cataloguing and grading of the pieces, adapt them to the needs of the market, and communicate the results of this work. The real problem for producers, artists, record companies and everybody else who contributes towards creating and making available a piece of music is not whether or not they still have a role to play, but how they are to be paid for the value they have created. At the moment, every time we buy a CD we contribute towards the payment of all of the actors involved in the creation of value; but if the music is available via the Internet, how can we guarantee that it is paid for? Record companies could allow the downloading of a file only after the payment of a certain sum, but what is there to stop users from reproducing hundreds of copies of the downloaded file (for which they have only paid once) or making it freely available on the network? It is questions such as these that explain the attempts of the record companies to obstruct the spread of the MPEG format. The people responsible for a number of sites that made musical pieces available on the network have been taken to court on the grounds of copyright violations and forced to close down. Nevertheless, despite their power, the record companies will not be able to resist the assault of the new technologies in the long term, not least because these allow a decidedly more efficient and effective system for creating value than that offered by the traditional system. They will need to find a way of continuing to play their role within this new technological context, possibly by limiting the reproducibility of the music downloaded from the network.

The example of the music sector not only helps us to answer the questions posed above, but also highlights some of the problems connected with the process of dematerialization. What goods are likely to be associated with a significant shift from realization to support activities, and what goods are likely to be significantly affected by the process of dematerialization? It can be said that the importance of this type of development is related to the *information* content of the goods, which is obviously greatest in the case of information products and services. A piece of music, a novel, a film, a word-processing programme or the results of a market survey are all essentially pieces of information. The physical products that we buy (CDs, books, videocassettes, floppy disks or market reports) are only the supports on or in which the information that interests us has been stored. Words, numbers, lines of code, sounds and images are pieces of information that previously required different physical supports; today, all of them can be digitalized, recorded on the same support, and transmitted as information. In other words, it has now become possible to transport information instead of the physical supports on which it is recorded. Information products, such as musical CDs, are therefore subject to the greatest changes in terms of economic activities and all of the consequences that these will have on cost structures, competitive strategies and customer involvement (as we shall see later).

However, it would be a mistake to think that the developments described above only affect information products. There are many products that have a large information content that cannot be digitalized; e.g. pharmaceutical products in general and biotechnological products in particular. The value-creating systems of these products are clearly characterized by the predominance of activities aimed at the management of information and the development of knowledge: R&D, clinical trials, obtaining marketing authorizations, and marketing/advertising activities. The health sector also provides a good example in the service area. A significant proportion of hospital costs are due to the need to manage information: patients' records, medical prescriptions, test results, surgical procedures, the results of the most recent medical research and, the documentation necessary to obtain payments and/or reimbursements are nothing other than pieces of information that need to be collected, stored and used in the best possible way.

It would not be correct to call pharmaceutical drugs and hospital services information products, but they are certainly products and services with a considerable information content. The process of dematerialization is related to the information content of a product. In the case of information products, the reduction in realization activities can reach extreme terms (as we have seen for the music sector). In the case of products that have a high information content, realization activities can never be completely eliminated, but they can be considerably reduced. Clinical tests can be supported by the use of sophisticated equipment that reduces or in some cases eliminates the need for human intervention; the results can be automatically transmitted by an information network, and visualized or printed at the time and in the place they are needed without the need for the time-consuming transfer of paper copies; a patient's records and the results of all the tests he or she has undergone can be stored in a databank or on a smart card, and thus facilitate any future intervention, and so on.

This shift from the realization of consumer goods to the production of instrumental goods and/or intangible support activities has a number of significant consequences:

- on the cost structure of economic activities;

- on the competitive strategies that can be pursued by enterprises (because it avoids the classical trade-off between costs and differentiation);

- and on the way in which final customers are involved in creating value.

Changes in Cost Structures

It is the move from realization to support activities that underlies the progressive shift from direct costs (typical of realization activities) to indirect costs that is going on in many companies in many different sectors.

The change in average unit costs as the volume of goods produced increases is strictly related to the type of activity prevailing in a given business (see Figure 1.3).

- Businesses characterized by a considerable emphasis on customised

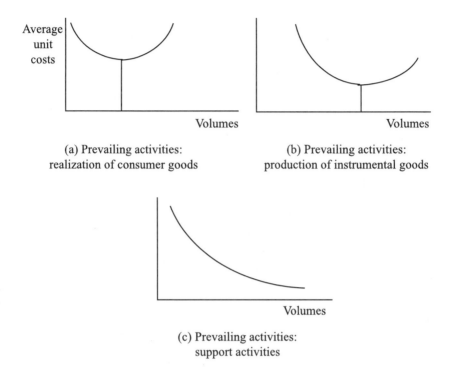

Figure 1.3   Average unit costs in relation to prevalent type of activity

production activities (artisan businesses) have relatively high average unit costs and low economies of scale.

- Businesses characterized by an emphasis on the production of instrumental goods (industrial businesses) have relatively low average unit costs and relatively high economies of scale;

- Businesses in which support activities prevail (intangible businesses) have decreasing costs as volumes increase.

As has already been underlined, the weight of a type of activity (and the consequent cost structure) depends on the type of product or service involved and the degree of technological and organizational development of the business. As can be seen in Figure 1.3, type a cost structures characterize labour-intensive service businesses (such as restaurants, bars, hairdressers) and customized production business (made-to-measure furniture, fitting out stands, tailoring); those of type b characterize the mass production of complex goods and those with a high material content (cars, white goods); and those of type c are typical of goods with a very high information content, such as applications software, videogames and data banks, and biotechnological products. Nevertheless, there are goods for which very different value-creating systems and cost structures can co-exist. One of these is footwear. Shoes can be produced by craftsmen, in which case there is a prevalence of production activities; as a consequence, the average cost is very high and the economies of scale very low, which is why no artisan producer can ever gain a significant market share. However, shoes can also be mass produced, in which case greater mechanization and automation makes it possible to use fewer resources for the production of individual shoes, whereas more resources are needed to develop an efficient production system. The industrial production of shoes leads to greater economies of scale and, if the volumes produced are sufficiently high, lower average unit costs. Finally, in some cases, even a traditional product such as a pair of shoes may have a high information content; for example, Nike produces footwear at an industrial level, but its strategy is based on product and process innovation, and on a very strong brand image. In this case, intangible support activities play a very significant role, which means that average unit costs continue to decrease as volumes increase to the extent that the ideal scale is global.

Why does this occur? Put very briefly, it can be said that the activities of producing consumer goods and those of producing instrumental goods are respectively directly and indirectly related to the volumes produced. The first are directly related to volumes insofar as they have to be repeated for every additional unit, whereas the activities connected with the preparation and maintenance of production and distribution structures are indirectly related to volumes because they are proportional to the production capacity desired. Furthermore, instrumental goods are subject to wear and need to be reconstituted after a certain number of units have been produced. Although conceptually different, the activities related to the realization of consumer goods and those related to the production of instrumental goods are both tangible and are therefore subject to the *economics of tangibles*. The average unit costs in businesses that have a prevalence of these types of activity tend to decrease as the volumes produced increase because economies of scale can be achieved. However, after a certain level, the average unit cost starts increasing again mainly as a result of an increase in the costs of co-ordinating and managing the complexity associated with greater volumes, and this establishes an internal limit on dimensional growth (which may be very low or very high).

The fundamental characteristic distinguishing support activities is that they do not depend on the produced volumes of goods destined for consumption. Intangible resources do not have any limitations in relation to their use and, in some cases (image or know-how, for example), can even increase with use. As the produced volumes of a given good increase, the costs of support activities are spread over an increasing number of units and so their average unit cost tendentially decreases towards zero. Instead of the economics of tangibles, they are governed by the *economics of intangibles*, a very different economic structure in which it makes no sense to speak of economies of scale because there is no sense in speaking of production capacity. Instrumental goods have a production capacity and are subject to wear; intangible resources have no production capacity (or rather, their capacity is infinite) and can increase with use.

This independence from produced volumes means that the complexity of the company does not significantly increase with the number of units produced and sold, thus containing the costs of complexity that accompany increasing volumes in the other cases. This implies the absence of internal growth limits and the fact that the bid to increase volumes can only be limited by external factors. In cases in which the market rewards the establishment of market standards (e.g. applications software), the conditions exist for an increase in sales volumes (achieved directly or by means of strategic alliances and production licences) until the market is saturated; on the other hand, if users express a demand for highly differentiated products (such as videogames) the increase in volumes is externally limited by the need for differentiation expressed by the market.

The prevalence of support activities (and their related costs) particularly affects high technology sectors, such as telecommunications, semiconductors, computers, software, industrial automation, and pharmaceutical and biotechnology products. In the case of some of these (particularly software and biotechnologies), almost all of the costs relate to research and development, whereas the costs of reproduction are absolutely marginal; for example, the first copy of a new, completely developed and tested software programme can cost tens of millions of dollars, whereas the reproduction of copies and manuals costs only a few, and even these costs can be eliminated if the Internet is used as the main distribution channel.

Although it is attenuated by the market demand for many alternative products, a somewhat similar situation exists in the case of products with a multimedia content, such as films, records and cassettes, television programmes, interactive CD ROMs, and electronic publishing goods in general. In the field of information providers, such as Reuters and Dun & Bradstreet, on the other hand, the situation is very similar to that of the high technology sectors. Almost all of the costs of these enterprises are related to the collection and organization of information, whereas their transmission costs are becoming increasingly less. Furthermore, rather than expressing a need for product differentiation, the users find it more convenient to be able to refer to a limited number of companies for the information they require and thus favour the success of just a few companies that hold the monopoly of their respective areas of specialization.

Although it is more marked in the high technology sectors, and among the producers of information and multimedia content, the growth in the incidence of initial research, development and planning costs is also significant in other sectors, such as the automotive and motorcycle sectors. In the first, for example, the complete design and putting into production of a new model can cost from 750 million to 6000 million dollars, whereas it has been calculated that production costs do not exceed an average of 1500 dollars. It is therefore hardly surprising that in the mid-1990s major manufacturers such as Fiat, Peugeot and Citroën formed a consortium to design the body of a new MPV. Initial development costs have clearly become so high that the individual manufacturers cannot adequately amortize them in the case of such a relatively little used car.

Overcoming the Trade-off Between Costs and Differentiation

The need to choose between containing costs and differentiating the goods produced is a golden rule presented in all strategic management textbooks. However, this dogma conflicts with the reality of an increasing number of products. For example, the quality of the service rendered by a bank is represented by the speed with which it carries out the various operations, the range of the services offered and the ability of the personnel to provide financial consultancy services. However, nobody would set off a good level of service against the need to put up with more unfavourable economic conditions; bank customers simultaneously demand a good level of service and competitive economic conditions. Software provides another example. Some of the most successful software packages (such as Microsoft's Office) do not have a premium price in comparison with similar products; on the contrary, they have been offered on the basis of highly aggressive pricing policies.

In the same way, it is not true that a leading magazine in its sector must necessarily cost more than alternative products, nor that a hit record must cost more than the others.

It can therefore be seen that the traditional opposition of differentiation and costs is really a phenomenon that applies only to some sectors. Making reference to the concepts introduced above, we can say that the trade-off between costs and differentiation becomes less significant the greater the information content of the goods concerned. The reason behind the different behaviours of businesses with a high content of information is their particular economic structures. In the case of goods with a high material content, better quality is generally accompanied by greater costs. A sophisticated dinner in luxurious and uncrowded surroundings offering a high level of service necessarily costs more than a dinner eaten in a fast-food restaurant. A high-powered limousine equipped with avant-garde technology, leather seats and particularly refined finishing inevitably has a higher average unit cost than a spartanly equipped runaround. In this type of business, it may happen that a technological innovation (for example, the change from metal to composite bumpers in cars) makes it possible to reduce average unit costs while improving the quality of the product. In such a case the trade-off between costs and differentiation shifts to a higher level (see Figure 1.4a) but nonetheless continues to hold good.

In the case of goods with a high information content, the trade-off between costs and differentiation only exists in relation to development costs. For example, the quality of a multimedia encyclopaedia on a CD ROM depends on the breadth of the subjects it covers, the number of illustrations and film sequences, the number

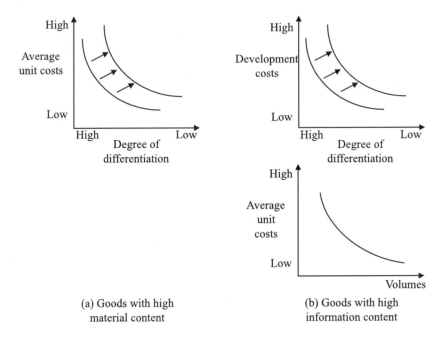

Figure 1.4 Relationship between costs and differentiation for different types of goods

and quality of animated drawings used to explain particularly complex concepts, the presence or otherwise of an online updating service, and so on. As all of these elements obviously have a cost, a better quality encyclopaedia requires more investments during the development phase. However, as can be seen in Figure 1.4b, the average unit costs depend more on the volumes sold than on the costs of development because, as the number of sales increase, the incidence of even very high initial costs will become minimal.

Changes in the Role of Consumers

One important trend that is ultimately due to the switch from realization to support activities is the growing involvement of consumers in the value-creating process. This has been encouraged by technological advances that have allowed users to carry out activities whose nature previously restricted them to the companies producing the goods. For example, let us take all the self-service activities made possible by automatic telling machines, self-installation programmes for packaged software or PC peripherals, online catalogues, online information or booking services, and electronic commerce systems.

However, the growing involvement of purchasers in value-creating activities can also be seen in the absence of any significant technological changes, as in the case of the spread of self-service facilities in the catering and distribution fields. A textbook example of how it is possible to involve purchasers in the creation of value is provided by Ikea, a company that operates in the furnishing and household goods sector using a chain of self-owned and franchised shops. Ikea can afford to charge its customers 20–30% less for products of the same quality as those of its competitors by allowing them to do a number of the activities that are traditionally carried out by resellers, such as the transport and assembly of the furniture. In order to obtain this result, Ikea had to make radical changes in its offer system by designing easy-to-assemble furniture, preparing instruction manuals, packaging the components in such a way that they can be transported without the need for a truck, and so on.

Irrespective of the contribution made by technology, these examples show that the involvement of end-users necessarily requires a simplification of realization activities that can be achieved by investing in support activities. A company that wants users to self-install software must make self-installation programmes available, just as a company that wants its customers to transport and assemble its furniture has to redesign the furniture itself and develop adequate packaging systems and instruction manuals.

The fundamental reason for which the involvement of customers in value-creating processes may, in many cases, be extremely advantageous is the fact that customers tend not to attribute a monetary value to the work they do for themselves. A freelance professional who takes home a new piece of software and spends an entire evening trying to understand how to install it takes into account only the purchase price and not the cost of his own time (even though he may make his own customers pay dearly for every minute he dedicates to them!). Likewise, an Ikea customer may spend six hours assembling the furniture that a specialized worker would have assembled in two, but he does not attribute a monetary value to these six hours; as he has avoided paying for the two hours of a specialist, he feels he has made a good bargain.

The changes in the role of the final customer described above highlight the importance of analysing value-creating systems by making explicit the activities that can be carried out by purchasers. This is particularly true in the case of those that may be influenced by the introduction of new technologies. Such an analysis, together with an analysis of the (real and perceived) costs of these activities, can provide some interesting clues when it comes to reconfiguring customer relations.

1.2.2 Connectivity and Unbundling

Towards the end of the 1980s the spread of standard-based open systems and the consequent spread of compatible equipment, together with the maturation of network technologies, led to the emergence of *client/server* or *network* computing. Network computing allows users to work with data, applications software and processing capacity without needing to worry about which computer actually contains these elements and what they have to do to gain access to them. In this type of system, each user has access not only to the resources of his own computer, but also to the resources of the entire network: to paraphrase an advertising slogan, *the network is the computer.*

During the 1990s, the connectivity of information systems has been qualitatively improved by the spread of the Internet and the consequent adoption of universal technical standards of communication that have made it possible to eliminate the information barriers between different organizations. The technical standards used on the Internet were rapidly accepted and are now also used by many internal company networks (intranets) and reserved inter-organizational networks (extranets). These evolutions delineate a scenario in which there is no technological difference between navigating within our own PCs, navigating within our own company's network or the extranets to which we have access, and navigating on the Internet. This is the era of universal connectivity.

The subject of universal connectivity involves the following aspects:

- the many faces of connectivity;

- the new economics of information arising from universal connectivity;

- the relationships between connectivity and business cost structure;

- the unbundling and rebundling opportunities arising from universal connectivity.

The Many Faces of Connectivity

The information systems of the past were prevalently inside the organization, and reflected the walls dividing one company from another. The information flows directed towards the outside (and often also internal flows) required the use of physical carriers (people or printed paper copies), which greatly limited the amount and richness of the information that could be transmitted. It often happened that data in digital form was printed on paper before being transmitted to a person who then had to re-enter it in the information system of his own company. Complex information could only be transmitted by means of costly personal contacts. However, the era of universal connectivity now finally makes it possible to reap the advantages offered by the possibility of directly transmitting digital data from one system to another. Information systems are beginning to be extended beyond company boundaries and can thus establish close information ties with suppliers, distribution channels and end-users (the last of which was impossible before the spread of the Internet). An insurance company, for example, can now establish stable connections with its agents; a bank customer can use his home computer to give instructions to his bank; inter-company systems allow companies to share information on-line with sub-contractors; and a private citizen who has sent a package by courier can track its progress by interrogating the courier's database via the Internet. The Internet also allows end-users to consult and compare the catalogues and offers of different suppliers of the same product, to ask for clarifications or additional information, to make use of electronic mailing, to make his own bookings or purchase orders without the intervention of a representative of the supplying company, to construct personalized offer systems, and to check the progress of a given order.

In some cases, instead of being between companies that handle different phases of a particular process, the connection may be with competitors or companies that operate in different sectors. Examples of this include the networks that allow the customers of one bank to obtain services using the automatic telling machines of another bank; the common booking systems of airlines or hotel chains; the shared databases of organizations which, although operating in different sectors (e.g. car hire companies, hotels and travel agencies), have the same customers and therefore find it useful to stipulate alliances and exchange information. The Tradenet System of Singapore provides a perfect example of connectivity between complementary and competing companies in that it has automated customs clearance in the port of Singapore in such a way as to interconnect Government and customs offices, and transport and insurance companies, with the result that clearance times have been reduced from 2–4 days to about one hour.

Another interesting example of the use of connectivity by competitors is Autonetwork, the first used car spare parts exchange network created in the United States, which consists of 400 carbreakers in Southern California who exchange requests for used spare parts by computer. Every day, Autonetwork transmits about 5000 requests to its members and allows them to handle the exchange of parts in a much more efficient way than the traditional telephone-based systems. The efficiency of this system has led to it being imitated at a local level throughout the country, and there is now also a national network.

By allowing the interactive electronic transfer of information, universal connectivity breaks down the information barriers between customers, suppliers and partners. It shortens the time needed to carry out activities at all levels of the value-creating system, increases the possibilities of personalization and significantly reduces costs. Universal connectivity changes the metabolism of value-creating systems. What does this mean in operational terms? What are the consequences of these developments for the economic structure of businesses and the characteristics of competitive systems? Which businesses will be most affected by these changes?

In order to understand the implications of universal connectivity, it is necessary to consider that information, as well as the means of transmitting it, not only has a significant impact on the running costs of a business, but also contributes towards defining the boundaries of an enterprise, the organizational solutions it adopts, the paths of material flows and even the configuration of value-creating systems. As Evans and Wurster (1997) put it: 'information is the glue that holds together the structure of all businesses'. Companies consist of a large number of activities co-ordinated by information flows. The way in which companies organize them-selves internally and define their boundaries is largely determined by the way in which information is transferred. For example, the classical hierarchical structure is based on the assumption that a superior can have a rich exchange of information with only a limited number of subordinates. It is no accident that the develop-ments in information technology have been the major factor that allows the redefinition of the span of control and the advent of lean organizations. The theory of transaction costs suggests that the boundaries of a company are defined by the way in which informa-tion is exchanged; inside a company, the information flows are rich (i.e. interactive, personalized, and involving complex information), whereas the exchange of information with external players is more limited. Setting aside the legal definition of the boundaries of a company, it can be said that operational boundaries are marked by a narrowing in the information flow. Let us take, for example, two companies that have a very close collaborative relationship, share the same information system, have mixed working groups and care-fully co-ordinate their respective activities. From the legal point of view, they are two distinct entities, but the same cannot be said from the strategic and organizational point of view.

A key assumption of traditional economics is that rich informa-tion flows can only exist among a limited number of counterparts: for example, standard products can be bought from hundreds of different companies, but for the supply of customized products (which require a richer information flow) companies generally rely on a limited number of partners/sub-suppliers.

The way in which information is collected and transmitted also has an effect on the physical flows of goods. One example of this is the resale of PCs and their related accessories. If we only consider logistical needs, it is probable that large city warehouses from which the products can be sent directly to purchasers would allow more economic stock management and a more efficient logistical flow. However, the distribution structure is actually more fragmented (and the goods follow a longer physical path) because the customers need information and assistance that centralized structures cannot adequately provide. Furthermore, decentralization allows the more efficient collection of information concerning the needs of individual customers, as well as their financial situation and solvency. In this case, as in many others, the size of the salespoints is therefore greatly influenced by the way in which information is collected and transmitted, even though this does not optimize material goods flows.

The New Economics of Information Arising from Universal Connectivity

By redefining the way in which information can be transmitted, universal connectivity can have a significant impact on the economic structure and configuration of value-creating systems. As the economics of these systems are greatly influenced by the economics of information, study of the latter can reveal the primary causes of many of the changes taking place in the former by connecting events that would otherwise be difficult to interpret in the form of a global picture.

How have information technology and universal connectivity changed the economics of information? What are the distinctive characteristics of the old paradigm that still determines the way in which the majority of value-creating systems are configured? What are the characteristics of the new economics of information?

The traditional paradigm has two main distinctive characteristics:

- the strict tie between goods and information flows;

- the trade-off between richness and reach.

As regards the tie between goods and information flows, in the past, much of the information remained incorporated in the goods and could not be transferred to other types of support. For example, the information relating to the defective nature of a hide destined for the production of bags resided by definition in the hide itself. Before information technology made warehouse accounting economically advantageous, the information concerning the goods in hand remained in the goods themselves: in order to check the availability of a product, it was necessary to check it physically by going to the warehouse. Information concerning the quality and aesthetic appearance of many products (clothes, cars, houses) was (and is) fully appreciable only by seeing and touching the goods. The fact that the majority of the information was incorporated in the goods, and could not be extrapolated and memorized on different supports, meant that the information flow was in many cases *embedded* in the physical goods flow. It is only recently that we have began to conceive of and perceive their separate existences. The strict tie between information and goods flows that was typical of the old paradigm meant that a lot of information followed the same path as the goods and, as we have pointed out above, the flow of goods was often adjusted according to information needs.

The trade off between richness and reach, in the past, even when it was separated from its related information could only be transmitted as a physical support. Much of the information was (and still is) memorized and transmitted on paper. Particularly rich and complex information could only be transmitted by means of personal contacts, in which case the physical carrier of the information was an individual: a salesman, a consultant, an instructor. When information is transmitted using a physical support, whether this is a product or an information support, it can only go where the product or support goes – and stops there.

As Evans and Wurster (1997) pointed out, the presence of a traditional physical carrier implies a trade-off between the richness and reach of the information: in other words, rich (interactive, personalized and complete) information can be transmitted to a limited number of destinees; as the richness of the information diminishes, a greater number of people can be reached. For example, a salesman can transmit rich information to a limited number of potential customers, whereas the direct mailing of less rich information can reach a very large number. A showroom can transmit rich information to a limited number of people, whereas a poster advertising campaign can transmit a limited amount of information to thousands.

The advances made in the field of telecommunications during the course of this century have made it possible to reduce some of the limitations affecting the transmission of information by making available large capacity and ubiquitous carriers such as telephone networks, and radio and satellite transmission technologies. However, telecommunication technologies did not significantly reduce the trade-off described by Evans and Wurster until just a few years ago. A telephone allows the transmission of interactive and personalized information, but the communication is one-to-one and so the reach is limited. Radio and television transmit an enormous amount of information to a large number of people but, because the relationship is one of 'one-to-many', the information is lacking in richness because it is not personalized and not transmitted in an interactive manner.

Information and communication technologies offer an opportunity to overcome the traditional economics of information by enabling:

- the separation of information from goods;

- new means of transmitting information.

As regards the separation of information from goods, the first qualitative leap in the method of handling information came when information technology provided the tools enabling much of the information relating to goods to be 'detached' from the goods themselves. Warehouse accounting software allows us to check the availability of a product without physically going to the warehouse. While recognizing that they cannot completely replace the perception of a physical good, multimedia catalogues do make it possible to visualize objects from different perspectives, turn and enlarge the image. Although their cost still limits their spread, virtual reality systems provide a complete sensory perception of the represented goods even when they are not physically present. CAD systems provide three-dimensional images of designed products even before they physically exist. In other words, information technologies have created the conditions for (at least partially) eliminating the embedding of information flows in goods flows. It is still true that a lot of information continues to be embedded, but a growing amount can now be separated and this means that goods and information flows can now theoretically follow distinct paths that optimize the flow of both.

However, value-creating systems cannot be radically reconfigured until this separated information can be easily transmitted. For example, a catalogue recorded on a multimedia CD ROM rather than being printed on paper does not change the economic structure of a distribution system if it needs to be delivered by a salesman physically visiting a customer. A real qualitative change only comes when digitalized information is networked and can be accessed by users in an interactive and personalized manner without the need for a physical carrier (be this a person, a piece of paper or a CD ROM). In the era of universal connectivity, the physical carrier becomes the network (or rather the infrastructure consisting of servers, PCs, cables, transmitters and satellites) on which information is universally accessible thanks to the presence of standard communication protocols.

It is the availability of this new type of physical carrier that is leading to a radical change in the economics of information. The new paradigm does not include the traditional trade-off between richness and reach because we now have the tools for interactively transmitting rich and personalized information to an unlimited number of people.

In order to highlight the significance of this change, we can take the example of the distribution of books (see Chapter 4), the traditional method of which clearly reflects the trade-off between richness and reach, as well as the embedding of information flows in physical flows; communication can be summary and reach a large number of people (e.g. direct mailing, an editorial or an advertising campaign), or rich and interactive but with a very limited reach (e.g. the suggestions and advice provided by a sales assistant in a specialized book shop). In the case of traditional distribution, the majority of the information necessary for the purchasing process is contained in the books themselves, and so it is essential to be able to touch them, leaf through their contents, read the index and look at the back cover. As a result, publishers are driven to distribute their titles to all the available salespoints. Although the consolidation of large-scale distribution chains has modified the competitive context, the configuration of the value-creating system has remained essentially unchanged: the books are printed, put on the shelves, leafed through by potential purchasers, and sometimes bought.

However, this apparently established situation has been radically changed by the introduction of virtual bookshops, the first of which to reach a critical mass on the market was Amazon.com. Founded in 1994, Amazon.com spent a year in setting up the necessary infrastructures and started selling books online in 1995 when it had a turnover of 511 000 dollars; by 1998, this had increased to over 600 million dollars. A visit to the Amazon.com site clearly demonstrates the absence of any trade-off between richness and reach, because it provides reasonably detailed information concerning something like two and a half million titles. The information includes the image of the cover and a brief description of the contents; in many cases, these are also accompanied by press reviews, the texts of interviews given by the author and/or the comments of other readers. Amazon.com is not a specialized bookshop but can become one: by means of search functions, we can visualize only the titles relating to a certain category of books and see everything (or almost everything) that has been printed about astronomy or angling. If you already know what you are looking for, the search can be made by author or title. By replying to some questions concerning books that we have enjoyed reading in the past, it is possible to receive suggestions as to which other books may interest us. If we have to choose a present, we can receive suggestions as to which books are appropriate for the birthday of a five-year-old, mother's day or Valentine's day. From the point of view of Amazon.com, the service offered to its customers is not personalized insofar as the online interface and information are the same for everybody but, from the point of the user, it is highly personalized because it is interactive and can be adapted to specific needs. Online bookshops also provide an excellent example of the division between information and goods flows: the information arrives directly in the houses of potential customers, whereas the goods (books in this case) remain in the warehouse of the wholesaler or Amazon until the time of purchase, when they are home-delivered. Wholesalers such as Ingram (the largest book wholesaler in the United States) have begun to supply online customers with a service that allows books to be home-delivered directly even without having to pass through the warehouses of virtual booksellers. In this case, the path followed by the information (publishers and reviewers → virtual bookshop → consumer → virtual bookshop → wholesaler → transport company) is radically different from that of the goods themselves (printers → wholesalers → transport company → final customer), and it thus optimizes both flows.

The Relationships Between Connectivity and Business Cost Structure

It is interesting to see that, in comparison with traditional methods, the transmission of information over a network leads to a clear shift from realization to support activities, as described in the previous section. Although they are distinct phenomena, universal connectivity and the change from realization to support activities are actually interwoven.

An example of this comes from brokerage services. Starting from zero in the mid-nineties, in 1998 20–25% of all retail trades in shares were online, and this proportion is expected to increase to 50% by 2001. The number of brokers providing access to their services via the Web increased from 20 in 1996 to 52 in July 1998. Online trading is a clear example of the new inappropriateness of the classical trade-off between richness and reach. The personal relationship with a relatively limited number of clients that characterized traditional brokers is being replaced by an online interface that makes it possible to deal with a practically unlimited clientele. Realization activities (consultancy, the execution of purchasing and sales orders) are being replaced by support activities aimed at developing increasingly user-friendly customer interfaces, online systems allowing consultation of the current situation of individual portfolios, and software programs designed to aid customers making investment choices. Online trading leads to a cost structure that is radically different from that of traditional finance brokering. The salaries of brokers (which are proportional to the volumes handled) are being replaced by the costs of developing the online service (which have little to do with the volumes handled). This increases the advantages associated with a large market share and has driven online operators to reduce their transaction commissions considerably: the commission charges applied by the traditional channels amount to an average of 75–100 dollars per operation, and are generally proportional to the size of the transaction; the average commission charges of the ten leading online brokers decreased from 53 dollars at the beginning of 1996 to 16 dollars at the end of 1997. In some cases, the commission for online purchases (which is usually fixed) has dropped to ten or even five dollars per transaction. At first sight, it could be thought that the strategy of online brokers is based on cost containment at the expense of the differentiation guaranteed by a traditional personalized service. However, online trading actually not only leads to lower costs, but in many ways also to better quality. In comparison with traditional brokering, online trading allows transactions to be executed more quickly and, in a world in which a delay of just a few minutes may lead to enormous losses or gains, this is a fundamental element differentiating the service. Furthermore, online brokers can enrich their service by offering information, financial analyses and portfolio management suggestions capable of adding considerable value to their trading services. As the management of the site and the development of online services mainly require support activities, online trading provides a perfect example of a business in which average unit costs are much more influenced by the volumes handled than by the quality and differentiation of the service, thus giving the lie to the classical trade-off between costs and differentiation. A structural problem in this sector is that when almost all of the costs sustained by an economic activity are development costs, and the marginal cost of the product or service tends to zero, the struggle for the acquisition of market share by reducing prices can become mortal, as shown by the vertiginous collapse of commission charges. The increases in the volumes handled have so far allowed many online brokers to compensate for the reduction in commission charges, but what will happen when growth rates begin to decline? It is likely that competition will put many marginal operators out of the game, and that things will only settle down when the few remaining competitors find a point of equilibrium. Nonetheless, the transparency of this kind of market will presumably continue to ensure that the pressure on prices is high. Although very different, the case of online trading once again highlights a problem that we have already considered in the case of the music sector: the problem of obtaining a payment that is proportional to the value created in a dematerialized context.

Unbundling and Rebundling

The separation of information flows from goods flows, and the new compatibility of richness with reach, gives rise to what may become a managerial watchword over the next few years: 'unbundle and rebundle'. Universal connectivity makes it possible to divide and re-aggregate activities, flows and goods, while taking into account the economic structure of the various elements and eliminating at least one part of the compromises that characterized the old economic paradigm. This means questioning consolidated operating methods and economic specializations that were apparently beyond discussion. Even in seemingly traditional and well-established businesses, the confines of companies and sectors shift and blur to such an extent that they can no longer be taken for granted.

Let us consider the unbundling of activities. According to Evans and Wurster (1997), 'Existing value chains will fragment into multiple businesses, each of which will have its own sources of competitive advantage. When individual functions having different economies of scale or scope are bundled together, the result is a compromise of each – an averaging of the effects. When the bundles of functions are free to re-form as separate businesses, however, each can exploit its own sources of competitive advantage to the fullest'. Retail banking provides an interesting example of this type of unbundling. The traditional retail banking model is characterized by large organizations producing, packaging and cross-selling a number of different financial services through proprietary channels. The wide-ranging scope of traditional retail banks is driven by distribution, the high costs of which can only be covered by selling multiple products. However, this is being changed by universal connectivity and financial innovations. There was once no question that banks should directly perform a number of different functions (offering payment services for their customers, gathering financial resources and pooling them to finance large-scale enterprises, lending financial resources, etc.), but these are now becoming increasingly severable. Nowadays, a number a financial institutions carry out limited sets of functions and activities (such as managing a credit card business, mortgage lending or gathering savings), whereas others continue to offer multiple products and services. The bundle of functions and activities is now a choice rather than a defined fact.

The unbundling of functions and activities is not only related to the presence of different economies of scale and scope, but also to the type of competence required to perform the various activities. It is in the perspective of activity unbundling that we can interpret some of the most recent managerial trends, such as focussing on core competencies and outsourcing. For example, logistics systems cannot be outsourced without a close informative connection between a vendor and its customers. The possibility of outsourcing entire company functions allows enterprises to use all their resources for the things they know how to do best. EDS deals 'only' in information systems and Federal Express 'only' in logistics systems, and this allows both the vendor and its customers to concentrate on their own core competencies.

In relation to the unbundling of different types of flows, we have already seen the example of virtual bookshops. In this type of unbundling the general rule is that information (the transfer of which has become simple and cheap) can travel a great deal and reach a very large number of people in an interactive manner. However, the transfer of physical goods has to be more linear and take the shortest possible route. An interesting example of this can be seen in the innovations introduced by Gucci in the phases of cutting leather for the production of its bags and shoes. The cutting of leather has always been an extremely critical activity insofar as hides are natural products, which means that they are not only expensive to produce, but also that their quality is difficult to predict and they may contain various defects at different points. For this reason, traditional cutting requires highly expert cutters who are capable of placing the shapes sent from the design and model engineering office in such a way as to minimize waste and avoid random surface defects. Cutting is critical because it not only has an effect on costs, but also on the quality of the finished product; given the difficulty of finding suppliers who offer adequate quality guarantees, this phase cannot usually be outsourced. In the traditional system, there is no way of separating the information concerning the defects of the hides from the hides themselves – it 'travels' with them. However, Gucci introduced some innovations which, by separating the information about the hides from the hides themselves, made it possible to manage the entire cutting phase in a more rational manner and facilitated the decentralization of the same to partners, some of which are even very distant geographically. The new method consists of the following elements:

• a CAD/CAM system for design and model engineering;

- the installation of digital systems for the analysis of hides and the detection of defects on the premises of supplying tanners;

- an automatic lay planning system which, by combining the information from the design office and the tanners, establishes the best way of making the cut;

- the installation of some automatic cutting systems in internal production departments and on the premises of some external partners.

Within the framework of the new system, the tanned hides follow the most rational course to the most convenient cutting centre, whereas the information (now separated from its physical support) is transmitted to Gucci where, with the help of the automatic lay planning system, it is established how the cut must be made in order to minimize costs and maximize quality. The processed information is finally sent to the chosen cutting centre.

The unbundling of activities and flows is often accompanied by a profound transformation of distribution systems. Universal connectivity allows many producers to come into direct contact with final customers, for whom they can interactively provide rich information and thus establish a more personalized and precise form of communication. In the case of a growing number of goods, this implies replacing mass advertising with cheaper and more efficient means of communicating with increasingly specific segments of demand. At the same time, increasingly powerful information systems make it possible for companies to follow an increasing number of customers efficiently and, in some cases, thus make the filter of commercial intermediation superfluous if not actually harmful.

One example of this is the sale of computer printers. The traditional channel involved them being sold by the manufacturers to retailers who subsequently accepted responsibility for contacting end users. In the past, the role of the retailers was fully justified by the advice that they were able to give consumers at the time of purchase, the difficulties that the same user may encounter when the printer is installed, the need to deliver the printer to the consumer's home, and the need to provide adequate after-sales assistance. Furthermore, thanks to their relative limited range of action, retailers could follow their customers in a personalized manner, evaluating their reliability and potential. However, current changes are undermining the position of the resellers of IT products at various points. End-users are much more informed than they once were and, in many cases, with the aid of the information that can now be easily found in the specialized press or on the Internet, are capable of choosing the product that best satisfies their needs by themselves. 'Plug and play' printers have become very easy to install correctly. Information concerning the reliability of enterprises can be obtained from service companies, such as Dun & Bradstreet, and the use of a computerized customer management system allows producers to handle an archive that contains not only the demographic and fiscal data of end-users, but also the products they have previously purchased, the technical problems encountered, the repairs carried out, and any needs that a customer may have expressed. In fact, so far as this last point is concerned, an inefficient intermediary could lead to a manufacturer not receiving precious information that may be useful not only in terms of customer management, but also in terms of the development of new products and markets. In this context, the role of a commercial intermediary would be reduced to a purely logistics function, which can be carried out more efficiently by a transport company at a cost that is only a fraction of a retailer's margin.

Although it is clear that the type of evolution described above will never represent the rule for all products and all market segments, the trend towards the elimination of inefficient intermediaries seems to be well under way. This is particularly true if we consider the growing pressure towards the reduction of margins that characterizes many markets and is driving enterprises to identify all the possible solutions that will allow them to make overall savings in this area.

However, even without considering extreme situations of 'disintermediation', the cases of virtual bookshops and the music sector widely dealt with above provide an illustration of how the role of the still-existing intermediaries has been completely redefined and the distribution system profoundly changed.

Finally, let us consider the unbundling and rebundling of the goods and services. In some cases, this type of unbundling comes directly from the unbundling of activities and functions, as in the example of retail banking described above; specialization by function implies the disjointed offer of individual services by different economic players. In other cases, the unbundling specifically involves the goods and services being offered. In the music sector, the online distribution of music and its recording on CDs or other supports by the users themselves imply that we will no longer have to buy all the tracks of an LP as we do today, but that we will have the possibility of choosing to buy only specific tracks. Similar developments may take place in the publishing field. Why should we need to buy an entire book when we are only interested in one of its chapters? Why should things become so complicated if, while respecting the laws of copyright, we want personalized material originating from a number of sources? McGraw Hill have recently started offering teachers an interesting service for the production of made-to-measure textbooks. Described very briefly, the system consists of a database of teaching materials divided by subject area (medicine, economics, jurisprudence, and so on), which may be articles, papers, teaching cases or various types of exercise, not necessarily originally published by McGraw Hill. The teachers interested in the service can gain online access to the database, select the material they consider most interesting, establish the sequence in which this material is to be placed, integrate it with their own material (papers on subjects not covered by the database, introductions, additional exercises, etc.), and define the title of the book. McGraw Hill then proceeds to print the number of books requested by the teachers, making them pay the authorship rights relating only to the material actually used.

1.2.3 Systemic Products and the Spread of Industry Standards

The last of the current developments affecting advanced economic systems that we shall consider here is the increasingly systemic nature of products and services. This may take various forms because it is possible to distinguish the following different types:

- at the level of finished products;

- at the level of users;

- at the level of components.

Finished Products

A systemic finished product or service must be used (or is better used) in conjunction with other complementary goods. Examples of systemic products include videorecorders and videocassettes; hardware, software and telecommunication products and services; CD readers and CDs; the different components of an industrial automation system; a drill and its various accessories, and so on. Less strong examples are furnishing systems; tourist packages including flights, hotel accommodation, a hire car and other services; lifts and related maintenance services, etc.

Users

This occurs when users find it advantageous to adopt the product that is most widely used by the people with which they have to interact. For example, the producers of spreadsheets find it difficult to undermine the predominant position of Microsoft, not so much because its Excel spreadsheet is technically superior to the others, but because it has become the most widespread and so its users have fewer difficulties when using applications developed by others or sharing files with other users. In the presence of strong systemic relationships among users, the existence of 'open systems' (i.e. those in which the products of different manufacturers are compatible and can interact with each other) becomes essential if one wants to remain on the market. However, in some cases, a guarantee of good compatibility may not be enough to make a product as attractive as that which is most widely sold. For example, it is possible to transform an application created in Lotus 123 into an Excel application, and so the two systems are open and compatible with each other; but despite this, users find it more convenient to adopt the more widely used software in order to ensure that their system is not only compatible, but identical in all respects to that used by their interlocutors.

Components

The systemic nature of a product may also lie in the fact that it incorporates complex elements based on different technologies.

Examples of such goods include the cathode tubes used to produce televisions; the various components of a personal computer (microprocessors, RAM memories, mass memories, other components); the gear systems used in the production of sports cycles; the control units incorporated in numeric controlled machines; and the advanced materials, such as carbon fibre, that can be used to improve the performance of a highly disparate range of products (boat hulls, tennis racquets, skis, and so on). The systemic nature of components is not a new phenomenon. However, what is changing is the increasing number of complex products containing complex components whose technological differentiation means that they are generally produced by distinct economic players.

The success of a single market standard, and the exclusion or marginalization of alternative systems, becomes more likely in the presence of systemic products and components; and this can lead to the creation of quasi-monopolistic situations if only one company controls the product in question (as in the case of Microsoft's PC operating systems), or the adoption of a sector standard on the part of different competitors. This latter has occurred in the case of the production of personal computers (WINTEL), videorecorders (VHS), CD readers, and so on.

As far as the systemic nature of components is concerned, it is important to remember that the increasing spread of widely accepted standards represents the prerequisite for an efficient division of work and greater customer satisfaction. An example of this comes from the advantages connected with the success of the GSM standard for cellular telephony in Europe, and the problems caused by the incompatibility between this and the D-AMPS system used in the United States.

The acceptance of a given standard can be encouraged by the company that originally developed the standard itself by means of internal growth, the creation of strategic alliances or the granting of production licences. In other cases, the enormous collective advantages associated with the introduction of sector standards may lead to national and international governmental interventions designed to define the technical parameters that need to be respected in order to ensure the compatibility and integration of components produced and used in different geographical areas.

In some cases, the standardization of a system's components is forced by the presence of an enterprise that plays a co-ordinating role for all of the companies belonging to a given network. One interesting example of this is that of Sikisui, a Japanese company that is capable of delivering personalized homes in only nine days thanks to an integrated network that goes from salespoints to component suppliers (McHugh et al., 1995). When Sikisui customers enter a salespoint, they are received by a salesman who defines with them the characteristics of the construction. Each agent has a terminal that is connected to Sikisui's design office by means of which first the general layout of the home is established and then the personalized details requested by the customers are defined. The various options chosen by the customers are gradually added to the display in such a way as to give an idea of what the final result will look like. Once the project is satisfactory, the computer prints a contract within the space of a few dozen minutes indicating the total cost and delivery times (which may vary slightly depending upon the chosen configuration). After the contract is signed, the central computer of Sikisui sends purchasing orders to a network of authorized suppliers with the understanding that, if one of the suppliers cannot guarantee delivery within three days of receiving the order, he is responsible for identifying another supplier in the network who is capable of fulfilling the order on time. The various components arrive at the headquarters of Sikisui two days before beginning the work on the chosen site, are assembled into modules and, within about ten days of the signing of the contract, the final construction of the home is begun. Aside from the incredible lead-times involved, the interesting aspect of this case is that the personalized components for each home represent something like 50% of the total, something that bears witness to the considerable personalization of the delivered construction. It is obvious that a system such as that of Sikisui can only function if all of the components, however diverse, are designed in conformity with highly precise standards that make them perfectly compatible and interchangeable.

The example of Sikisui also reminds us of the close tie existing between the standardization of components and co-production. The greater the systemic nature of a good, the more difficult it is for an individual company to take responsibility for all of the components in the final product. The greater the importance of co-production the greater is the need for integration and standard sharing.

1.3 EVOLUTION AT COMPANY LEVEL: FROM ENTERPRISES TO VALUE-CREATING SYSTEMS

The changes taking place in the economic environment are fostering a new enterprise model. Universal connectivity is drastically reducing the costs of gathering information, controlling and co-ordinating transactions with other economic operators. This reduction in external transaction costs is accompanied by greater environmental turbulence and a need for flexibility that undermine the capacity of large, integrated and diversified companies to withstand the growing competitive pressure. At the same time, isolated small companies are finding it difficult to compete in such an environment as they lack the financial and human resources necessary to sustain the accelerated rate of innovation.

All these changes seem to be leading to the disaggregation of large, integrated and diversified companies, and the greater co-ordination of the activities of small, independent enterprises. As a result, competition increasingly takes place between networks or, to use a more generic term, value-creating systems (VCS). As seen below, a large number of authors and economic observers are beginning to consider shifting the focus for strategic analysis from enterprises to value-creating systems.

'An industrial enterprise will no longer be an activity of isolated production, but rather one node in a complex network of suppliers, customers, engineering activities and other service functions'. (Earl Hall in Davidow and Malone, 1992).

'The new model is derived from Michael Porter's concept of the value chain, but extended into the notion of a *value network* ... The provision of value is not something chained in a linear way, but rather something generated through an ever-changing open network.' (Tapscott and Caston, 1993).

'What will a virtual company be like? There is no single answer. To an external observer it will appear almost boundless, with permeable and continuously changing interfaces between the company, its suppliers and its customer. Seen from the inside, it will be no less amorphous, with the traditional offices departments and operating divisions being continuously redefined on the basis of needs'. (Davidow and Malone, 1992).

'A holonic network is a set of companies that acts integratedly and organically; it is constantly re-configured to manage each business opportunity a customer presents. Each company in the network provides a different process capability ... Each configuration of process capabilities within the holonic network is called a virtual company.' (McHugh *et al.*, 1995).

'Increasingly, successful companies do not just add value, they reinvent it. Their focus of strategic analysis is not the company or even the industry but the value-creating system itself, within which different economic actors – (suppliers, business partners, allies, customers) – work together to co-produce value.' (Normann and Ramírez, 1993).

'It used to be relatively easy to determine where the boundaries of a firm began and ended. No more. Deverticalization, a focus on core competencies, and a greater reliance on partnerships are redrawing the boundaries of the firm. The 'extended' or 'virtual' enterprise, enmeshed in a web of alliances and long-term supplier relationships, gives rise to a host of new management issues. The emerging questions include: how to determine which strategic assets are worth owning and which are not? How do we control 'critical resources' that lie outside the legal boundaries of the firm? What determines the division of power and influence within coalitions and networks? Is the coalition, rather than the single firm, that should by the unit of analysis in competitive battles? How are collaborative and competitive impulses balanced when competitors are also partners? What are the limits to co-ordination within the networks?' (Hamel and Prahalad, from the Call for Papers of the 1996 annual Conference of the Strategic Management Society).

Despite their differences in emphasis, all these comments come together in delineating a new economic model. Although they continue to exist as legal and decision-making subjects, individual companies are no longer the focal point of strategic analysis. This change in perspective makes it necessary to reconsider all of the tools of strategic analysis developed over the last few decades, and raises questions concerning methods and models that were taken for granted until just a few years ago. In particular, we need to think of strategy in terms of value-creating systems rather than individual companies.

In the search for new instruments of strategic analysis, it may be useful to draw up an identikit of the new company model. The company profile that seems to be best suited to respond successfully to current environmental changes includes the following elements:

- focus on core competencies;

- the ability to participate simultaneously in more than one value-creating system;

- the ability to ensure organic connections with the other economic players participating in the value-creating systems to which it belongs (interconnected companies);

- a high degree of internal integration (integrated company) and a streamlined organization (lean companies);

- internal and external flexibility.

1.3.1 Focus on Core Competences

Growing technological complexity and accelerated innovation processes make it increasingly difficult for companies to maintain excellent performances in relation to a large number of activities involving different technological and organizational characteristics. In this context, large diversified companies managed as a complex of autonomous business units that fundamentally lack any common distinctive competencies are destined to produce increasingly disappointing and inadequate results. As Prahalad and Hamel (1990) pointed out, within a continuously changing environment in which competitive advantages are subject to continuous erosion, the winning companies will be those that manage to invent new markets, rapidly enter emerging markets and even radically change the way in which they present themselves on consolidated markets. However, such a proactive approach is only possible when the management of a company is capable of developing its technological and production know-how, strengthening the competencies underlying its offer of individual products and services, and reinforcing the company's ability to share common skills. A good example of this is Canon, an apparently highly diversified company that operates in sectors ranging from photographic equipment to videocameras, printers to photocopiers, and fax machines to image scanners. However, more careful analysis reveals the fact that, although they are aimed at different markets and have different functions, Canon products are actually highly homogeneous in terms of their critical underlying technologies, and the fact that the company has founded its competitive success and innovative capacities on its distinctive competencies in the fields of optics, the treatment of images and microprocessor-controlled equipment. Rather than considering it a highly diversified company, it would perhaps be better to see Canon as a company that concentrates on its distinctive competencies. Returning to what has been said concerning the changes taking place in a company's cost structure, among other things, an emphasis on distinctive competencies makes it possible to concentrate investments in the areas of research, development and design, reach the increasingly greater critical mass necessary for the achievement of satisfactory results, and spread initially high development costs over a wide range of final products.

1.3.2 Participation in More Than One Value-creating System

The transversal character of many technologies means that companies often have to participate simultaneously in more than one value-creating system in order to make the most of their distinctive competencies. Depending on the situations and opportunities that arise, they interconnect themselves with different economic players capable of offering other skills useful for satisfying customers' needs.

The VCSs in which a company takes part may have many affinities or common aspects, or may be very different from each other. For example, leveraging its ability to produce editorial economic/financial contents and its reputation, the *Financial Times* can participate in VCSs leading to the production of daily newspapers, electronic publishing products (CD ROMs, online databanks, information on the Internet), economic and financial publications, and so on, because there is a clear affinity in terms of content and targets between the market segments in which the company operates. For each of these different VCSs, the *Financial Times* has to integrate itself with players offering specific competencies (printers, newspaper distributors, CD producers, software companies specialized in multimedia products, variously configured retail sales points, transport companies, direct mailing agencies, etc.).

The opportunity of participating in more than one value-creating system often goes together with the presence of intangible resources which, precisely because they are intangible, are not exhausted by use and can be applied to different fronts. An example of this could be a public library that has developed a particularly efficacious and easy-to-use internal cataloguing system, and which has used this system to catalogue almost all of a certain branch of literature (let us say European literature from the nineteenth century onwards). Its competence in cataloguing and the resource represented by its database could be useful in other value-creating systems. The library could sell its database and updating service to an electronic publishing company, which could publish it together with other contents online or on CD ROMs.

1.3.3 The Interconnected Company

An 'interconnected company' is capable of organically connecting itself with the other economic players involved in the VCSs of which it is a part. As was pointed out in our discussion of connectivity and unbundling, these connections can link a company not only with its suppliers and customers, but also with its competitors or similar and complementary companies. Increasingly important competitive factors, such as time-to-market and lead times, are very much influenced by the information compactness of the value-creating system, that is, the ability of upstream activities to transmit information quickly and rapidly receive a feedback from their downstream counterparts. In the same way, only by having close connections with suppliers on the one hand, and distribution channels and final customers on the other, can a production company create a strategy of mass personalization, improve its understanding of the needs expressed by purchasers, and rapidly adapt to the ever-changing demands of the market.

In a certain sense, it is possible to relate interconnection capacity to the 'intelligence' of a VCS. Just as human intelligence is closely related to the number and speed of neuronal synapses and the interconnections of different parts of the brain, the intelligence of a value-creating system is greatly influenced by the extent of the connections between economic players/activities (in terms of its capacity to exchange information) and the ease with which the system is capable of establishing new connections by replacing inadequate players and adding or removing activities from the configuration.

Interconnection makes it increasingly easy for different companies to carry out interdependent activities regardless of their geographical separation. For example, Nike can be described as the brain of a broad value-creating system that internally carries out only some key activities (such as design and marketing), and outsources almost all of the production activities. One of the most interesting aspects of the Nike case is that, although the company has delegated its production to a number of widely dispersed companies mainly located in South-east Asia (in order to take advantage of lower labour costs), it manages to control the progress of these activities very closely from its Headquarters in Beaverton (Oregon). Nike's sub-contractors are given precise instructions concerning the configuration of their production processes, as well as the work that needs to be carried out, mainly thanks to the permanent consultancy offered by its locally resident quality and technical managers. It also manages to influence and control production processes directly by means of the use of electronic connections, which send production orders directly to the information systems of the sub-contractors and provide the electronic information necessary to ensure that their machines can be converted to produce newly introduced models. Given the type of production, such a relationship can obviously only be established with technologically advanced suppliers and in relation to those phases of the production process that are most susceptible to standardization; nevertheless, it allows Nike to take advantage of low production costs while simultaneously continuing to have direct control over the good functioning of the production processes involved.

The examples of interconnected companies often make reference to technological innovation, but it is worth remembering that technological progress simply makes available the tools by means of which different companies can establish efficient low-cost connections. In the absence of a common strategic design and company willingness to change its organization, no connection of this kind could ever work.

The establishment of stable connections above all means creating a lasting alliance with other economic players aimed at ensuring that one system is more competitive than alternative systems and, by definition, a strategic alliance can be created only if all of the players involved believe that they can benefit from this type of co-operation. However, this is only possible if the companies have the same opinion concerning the value that they are to create together, are convinced that they need each other in order to create it, and have come to an agreement as to how the created value is to be divided. Unless these conditions exist, there is no chance that distinctly separate organizations will agree to exchange information and commit themselves to the pursuit of a common objective. By the same token, the absence of a shared objective means that the companies will continue to operate as a chain of independent entities, each of which will limit itself to add value to the goods acquired from others and then sell its own goods to the best buyer.

1.3.4 Integrated and Lean Companies

Competitive pressures are forcing companies to review not only their external relations, but also their internal organization. Instead of being a set of business units and specialized functions, companies must begin to operate as single, large (even if diversified) enterprises that often have to operate on a global scale. An increasing number of companies are becoming aware of the technical, structural and organizational barriers that prevent or hinder their internal infor-mation flow, and the need to overcome them by creating direct channels between the source of the information and the people who use it, as well as by identifying the way in which information can be shared by the entire organization.

In many cases, the trend towards greater company integration takes the form of bringing together what were once distinct func-tions: for example, the multinational food company Nestlé has established an 'Innovation Division', which includes the functions of research and development, engineering, marketing, and organiza-tional development; and another example is that offered by Mercedes, which has overcome the traditional separation of purchasing and production activities by incorporating them in the same division. In other cases, although without going so far as uniting different functions, companies have worked on strength-ening between-function connections by, for example, introducing process managers alongside functional managers.

The interest aroused by interventions aimed at guaranteeing

greater company integration is confirmed by the fact that many of the most interesting contributions published in the literature during the 1990s support the importance of integration and the danger of excessively autonomous (and consequently uncoordinated) business units and company functions. In the former case, the most relevant contributions include studies on core competencies (Prahalad and Hamel, 1990), that have underlined the dangers connected with the vision of an enterprise as a set of autonomous business units and the importance of core competencies as an element of unification. In the case of the integration of functions, it is sufficient to consider the numerous contributions that have been made in the field of process re-engineering (Hammer and Champy, 1993).

The focus on core competencies, the incorporation of once distinct functions, the potential of the new information technologies and the related decline in the importance of the informative and controlling role of intermediate hierarchical positions, are presuppositions for the creation of lean company structures characterized by a very limited number of hierarchical levels, the broadening and integration of organizational units, and less formalized and more flexible operational mechanisms than those found in traditional organizations. Growing competitive pressures and the economic difficulties associated with them have driven many companies to adopt the logic of lean management as a means of reducing company structures whose economic costs have become unsustainable. However, rather than its effects on cost structures, the strategic advantage of lean management should be looked for in the greater compactness, flexibility and strategic agility of a lean structure, and the greater capacity of lean companies to react rapidly to market opportunities.

1.3.5 Internal and External Flexibility

The internal and external flexibility of an organization, or rather its ability to modify its external relationships and internal configuration, is the only possible response to the increasingly dynamic changes taking place in the environment, and brings all of the elements described above together. By considering their core competencies, companies must be able to connect themselves flexibly to different value-creating systems and be capable of rapidly and efficiently establishing new connections with other players. The integration and leanness of an organization are fundamental if it is to perceive the need for change quickly enough and then make the necessary changes in its own configuration.

1.4 ENVIRONMENTAL DEVELOPMENTS AND THE EVOLUTION OF MANAGERIAL DISCIPLINES

Precisely because of their lack of continuity with the past, the structural changes described above require new models for interpreting companies and competitive systems. What are the characteristics that a strategic analysis model must have if it is to be capable of correctly interpreting the new economic context? What help can we expect from management studies and the economic literature in general?

1.4.1 The Evolution of Economic Studies

Management studies have partially reflected the evolution of the environmental context through the development of areas of research such as process re-engineering and inter-firm networks, and environmental changes are also reflected in a series of contributions describing the new economic reality. Nevertheless, however interesting these may be, it is still hard to find new strategic analysis models suited to the new reality.

As regards the process approach, the interest of managers and academics in processes, rather than functions and activities, as a criterion for the aggregation and organization of company operations has been growing over the last few years. A good part of this interest has been triggered by the potential for improving the processes connected with technology developments. By strengthening the information flow between activities of different kinds, the new technological paradigm is bringing to the forefront the processes that transversally cross companies and value-creating systems, and gradually reducing the barriers that have traditionally divided different classes of activity.

Since the beginning of the 1990s, the process approach has been

Processes

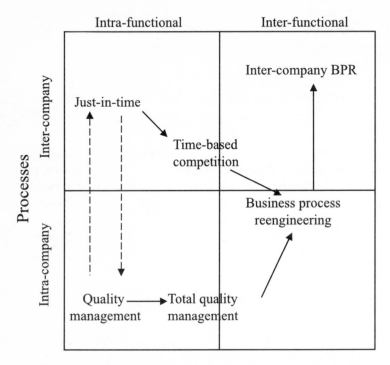

Figure 1.5   The managerial theories linked to the process approach

diffused by publications on business process re-engineering (BPR), such as those by Davenport and Short (1990), and Hammer and Champy (1993). However, when considered in a broader perspective, many of the management 'fashions' of the last few years can be linked to the process approach: from 'just-in-time' to 'total quality' and 'time-based competition' (see the matrix in Figure 1.5).

The BPR approach (Davenport and Short, 1990, Hammer and Champy, 1993, and Davenport, 1993) emerged at the beginning of the 1990s as an almost natural development of the studies of time-based competition (which essentially dealt with the containment of times and costs by means of the reconfiguration of inter-functional processes) and total quality management (which, among other things, supported the search for continuous improvement by means of the reconfiguration of processes, albeit generally within the ambit of a particular function). Although process reconfiguration was not extraneous to previous approaches, it was only with the affirmation of BPR that the term 're-engineering' began to be widely used in reference to company processes. The qualitative leap made by BPR studies can be essentially attributed to their highly inter-functional perspective which, for the first time, directly considered the subject of functionally transversal processes. By working on transversal processes (with respect to traditional company functions), BPR drew the attention of managers towards areas of intervention that offered possibilities of radical improvement precisely because they had long been neglected. It suggested that companies could significantly improve the times and costs of their activities, their customer relations and their capacity to respond to the needs of the market. Furthermore, the BPR studies were the first to incorporate the evolution of information technologies in an organic manner by highlighting their role as a central element of organizational and strategic change.

Although they did not deny but actually stress the importance of inter-company processes, the first contributions in the field of BPR concentrated on process re-engineering at company level; more recent contributions have underlined the need to conceive and re-engineer processes by overcoming not only the barriers between different functions and different areas of responsibility within individual companies, but also by reducing (if not eliminating) the barriers that exist between the different companies belonging to a given value-creating system. In particular, McHugh et al. (1995) pointed out that the BPR studies carried out up until that time had restricted themselves to considering what happens within the four walls of a specific company, and thus did not explicitly extend re-engineering interventions to the other companies making up the wider value chain or consider them as an integral part of the processes upon which to act. Inter-functional re-engineering has led to radical improvements in the way processes are carried out at individual company level; at an inter-company level, BPR can also be considered an important tool for the reconfiguration or re-engineering of value-creating systems as a whole.

At a time in which process re-engineering also involves inter-company processes, it becomes intertwined with what we have previously identified as one of the other elements affecting the economic environment: inter-firm networks. As Lago (1995) pointed out, the theoretical publications concerning inter-firm networks can be divided into two broad categories. The first consists of prevalently empirical contributions that describe the configurations of particular inter-firm networks and, on the basis of these observations, attempt to establish significant classifications and draw generalizations which, in many cases, also include analytical and behavioural rules. Precisely because of their empirical origin, these studies are greatly influenced by the characteristics of the inter-firm networks that are most common in the geographical areas analysed by the authors. It is therefore not surprising that the large numbers of Italian studies, including those of Varaldo (1988), Lorenzoni (1992) and Lipparini (1995), have concentrated on the analysis of aggregates of small companies often situated in industrial areas, whereas Japanese authors have concentrated on sub-contracting networks and those from the USA have given more attention to networks of large companies, particularly in high technology sectors.

The second category consists of studies whose authors have used the transaction costs approach to investigate networks from the mainly theoretical point of view of asking themselves whether aggregates can or cannot be considered an intermediate or hybrid form of the management of transactions between the market and the hierarchy.

As has already been pointed out, the relationships among the activities making up value-creating systems may be governed by the hierarchy, the market or other more or less close collaborative or co-ordination relationships. It is therefore not necessarily true that the relationships between the players making up a value-creating system are such as to represent an inter-firm network even in the broadest sense. Nevertheless, many of the developments described in the present chapter show that inter-firm networks represent a very interesting governance model. The literature on this subject can therefore provide a large number of starting points for classifying the co-ordination structures and mechanisms of value-creating systems, as well as for identifying the most suitable configurations in different competitive contexts.

Despite the interest aroused by the process approach and inter-firm networks, however, there is still a lack of published strategic management studies including analytical schemes that are consistent with the changes described in this chapter. Many authors have begun to examine the consequences of the current changes and have suggested interesting starting points for further studies, but none have yet illustrated strategic analysis techniques that go beyond those developed in the 1970s and 1980s.

The analytical instruments and methods that we still use are fundamentally based on concepts of firms and industries that are beginning to show their limitations as a result of the general blurring of borders and the weakening of barriers between different firms and different industries, and the general increase in inter-relationships.

It is in relation to the industry concept (intended as a set of companies producing similar goods) that the techniques for analysing competitive systems, competitors and the market have been developed.

Likewise, the concept of a firm is still considered as a fundamental focus of analysis and a number of instruments have been developed around it, including the business idea model, the value chain, the methods for business definition and the construction of portfolio matrices.

It is certainly not our intention here to say that such concepts are now out of date and of little use, as they represent two elements that are indispensable to economic studies. In particular, the concept of the firm is and will always remain a cardinal element in the analysis of economic systems: successful competitive strategies are not sought by abstract entities, company networks or 'virtual enterprises', but are defined by managers and entrepreneurs who identify themselves with a company as an autonomous and lasting organization.

Nevertheless, it is worth pointing out that our focus on industries, companies and company functions is the fruit of a vision aimed at cutting economic activities in a 'vertical' manner that highlights the distinction between operations of different kinds, as opposed to a 'horizontal' view that spotlights processes and operational inter-relationships. The limitations of a vertical vision are not apparent when industries, enterprises and company functions are separated by well-defined borders and substantial physical and information barriers. However, the evolution of economic systems that we have tried to describe in this chapter, is gradually leading to a progressive blurring of such borders and a reduction in such physical and (above all) information barriers. Companies remain fundamental decision-making bodies, but they must increasingly come to terms with the general increase in the inter-relationships described above. The growing inter-relationships between functions are removing companies' internal barriers, and the growing inter-relationships with other economic players are forcing companies to deal with a structural instability and a closer interdependence with other economic players.

An analysis of the most recent strategic management studies shows that many authors have already confronted the need to adapt strategic management to the changes that have taken place in the environment, including Drucker (1992), Davidow and Malone (1992), Quinn (1992), Abell (1993), Prahalad and Hamel (1990), Normann and Ramirez (1994), D'Aveni (1994), Nonaka and Takeuchi (1995). However, although they offer some interesting perspectives, they have not led to the emergence of any precise strategic tools capable of replacing or supporting models such as those of the five competitive forces, the business idea and the value chain. In other words, progress has been made in terms of describing and analysing such changes at a mainly qualitative level, but there is a lack of operatively applicable models of analysis and mini-theories. This limitation is all the more evident if we bear in mind that the existence of operational models united with a solid conceptual basis is a determining factor in ensuring that strategic management theories are accepted not only by academics, but also by practising managers: it is enough to think of the portfolio matrices of the Boston Consulting Group, the strategic analysis models proposed by Porter (particularly the model of the five competitive forces and the value chain), and the business idea model developed by Normann (1977) and Coda (1984).

The following chapters will attempt to describe the approaches that can be adopted in order to develop strategic analysis models with reference to the emerging environmental context. However, before concluding this chapter, it is perhaps worth providing a sort of 'identikit' of the type of models we are looking for.

1.4.2 Strategic Analysis Models for the New Economic Paradigm

The examination of the environmental context that has been made in this chapter makes it possible to outline the characteristics that a strategic analysis model should have in order to allow strategic objectives and the sources of competitive advantage to be identified more easily. These characteristics can be summarized as follows:

- an orientation towards final customers;

- the capacity to describe multiple relationships among activities;

- the capacity to describe systemic products and co-production phenomena;

- the capacity to describe the variability in the configuration of companies and value-creating systems;

- the capacity to illustrate strategic choices of inter-firm networks;

- an orientation towards innovation.

Let us consider each of these characteristics in turn. The growing competitive pressures characterizing many sectors are forcing companies to adopt the perspective of their final customers in an attempt to understand what they consider to be the key elements in a supply system and thus determine the value received. Tolerance of procedures and activities that are not justified from the point of view of the creation of value for customers is becoming increasingly limited. This perspective not only implies greater attention towards direct customers, but is driving the companies that intend to play an active role in a given value-creating system to adopt the point of view of the final purchaser of a product (or of significant inter-mediate customers) whose purchasing decision justifies all of the activities carried out by the system as a whole.

In the past, the relationships between economic players were principally bound by the downstream transmission of the value incorporated in the goods. As Normann and Ramírez pointed out (1993), 'Our traditional thinking about value is grounded in the assumptions and the models of an industrial economy. According to this view, every company occupies a position in a value chain. Upstream suppliers provide inputs. The company then adds value to these inputs, before passing them downstream to the next actor in the chain, the customer (whether another business of the final consumer) ... Today, however, this understanding of value is as outmoded as the old assembly line that it resembles and so is the view of strategy that goes with it.'

Although perhaps excessively drastic in their judgements, Normann and Ramírez pick up a very important change in the relationships among activities (and economic players). Sequential relationships connected to the flow of goods along a value chain (or system) are always present and highly relevant, but these are now accompanied by other types of relationships and flows that the traditional models are incapable of identifying. First of all, the spread of systemic products has led to the greater importance of simultaneous or parallel activities. Secondly, the weight of support activities that do not represent part of a sequence of activities from up to downstream has increased. Finally, in a growing number of cases, the goods flows are beginning to detach themselves from other types of flow (especially information flows), thus making it necessary to consider them separately. A good strategic analysis model should adequately represent all these flows and relationships.

As regards systemic phenomena, the models of strategic analysis developed during the 1970s and 1980s were created in the light of what were essentially stand-alone goods and companies that were capable of controlling a considerable portion of the value received by the final users of the goods themselves. The growing importance of systemic products, consisting of various elements based on different technologies and complementary to other products, is tending to diminish that share of the value for the final user that any one company can directly control, and this underlines the importance of co-production and co-participation in the creation of such value. It is therefore necessary to have analytical models that are not just capable of representing the value created by sequences of activities, but also the contribution made by parallel and non-sequential activities belonging to other production processes.

In a period of structural change, it is important to have instruments that make it possible to separate the analysis of value-creating systems from that of the configuration of individual companies. One thing is the reconfiguration of the systems (e.g. the difference between traditional and online book distribution), whereas the make, buy or connect choices that different economic players can make is something else again (e.g. a chain of bookshops that sets up its own publishing activities).

With reference to the strategic analysis of networks, if it is true that, alongside the traditional options of make or buy, the connection option is becoming increasingly frequent, and that a growing number of companies find themselves participating (sometimes exclusively, sometimes not) in inter-firm networks, it is obvious that there is a need for instruments designed not only for the analysis of individual companies, but also for the analysis of sets of companies that are strategically co-ordinated.

As regards the orientations towards innovation, models of strategic analysis are developed on the basis of observations of the real world and attempts to interpret and classify economic phenomena. Precisely because of the way in which they are conceived, it is rare to find strategic analysis models capable of providing any real clues for innovation; at most, they can help users to adopt strategies that are consistent with the analysed reality, but they are unlikely to provide indications as to what should be done to overcome the problems arising from the reality on which they are based.

Nevertheless, this limitation (which is part and parcel of any model, however well conceived) can be at least partially overcome by adopting certain techniques. First of all, the model must be developed on the basis of the analysis of the most advanced and innovative economic realities, even though these may not have much weight at the time it is being developed; it is this that justifies the interest of many authors in the strategies characterizing the information technology sector. It is likely that, precisely because they are in close contact with the technologies that can change our future, the companies operating in this sector more rapidly identify organizational and strategic solutions that are consistent with the new technological paradigm, and that the study of these solutions may be enlightening for many other sectors. Similarly, the so-called 'virtual enterprises' may now account for only 0.01% of all companies but, given that they are the fruit of innovative strategies that are going in the 'direction of history', they also represent an extremely interesting model.

Secondly, a greater orientation towards innovation can be obtained by basing the model on elementary (and where possible universal) units of analysis. In other words, it is necessary to think of the model in terms of economic structures that are not destined to undergo continuous modifications in time and space; it should be based on those elements that are most likely to remain relatively unchanged despite the constantly changing environment of which they form a part.

Finally, it is very important to ensure that the model concentrates on the fundamental objectives pursued by the analysed system. In the case of models of strategic analysis, a fundamental objective can be the satisfaction of the needs of final users, the approval of whom justifies the very existence of value-creating systems.

The characteristics described above require a different approach from that traditionally adopted. It is necessary to assume a strategic perspective that is broadened to include value-creating systems and based on the strategic analysis of economic activities rather than on dishomogeneous aggregates of activities such as those represented by firms or industries.

2

The Value Net

The evolutions described in the previous chapter require strategic tools that are capable of helping companies to define themselves and their competitive environments in a simultaneously wide ranging and flexible manner. In this chapter we shall attempt to respond to this need by suggesting a model (the value net) that assumes value-creating systems as the fundamental object of investigation and activities as the basic units of analysis.

We shall begin by considering the definition of a value-creating system, and then go on to describe the elements in the value net model.

2.1 VALUE-CREATING SYSTEMS

Each time we buy a product or service, we are taking advantage of a value that has been created by a large number of players. The value we receive if we buy, for example, an Alias flowered silk blouse, has been created by the producer of the fabric, the fabric printer, the stylist, the clothing manufacturer, the advertising campaign manager responsible for giving the trademark Alias an image of prestige, and the boutique owner who has suggested how to make the most of the blouse by wearing it with other garments. Our blouse is the sum of the activities of a large number of different companies, even though it is likely that we only know the name of the shop in which it was bought and the company associated with the Alias trademark. Despite this, we actually make a global judgement when we evaluate the blouse. If inadequate finishing or a mistake in the printing means that the flowers fade after just a few washes, we tend to blame the value-creating system as a whole. Our opinion of all products bearing the Alias trademark tends to go down, as does our trust in the shop where the blouse was bought. A mistake made by just one of the players involved in just one of the activities leading to the creation of a silk blouse compromises all of the work done by the entire value-creating system, damaging the image (and, over the long term, also the business) even of those who have done their part properly.

When we buy a technologically complex systemic product, the value-creating system behind it is particularly broad and articulated. The value of a desktop computer is determined by a very large number of activities: the design and production of the microprocessor, the production of the semiconductors and memories, the design of the PC architecture, the styling of the product, the production of the modem allowing network connections, the design of the operating system, the distribution activities involved in bringing the computer to the shop, and the purchasing advice provided by the sales staff. As average users, we know that these activities have been carried out by different companies, even if we only know the names of some of them. However, once again, the judgement we make of the received value is a global judgement. For example, if we have to wait more than a month after being told that the computer would be delivered in a week and then, when it does arrive, we find that it has a different configuration from the one we ordered, we end up judging the whole value-creating system negatively. It does not matter to us whether the delay has been caused by the microprocessor producer, the assembler or the computer shop, nor who was responsible for the wrong configuration. We only know that the system as a whole has not lived up to our expectations.

Furthermore, in the case of a systemic product such as a personal computer, the value associated with it depends not only on the product itself, but also on the availability and quality of a wide range of complementary goods. In other words, the value we receive from the hardware does not depend only on the quality of the hardware itself, but also on the availability of software suitable to our needs, on the presence of service companies that will help us to resolve any problems we may have with our modem and permit us to connect online with the data banks we want to use for our work, on the activities of whoever is responsible for keeping those data banks updated, on the presence of adequate telecommunication infrastructures, and on the quality of the telecommunication services to which we can gain access. The individual companies operating in this enormous value-creating system may be able to decide to concentrate on specific and well-defined activities, but they cannot avoid asking themselves how the activities carried out in the other parts of the system affect the value of what they can provide to the final consumer, or what it is that they can do to change the situation to their own advantage.

Although it is more evident in the most complex competitive systems, the need to insert the activities of one company into a larger value-creating system is the same in all contexts. Whoever produces burglar alarms should consider their installation. The manufacturers of household appliances should consider their repair. Drug wholesalers should be concerned with the competitiveness of independent drug stores. Shoemakers who outsource part of their production should help improve the efficiency of their sub-contractors. When companies concentrate exclusively on themselves and fail to consider their role in the value-creating system in a broader perspective, or the competitiveness of their system in comparison with others, they run a series of risks. They may well find that their efforts to improve their own position within a system are wasted because the system they have chosen is a loser, or that they are creating a value that end users cannot receive or perceive, or that they have simply become pawns subject to the decisions of their more influential and far-sighted system partners.

2.1.1 A Definition of Value-creating Systems

The examples given above highlight the fact that, in the majority of cases, consideration of the activities of individual companies only makes it possible to understand a part of the value received by final customers. They also demonstrate that these customers tend to make judgements at the level of the value-creating system as a whole, rather than at the level of the companies making it up. It is therefore clear that the perspective of strategic analysis needs to be broadened from individual companies to value-creating systems.

The concept of value-creating systems is not new. Albeit with different shades of meaning, it has been used by many authors working in the field of strategic management. Furthermore, it is very clear to those executives who have been able to establish the strategy of their companies within the framework of a broader perspective and have therefore taken care to define the elements determining what the purchasers they are interested in consider to be overall value. It is a concept that has recently been adopted by authors interested in pointing out that the sequential approach based on individual companies, which is typical of the traditional instruments of strategic analysis, only provides a very limited view of new competitive contexts (see sections 1.3 and 1.4). In particular, Normann and Ramírez (1993) have underlined the fact that 'in so volatile a competitive environment, strategy is no longer a matter of positioning a fixed set of activities along a value chain. Increasingly, successful companies do not just add value, they reinvent it. Their focus of strategic analysis is not the company or even the industry but the value-creating system itself, within which different economic actors (suppliers, business partners, allies, customers) work together to co-produce value'.

However, unlike other key concepts in strategic management, the concept of a value-creating system has never been clearly defined. This is probably because it has only very recently been taken into serious consideration as a key element in the development of strategic analysis models. We shall therefore try to make up for this lack by proposing the following detailed definition:

- a value-creating system (VCS) can be defined as a set of activities creating value for customers;

- these activities are carried out using sets of human, tangible and intangible resources;

- they are linked by flows of material, information, financial resources and influence relationships;

- VCSs also include consumption activities, insofar as the value that final customers enjoy is also a function of the way they use and consume the potential value received;

- final customers not only receive and consume the value created, but can also participate in value-creating activities;

- activities may be governed by the market, a hierarchy or intermediate forms of co-ordination (company networks);

- various economic players may participate in a VCS (companies, families, public bodies, non-profit organizations) by taking responsibility for one or more activities;

- an economic player may participate in more than one VCS.

Strategic analysis can be made with reference to a typical VCS (e.g. the PC VCS) by describing the typical characteristics of the companies operating in this competitive context. In other cases, the analysis can be made by describing a specific VCS; for example, the system in which IBM's PC Strategic Business Unit is involved.

Reference to a concrete example may help to clarify the proposed definition. Let us suppose that we want to describe the VCS of a given brand of multimedia PCs (IBM), equipped with modems and sold by the network of IBM concessionaires.

A VCS is a set of activities creating value for customers: the value received by the final purchasers of multimedia PCs is created by means of a long series of activities: microprocessor research and production; the production of semiconductors, memories, modems and other electronic components; computer assembly; video and keyboard design and production; the development of the operating system; the advice given by the concessionaire at the time the machine is chosen and purchased; the installation of the computer ... and so on. Taking a broad perspective, the received value also depends on a series of activities that, although not directly connected with the hardware, significantly affect its usefulness. These activities include the development of software applications, software retail sales, training services related to both the hardware and software, data banks updating, the production of CD ROMs, the supply of online data banks, telecommunications services, etc. It is the combination of all of these activities that makes possible the activity of consumption and the satisfaction of the needs for which the product was bought.

Activities are carried out using sets of resources: the activities listed above can be carried out using sets of human, material and intangible resources. For example, the advice given when choosing a computer is offered by the sales staff of the concessionaire using the support of illustrative material and demonstration software, as well as the concessionaire's premises and equipment (offices, showroom, computers for demonstration purposes, etc.). As we shall see more clearly in Chapter 4, the characteristics of a given activity and the resources necessary for performing it determine its structural attractiveness, which is linked to its capital requirements, cost structure, distinctive skills, entry barriers, the degree of differentiation of its output, and so on.

Activities are linked by various kinds of flows: all these activities are more or less strictly related to each other. Production and distribution activities are connected by the physical flow of goods. It is worth noting that many of the activities linked by physical flows are carried out in parallel (e.g. the production of the video, keyboard and computer base) and only come together at the time of installation.

The entire VCS is also influenced by information flows that go both downstream (e.g. information concerning new products) and upstream (e.g. information relating to problems in using the machines, customer requests, sales data, etc.), or transversally between different activities (e.g. information about innovations relating to the operating system are transmitted well in advance to both hardware and applications software producers).

Other activities, such as research and development, involve relationships of reciprocal influence that are neither sequential nor concerned with the flow of goods, as in the case of the reciprocal influence between Intel and Microsoft, which is intended to ensure the co-ordinated market entry of compatible products. Despite the fact that they are parts of different production processes, the two companies have a close relationship and common interests, as can be seen by the fact that Microsoft launched Windows 95 (software requiring PCs equipped with very powerful microprocessors) immediately after Intel's launch of the Pentium microprocessor. The two actions initiated a process that upgraded the existing PC base in terms of both hardware and software.

VCSs also include consumption activities: consumption activities form part of the VCS because the amount of value customers obtain may depend on how they consume the potential value created. For example, a PC user could use his PC at one-tenth of its potential because of a lack of training on the software used: this could be due to a lack of suitable training courses on the market, to software unfriendliness, or to a general inability to use the PC.

Final customers can participate in value-creating activities: final customers not only consume value, but can also participate in its creation. For example, families and individuals carry out value-creating activities insofar as their purchase of a computer directly involves its transport and installation, and the installation of the software.

Activities may be governed by markets, hierarchies or networks: the different activities may be controlled and co-ordinated by the market (e.g. in the case that IBM buys electronic components on the market without having any preferential relationship with a particular supplier), by a hierarchy (when one player manages and co-ordinates more than one activity), or by means of long-term relationships involving various players. This last situation occurs when the different players establish stable alliances, strategic partnerships, joint ventures, subcontracting agreements, production and distribution licences, networks or outsourcing agreements.

Various economic players may participate in a VCS: the PC VCS involves a large number of different participants, the majority of which are usually but not necessarily companies. Besides final users (families and individuals), the VCS may involve public bodies and non-profit organizations. For example, even if they are managed by private companies, telecommunications services imply the involvement of a large number of public bodies for purposes of authorization, regulation, the allocation of network wavelengths, and so on.

The concept of a VCS is therefore neutral in terms of the relationships that the various players may establish in order to create value. It is possible to have systems in which one single and highly integrated company is directly responsible for almost all of the activities necessary for the creation of value; systems in which value is created by a group of closely co-ordinated companies; systems in which different companies share in the creation of value by interacting with each other via market mechanisms, without establishing any particular collaborative relationships; systems in which final customers actively contribute towards the creation of value and systems where no such participation takes place at all.

An economic player may participate in more than one VCS:

finally, individual players may be involved in more than one VCS, sometimes playing different roles. For example, IBM produces personal computers (mainly by carrying out activities related to designing its PC architecture and assembling the chosen electronic components), but also uses its name and sales structure to operate in sectors ranging from mainframes to computer consultancy services.

2.1.2 Subjectiveness of the Boundaries of Value-creating Systems

Relating the overall value received by an end-user to the VCS rather than the activities of individual companies is clearly useful, but the adoption of this broader perspective immediately raises a number of doubts. Focusing strategic analysis on VCSs could lead to the identification of activity systems that are too large and complex to be analysed; furthermore, from the point of view of individual companies, the adoption of such a broad perspective may mean wasting time on the analysis of activities that the company itself cannot influence in any way.

These risks exist. Pushed to the extreme, the concept of a value-creating system would lead to the identification of sets of activities that are too broad for analysis, and it is also likely that any individual company for which such an analysis is made can play an active role only in relation to a more or less restricted sub-set of activities. Although they undergo continuous changes, and are crossed by flows and relationships of various types, individual companies have boundaries that can be precisely defined (at least in legal terms), whereas those of VCSs are not clearly definable. For example, when we sit in front of a computer and use a CD ROM to consult all of the issues of an international economics journal published over the last ten years, we are making use of a value created by an enormous number of activities: the preparation of the articles and the production of photographs; the research involved in the digitalization of the texts and images; the production of the CD ROM; the research and production activities involved in making the computer and its components; the development of the database search engine and consultation software; and the development of word-processing software for cutting, memorizing and re-processing the parts that interest us. All of this has been made possible thanks to the work of thousands of people in hundreds of companies: journalists, photographers, researchers, salesmen, and skilled and unskilled workers have made use of material and intangible resources in order to allow us (and many other consumers) to consult thousands of articles easily.

However fascinating it may be, a perspective of this kind is of little practical use when it comes to strategic analysis. It is true that VCSs do not have any boundaries, but it is also true that strategic analysts have to define how far they want to go, where to cut the relationships, which activities need to be explored in detail and which can be considered in a more summary manner.

Staying with our example of the personal computer, upstream of the production of the video screen lies the production of cathode tubes, and upstream of this there is the production of cathode tube components, and then the production of the raw materials (glass, special materials, plastics, and so on). We can even go further and consider the production of the machines needed to produce the raw materials and components. However, it is clear that, if the analysis were being made on behalf of a PC assembler, it would be absolutely useless to go so far. It would probably be better to stop with the production of the screens, and leave aside everything upstream of it. In this way, what we are defining is not an objective but a subjective border, which depends on the point of view of the analyst.

In other cases, the same type of considerations may lead to the interruption of the analysis before arriving at the end-user. Let us suppose, for example, that we want to analyse the VCS in which a machine tool producer is involved. In this case, it is obvious that it would be excessive and useless to push the analysis to the point of the consumption of goods containing the metal components produced; it is enough to arrive at the intermediate users.

Furthermore, and thinking once again of our PC manufacturer, it is important to consider the contribution made by the production of software applications or CD ROMs to the creation of value for the final consumer; but the analysis of these macro-activities does not need to go into great detail. In other words, it is important to have an overall reference model but, within the framework of this model, the magnifying glass needs to be used to scrutinize only those parts of the system that the company under investigation can influence in some way.

In conclusion, the absence of objective boundaries means that analysts have to define the 'subjective' borders of a VCS by adopting a position from which the system itself can be observed. Furthermore, the choice of the activities to investigate, as well as the degree of detail of the investigation, not only depend on the point of view of the company for which the analysis is made, but also on the company's strategic objectives. If, for example, our personal computer company intends to act directly or indirectly on the production of software applications, it is necessary to examine in more detail some activities and relationships that would otherwise be considered together.

2.2 THE VALUE NET: A TOOL FOR THE ANALYSIS OF VALUE-CREATING SYSTEMS

Now that we have defined VCSs as sets of activities that co-participate in the creation of value and lead to activities of consumption, and suggested that such systems are objects worthy of investigation, we can describe what we have called the value net: a model specifically developed for such investigations.

The purpose of the value net is to describe VCSs in such a way as to illustrate as clearly as possible:

- the overall VCS in which the individual economic players operate (the perspective is enlarged to include all of the activities and supply chains involved);

- the make/buy/connect choices that the players in the system have made or can make;

- the activities whose control ensures the greatest profitability;

- the activities that add insufficient value in relation to the resources required, or which even subtract value from the system;

- system bottlenecks;

- the possibility of reconfiguring the role of final customers and their involvement in value-creating activities;

- the possibilities for innovation in the system.

On the basis of our definition of VCSs, and the objectives given above, the value net model is characterized by:

- a broad vision of the system as a whole (or a significant part of it) and the fact that it adopts the point of view of the final customer (or a significant intermediate purchaser);

- the use of activities as key elements, regardless (at least in the first instance) of how such activities and resources are divided among the economic players involved.

2.2.1 The Broad Perspective of the Value Net

The development of a competitive strategy in an economic environment that is characterized by highly dynamic changes in the configuration and inter-relationships of the players involved must necessarily begin with an analysis based on a broad perspective. This analysis must be designed to consider not only the activities that are under the control of a given company at a given moment, but also all of the activities involved in the VCS of which that company forms a part (within the limits outlined above). In terms of innovation, it is also very important to look at the system from the point of view of the final customers of the goods it produces, because this makes it easier to identify the real sources of value for the purchaser, as well as any bottlenecks or inadequacies.

This approach makes it possible to overcome the limitations of models that, though they assume a broad perspective, try to describe chains or sets of activities using the traditional concepts of the *firm* and of *industry*, with all the difficulties that this implies in terms of representing the new economic paradigm. In order to highlight the specificity of the value net approach, it may be useful to compare it to Porter's supply chain analysis.

Porter's Perspective in Value System Analysis

One of the most widely used strategic tools is the value system model proposed by Porter (1985) and shown in Figure 2.1.

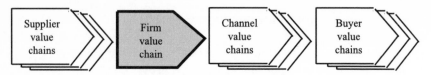

Figure 2.1   The value system. Taken from Porter (1985)

Porter says: 'a firm's value chain is embedded in a larger stream of activities that I term the value system ... Suppliers have value chains (upstream value) that create and deliver the purchased inputs used in a firm's chain. Suppliers not only deliver a product but also can influence a firm's performance in many other ways. In addition, many products pass through the value chain of the channels (channel value) on their way to the buyer. Channels perform additional activities that affect the buyer, as well as influence the firm's own activities. A firm's product eventually becomes part of its buyer's value chain ... Gaining and sustaining competitive advantage depends on understanding not only a firm's value chain but how the firm fits in the overall value system'.

Figure 2.1 and the paragraph quoted above show that Porter's value system refers to a more limited set of activities than our VCS: for example, it does not include those activities that contribute towards the creation of value for the final purchaser, but are not included in the value system itself. The value system model attempts to broaden the strategic perspective and to consider links with both upstream and downstream value chains, but it clearly takes the viewpoint of the company making the analysis, without ever fully considering the end-user's point of view. Furthermore, Porter describes value systems as sets of value chains; i.e. sets of economic players (companies, the business units of diversified

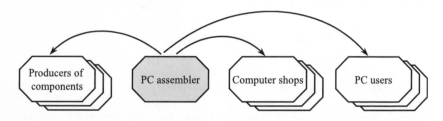

Figure 2.2   The value system perspective

companies, final purchasers). This perspective is schematically illustrated in Figure 2.2, which is based on a value system involving a
PC assembler.

The Value Net Perspective in VCS Analysis

As can be seen from Figure 2.3, the approach of the value net
model is fundamentally different from that of Porter's model. VCSs
are viewed as sets of activities (rather than companies), and these
activities are defined from the final customer's point of view.

Taking the VCS as the focal point of strategic analysis is of
utmost importance for those companies who want to avoid being
trapped in outdated perspectives as to how to compete in their
particular industry, and which understand that there is little sense
in enjoying a strong competitive position and having a high
bargaining power in relation to their direct customers, if they (and
their customers) form part of a losing system.

An interesting example of this is given by McKesson (Normann and
Ramírez, 1995), a major distributor of pharmaceutical drugs to

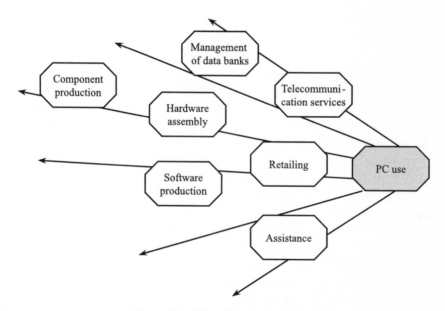

Figure 2.3   The value net perspective

independent pharmacies, which found itself having to redefine its strategy radically at the end of the 1970s. The system of distributing pharmaceutical products in the United States entered a phase of transformation in the 1960s that eventually undermined the previously good competitive position of the company. A growing number of pharmacies had been taken over by chains of drug stores which bought their supplies directly from the manufacturers, thus eliminating the need for a wholesaler. Although it continued to be favoured by the independent pharmacies, McKesson realised that its potential market was rapidly shrinking and that it would have to change its role or resign itself to leaving the business. The company decided on the first option, essentially on the basis of the following proposition: if our customers are not strong enough to survive against the competition, this generally means that the distribution system made up of our organizations is not an efficient system. With this conviction in mind, McKesson decided to offer its customers a set of services and products that would allow them to survive as independents, and adopted the slogan 'Your success is our success'. McKesson put itself in the shoes of the independent pharmacies by analysing their resources, markets and competitive situations. As a result, they realized that in order to provide a useful service, they would have to put the pharmacies themselves in a better position to interact with their own customers, the final purchasers of pharmaceutical products. The company therefore decided to start supplying independent pharmacies with a series of services (information technology solutions, marketing support, the personalization of product labelling, tools for sales analyses, support on shelf positioning, etc.) that were to make a significant contribution towards their competitiveness and help them to match up to the drug store chains. During the 1980s McKesson's moves enabled its VCS to withstand the competition of the chains, although the last decade has seen a further increase in the competitive advantage of the latter and growing difficulties for independent drug stores and their wholesale suppliers. Nevertheless, the McKesson case is an interesting example of what 'assuming a VCS perspective' really means.

Taking the view of the final purchaser inevitably means broadening one's horizons to value systems that may have little to do with the analysed company, but play an important role in the overall creation of value. Particularly in the case of systemic products, this breadth of view makes it possible to highlight bottlenecks, lacks or problems of integration between the offers coming from the various complementary supply chains converging on the activity of consumption. Furthermore, this type of perspective brings any changes in the relative importance of the various activities to light, and thus provides a significant basis for evaluating hypotheses of diversification and alliances.

In this sense, it may be useful to compare two opposed cases: Illycaffè and Apple.

Although taking the point of view of the final customer is particularly important in the case of systemic and complex products, it can also provide an interesting strategic opening even in the case of simple products. Let us take the example of a cup of *espresso* coffee. You probably do not know it but, if you ask for an *espresso* coffee in a high-class restaurant in the United States, you have a 30% possibility of being served coffee produced by a small Italian roasting company. In a market in which sales have been contracting in real terms, Illycaffè doubled its sales between 1993 and 1997; furthermore, despite the fact that Illycaffè coffee costs almost twice as much as the average of its competitors, it is continuing to increase its market share particularly in the upper band of the hotels, restaurants and cafés (Ho.Re.Ca.) segment. What is the reason for this success? One important element is certainly the company's broad strategic perspective, as testified by its company mission statement: 'Our mission is to delight *espresso* consumers throughout the world with a cup of excellent coffee'.

What is it that makes a cup of *espresso* excellent? First of all, it is necessary to use excellent raw materials. The coffee market is dominated by large importers who act as intermediaries between coffee producers and roasting companies. In order to have greater control over the quality of the coffee it buys, Illycaffè has decided to by-pass intermediaries and deal directly with the producers. It has also established collaborative agreements with some selected suppliers with the aim of improving cultivation methods. As the producers of coffee are highly fragmented and difficult to select, Illycaffè organizes an annual prize competition to select the best Brazilian harvest from more than 500 producers. In addition to receiving a cash prize, the winner is also awarded a contract with Illycaffè, a mechanism that allows the company to come into contact with the best producers and evaluate their harvests.

Once having obtained the best raw material, it is then necessary to roast the beans to perfection. A critical phase in this step is to select the beans that enter the production process, because even a small quantity of spoiled beans can compromise the quality of what would otherwise be an excellent batch. Given that there were no machines on the market that could make this selection automatically, Illycaffè developed with Sortex (a British company that specializes in producing sorting machines) an automatic spectrophotometric sorter.

An excellent cup of *espresso* coffee also needs a suitably structured and regulated coffee-making machine. In collaboration with University research centres, Illycaffè studies the process of percolation, with the aim of defining the best methods of grinding and packing the coffee bed, as well as the best water temperature and pressure. Furthermore, the company offers a repair and maintenance service in those parts of the world where the machine producers are not capable of guaranteeing adequate post-sales assistance.

Finally, in order to produce an excellent cup of *espresso*, it is necessary to ensure that the barman uses the coffee machine properly. To guarantee this, Illycaffè carefully selects its sales points in the Ho.Re.Ca. segment, organizes 'coffee master' courses for barmen, and carries out on-site inspections in order to check and support the quality of the service rendered. However, what can you do to guarantee the 'touch' of a skilled barman in Ho.Re.Ca. sales points that cannot be reached by courses or which are characterized by a high staff turnover, and what about those people who use their own small machines for themselves? For these situations, Illycaffè has developed and patented Easy Serving Espresso (ESE, pronounced 'easy'), a single measure of already ground, dosed and packed coffee that is ready to use. Since the beginning, Illycaffè has promoted the use of its own pads (in preference to those of its competitors) by granting coffee machine producers the right to use the ESE patent without charge, asking in exchange only that they respect some technical specifications in the configuration of their machines. This strategy has produced the hoped for fruits and led to the creation of the ESE consortium, which brings together a large number of *espresso* machine producers and roasting companies at international level. The patent has been freely transferred to the consortium, which was constituted with the aim of establishing ESE pads as the market standard. Acceptance of the ESE system is strategically important for Illycaffè insofar as it is essential for the affirmation and penetration of its coffee in markets, such as that of the United States, in which the turnover of barmen is high. Illycaffè says that a good cup of *espresso* depends on the 4 M's of *miscela* (blend), *macinadosatore* (grinder-dispenser), *macchina da espresso* (*espresso* machine) and *mano dell'operatore* (the hand of the barman). Illycaffè's ESE pads guarantee the *mano* of even the least experienced barman.

However, not even all of this is sufficient. According to Illycaffè: 'Good coffee is not enough: a banal cup makes for a banal coffee break', and it was this that led to the idea of the Illy Collection of coffee cups designed by famous designers and intended 'to make an *espresso* break a perfectly expressed aesthetic moment'.

The Illycaffè case is very interesting insofar as it shows that, even in the case of a simple product such as a cup of *espresso*, adopting the point of view of the final consumer can drive a company beyond the borders of the value system to which it belongs. Illycaffè did not limit itself to acting on the coffee value system, but extended its activities to support the value systems involving the *espresso* machine and coffee cup producers that participate in the creation of value for the final customer. In other words, Illycaffè considers and tries to act on all of the value systems converging on *espresso* consumers. This gives us an opportunity to define the concept of a value-creating system in terms that are different from those used above: a VCS can be defined as the set of value systems converging on the final consumer.

A classical example of the difficulty of considering one's own VCS in a broader perspective is given by Apple. Despite the fact that it was for a long time the competitor to look at in terms of quality standards, over the last few years it has continued to lose ground against products based on Microsoft operating systems. If we look at its strategic decisions, it is clear that the company defined itself as a hardware producer and neglected whatever did not fall within the scope of this line of activities, despite the fact that it also possessed an advanced proprietary operating system. This approach, which may have made sense up until the mid-1980s, has proved to be increasingly inadequate. At the beginning of the 1980s Apple chose to develop its own proprietary hardware rather than to adopt the IBM architecture on the grounds that the latter was based on less advanced technology than that which it had developed internally. The company also decided to produce its own computers, not to grant any licences, and to obstruct the birth of clones. This strategy was highly profitable for a few years, and guaranteed Apple high growth rates and the absence of competitors offering products with similar performances.

However, it contained in itself the germs of the subsequent problems of the company. The performance of IBM-compatible computers, originally far behind that of Apple computers, rapidly improved as a result of the efforts and investments made by all the competing companies that had opted for the IBM standard. Within the IBM-compatible world, Microsoft and Intel began to emerge as key companies for the system, up to the point that these two companies now define the Wintel PC standard. Thanks to the considerable progress being made on the hardware front, Microsoft could begin to imitate some of the most appreciated characteristics of Apple systems, and the introduction of Windows and Windows 95 significantly reduced the previously existing gap. However, the most deleterious factor for Apple is the fact that, precisely because of the efforts of dozens of competing companies, the Wintel world now covers more than 90% of the installed base, thus making it much more advantageous for the thousands of small and large software houses in the world to concentrate on products for Wintel rather than Apple PCs. The same can be said for all of the companies that produce PC hardware components.

From the point of view of the final customer, the limitations of the offer of the VCS associated with Apple are clear. The users of Wintel PCs have a virtually unlimited choice in terms of hardware prices, size and performance, the availability of accessories and complementary products (modems, mouses, CD readers, etc.) and software, as well as in terms of services and training courses. Furthermore, Wintel computers satisfy the preference of consumers for perfectly compatible products, as described in the first chapter. On the contrary, Apple users find a decidedly more limited range of hardware and software products on the market place, and this situation is aggravated by the fact that the performance of Apple computers is no longer so much greater than that of Wintel machines.

If we interpret the errors made by Apple in terms of the categories presented in this chapter, the company became the leader of a losing VCS. In the short term, its refusal to grant licences increased its contractual power in relation to its customers but, in the long term, led to an increasingly apparent lack in the supply of Apple-compatible software, accessories and complementary products. The advantages of the hardware line were sufficient to compensate for the differences on the other fronts for a certain period but, once this advantage had become smaller, a growing number of final consumers began to see the Apple system as no longer competitive.

The example of Apple shows that broadening the strategic perspective from the point of view of an individual company instead of that of the final consumer may lead companies to concentrate only on the value system to which it belongs and to neglect all of the complementary value systems converging on the final user. This can be very dangerous insofar as the value actually received by the final consumer is not the equivalent of the potential value created by each complementary system, but depends on the interaction of complementary products and services. For example, in the case of Illycaffè, the potential value of an excellent blend of coffee would be lost if no suitable *espresso* coffee machines were available on the market. Similarly, the enormous potential advantage of Apple's hardware and operating system is partially annulled by the absence of a sufficiently wide offer in terms of software applications.

2.2.2 Unbundling Strategic Thinking: Activities as Key Elements of Strategic Analysis

Adopting a broad strategic perspective does not mean that it is necessary to control all the activities making up a VCS. It is in fact very unlikely that any individual company possesses all the skills and resources necessary to deal with an entire system regardless of whether it is intended to satisfy simple (a cup of *espresso*) or complex consumption activity (a networked multimedia PC). Even if it did, it may in any case choose to concentrate on only some of the activities involved. Having identified a VCS, it is therefore necessary to identify the activities that a company intends to control directly, those it prefers to leave to others, and those it decides to control indirectly or in partnership with others. In other words, it is necessary to choose whether to make, buy or connect. One starting point in this respect is certainly the history and skills of the company, but what are the considerations governing the broadening or reduction of its strategic scope?

Let us return to the case of Illycaffè. Starting from the nucleus of its coffee roasting activities, this company has selectively extended its strategic scope in such a way as to control (directly or indirectly) other activities considered to be critical to the creation of value for the final user. Within this framework, and often in collaboration with other specialized players, Illycaffè conducts research studies concerning cultivation techniques and the technologies incorporated in roasting and *espresso* machines. It organizes training courses for barmen. It inspects and supports the activities of its sales points. It has conceived and organized the idea of the Illy Collection, turning to external designers and manufacturers in order to produce the cups. This is therefore not a case of vertical integration, but a selective extension of the strategic scope focused on those activities that were poorly performed but critical for the creation of customer value. In many cases, this induced Illycaffè to undertake support activities (research and training) in order to sustain other value-creating activities (the production of *espresso* machines or the preparation of a cup of coffee). At other times, Illycaffè has intervened by replacing other players (by providing post-sales services for *espresso* machines) or modifying its own offer (by marketing its ESE coffee pads). In relation to the ESE pads, it is worth underlining the fact that these incorporate not only the roasted product, but also the knowledge and skills used by an expert barman when he grinds, doses and compacts the coffee mixture as he should. This selective extension of the strategic scope of Illycaffè is illustrated in Figure 2.4, where the grey nodes represent the activities carried out by Illycaffè in its VCS.

The case of Illycaffè clearly shows the importance of what can be called unbundled strategic thinking. The company did not allow itself to be trapped by conventional ideas as to what a coffee roasting company should do, but decided to leverage on its competencies by undertaking selected activities usually controlled by the other players in the VCS. Cultivation techniques are usually considered to be the responsibility of growers; the technology relating to *espresso* machines is the responsibility of the companies that produce them; the quality of bar services is normally something

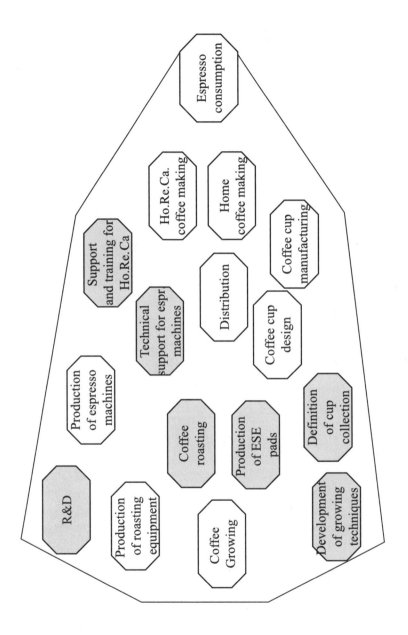

Figure 2.4   Illycaffè's VCS

that is left to bar managers; and the design of cup collections is certainly not a typical activity of coffee producers. However, Illy-caffè clearly does not take what others should do for granted. It conceives its VCS as an unbundled set of activities rather than a set of players, where 'who does what' is not taken for granted; the borders between the players are the point of arrival and not the starting point of strategic analysis.

It should now be clear why the value net model takes activities rather than companies as the key elements of strategic analysis. Management studies have included activities as the objects of strategic analysis for some time, but the traditional models concentrate on bundles of activities (regardless of whether these are represented by companies or industries), and it is only when a detailed analysis is made that they are capable of identifying the value-creating activities existing inside a company. The fact that the starting point of traditional models always conceives these activities as part of a bundle means that they are putting the cart before the horse: the definition of the bundle of activities that a company intends to carry out should be the final and not the starting point of a strategic analysis.

In addition to proposing a broader strategic perspective from the point of view of the final consumer, the value net therefore proposes a change in method. Instead of conceiving economic activity in terms of a set of economic players who internally perform a set of activities, it considers it in terms of the set of activities that create value for final customers. It is obvious that these activities are carried out by a number of interacting players, but 'who does what' is only considered afterwards. This is why we suggest that our method offers a means of making a strategic analysis that is free of pre-established assumptions.

2.3 THE ELEMENTS OF THE VALUE NET MODEL

We have described VCSs as sets of activities that jointly participate in the creation of value by using sets of tangible, intangible and human resources. We have also shown how these activities are tied to each other by flows of material, information, financial resources and influence relationships.

Using the forms of representation and conventions elaborated by

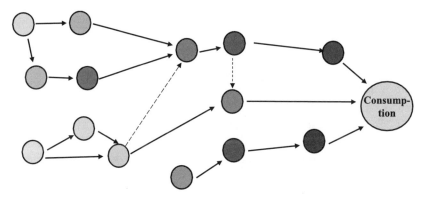

Figure 2.5　The value net

the theory of graphs, the activities of the value net can be seen in the form of nodes, and the relationships between them in the form of arcs. In the value net model, the nodes represent value creation or consumption activities, each of which may have its own specific resources or share them with others. The arcs describe the significant ties and relationships between the activities and, at various times, may represent flows of materials or services, flows of information, or more generic influence relationships between the nodes.

Starting the representation of a VCS from the activities that make it up (and their related resources), instead of beginning with the value chain of the players participating in it, can encourage a greater degree of strategic innovation, because it can avoid the risk that the institutional and organizational boundaries in which the nodes or groups of nodes find themselves at any particular historical moment are taken for granted.

From the point of view of analysis, this approach has the further advantage of making it easier to compare the choices made by the different competitors in a given market, and thus clarifying whether the differences are due to a different VCS configuration or differences in positioning within substantially similar VCSs.

2.3.1　Value Net Nodes

Every VCS can potentially be divided into a practically unlimited number of nodes because of the large number of activities involved in the creation of even relatively simple goods. However, in order to make a strategic analysis, it is obviously important to work at an appropriate level of aggregation. This means grouping together all the activities that can be considered as a unitary set insofar as, from a strategic point of view, it is not useful to distinguish them even if they may be technically different.

At the highest level of disaggregation, one node in the value net represents a set of economically inseparable activities that are worth considering as a whole in terms of economic analysis because they can be more conveniently carried out jointly, whatever the strategy adopted by the economic player in question. In this regard, it is worth clarifying the difference between our approach and that used by transaction cost theory, which assumes that transactions are elementary units of analysis. In the theory of transaction costs, a transaction is defined as the transfer of a product through a technologically separable interface and, from this definition, it follows that activities which cannot be technologically separated exist between transactions. Although analogous, our definition of a node is different. At the highest level of disaggregation, a value net node represents a set of activities that cannot be separated economically. In other words, although they may be technologically separable, these activities are worth considering as a whole in terms of economic analysis because they can be more conveniently carried out jointly whatever the strategy adopted by the economic player in question. Let us suppose that, among other things, the production of tin cans involves cutting the metal sheets and welding together the cut shapes. Cutting and welding can be done using different machines in different phases of the working process, and can thus be considered technologically separable activities. However, it is not worth separating them from an economic point of view if the only way of performing them economically is to join them in a single and continuous production process. They are technologically separable but economically inseparable, and should therefore be considered jointly in VCS analysis.

The separability (or aggregability) of activities may change over time in both technological and economic terms, particularly as a result of organizational and technological evolutions. This means that activities which can be distinguished at a given moment may well need to be subsequently aggregated or further broken down.

The identification of all economically separable activities represents the highest level of disaggregation in the analysis of a VCS. However, in many cases, it may be more appropriate to group them further by making one node of economically separable activities. VCSs are very broad and extended, which makes aggregated analysis inevitable in the case of those activities that are of no direct interest to the company making the analysis. For example, a semiconductor manufacturing company may decide to undertake a detailed analysis of all of the activities of semiconductor design and production, as well as all of those that are contiguous to them, in such a way as to distinguish all of the economically separable activities in this part of the VCS. This disaggregated analysis can then be put in a much broader framework aimed at describing the entire system, including those activities that are described in a more aggregate manner because they are more distant from the company's sphere of interest.

What we have said above makes it clear that nodes cannot be defined objectively, because their definition necessarily depends on the subjective choices made by whoever carries out the analysis. This underlines how delicate and crucial this phase is if we want to make more than a superficial analysis of a VCS. In general, it can be said that nodes must be:

- sufficiently disaggregated to allow the identification of the fundamental choices of internalization, externalization or connection that the players in a system can make;

- sufficiently aggregated to ensure that the representative model of reality does not become too complex and therefore hardly usable.

Particularly in the case of those parts of the VCS for which we want to make a detailed analysis, it may be useful to bear in mind the following suggestions for ensuring the appropriate degree of disaggregation:

- separate the activities carried out by different players in the system or those that are carried out by economically distinct players in analogous VCSs;

- separate the activities leading to the creation of a finished good (a product or a service) that is at least potentially sellable (even if not usable) on its own (e.g. car headlights, computer microprocessors, quality control of cloths);

- separate the activities which, although difficult to associate with specialized players, can be carried out by different players operating in the system (e.g. supermarket shelf management, which can be carried out by an external supplier or the supermarket itself);

- separate distinct activities that have a different nature (e.g. the design and production of microprocessors);

- separate distinct activities that have different structural characteristics: for example, the activities of shoe assembly may be separated into different groups (and therefore different nodes) depending on the complexity of the assembly, because this affects important structural features, such as the degree of specialization of machinery and know-how, economies of scale, the possibility of differentiating the offer on the part of specialized players and so on;

- aggregate those activities that are not included in the above.

As we shall see in section 2.4, VCS activities can be of various kinds. In order to make the representation of the system more legible, the different types of activities are represented by graphically different nodes. We shall discuss this after having described the value net arcs.

2.3.2 The Arcs in the Value Net

The majority of traditional strategic management models have been conceived by thinking above all of the physical flow of goods linking different economic players. However, in this 'era of information', the acquisition of competitive advantages is increasingly tied not so much and not only to a different configuration of the flow of goods, but also and above all to differences in the way in which information and information flows are managed. The value net model is not based on a particular type of flow, therefore it is possible to represent simultaneously all the flows that are important for the analysis, whether these are of goods, information, money or reciprocal influence relationships.

After having used nodes to represent the activities making up the analysed VCS, it is worth connecting these nodes by means of arcs representing their significant relationships. It is not necessary to represent all the flows existing within a given system simultaneously, but only those that are important for the particular analysis that is being made. When we are comparing two alternative systems that differ in ways in which they manage information flows, it is interesting to highlight them and the paths taken by the information. On the other hand, if the information flows existing in the system are of no particular interest (or do not form a part of the analysis that is being made) they do not need to be represented.

In general, it is possible to make suggestions concerning flows that are similar to those already made in relation to the degree of disaggregation of the nodes:

- highlight the flows that determine a competitive advantage;

- highlight the flows that have a different configuration in alternative VCSs;

- highlight the flows corresponding to a bottleneck in the system, or which are difficult to perform or lead to a loss of value;

- try to ensure that the model does not become too complex, and thus avoid representing flows that are not significant.

In order to make it easier to interpret the representation of the VCS, it is also worth using different ways of representing the different relationships between activities. Figure 2.6 shows the symbols that will be used in this book.

It is worth underlining the fact that influence relationships can be traced to a combination of information flows capable of influencing other flows or activities. One example of this is the manner in which Microsoft can influence the development of software applications by independent software houses. Microsoft provides software developers with information and the technical specifications of all of the variations made at the level of the operating system in such a

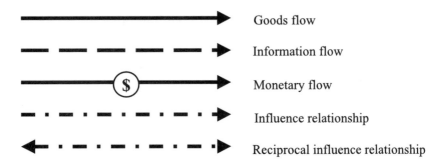

Figure 2.6   The representation of the relationships between value net activities

way that these can be taken into account in the design of applications. In this case, the information flow is not one-way because the
software houses can ask Microsoft for clarifications, provide
feedback and draw attention to any problems that may exist in
relation to the way in which the operating systems function.
However, the influence that Microsoft has over software producers
is not limited to the exchange of technical information. For
example, for months before the launch of Windows 95, Microsoft
stimulated interest by means of indiscretions, publications and
advance news in the specialized press and at congresses in an
attempt to transmit to the operators in the industry a sense of the
importance of the new system, thus driving them to develop compatible software applications well before it was actually put on the
market. In addition to various technical problems, the repeated
postponement of the launch date can be explained by Microsoft's
clear intention to arouse interest, create expectations and give the
independent software houses the time to complete their own
projects on this platform.

This example highlights how slight is the difference between
information flows and influence relationships. In the rest of this
book, we will use the term information flows to identify continuous
and relatively structured transmissions of information (e.g. the
transmission of sell-out data from a salespoint to production activities), and influence relationships to indicate the often interactive
and generally destructured exchange of information carried out not
only to communicate, but also and above all to influence the non-
routine decisions of the people it is intended for.

2.4 THE CLASSIFICATION OF ACTIVITIES

In order to obtain an economically meaningful subdivision, the activities in a VCS, should be classified on the basis of their nature. In this regard, the value net method proposes a classification that is partially different from those that have so far been most widely used in the field of managerial economics and strategic management studies. In particular, it is different from the classical division between direct and indirect activities, as well as from the classification based on the separation of primary and support activities proposed by Porter (1985). The reason for this diversity is not only a different interpretation of the nature of the activities themselves, but also and above all the use of a different analytical perspective. All of the classifications so far proposed in the management literature have been developed by making reference to individual companies. For example, the classification of primary and support activities proposed by Porter (1985) is based on the value chain of firms and distinguishes the activities relating to production, distribution, sales and after-sales services from those designed to support these activities. This approach is illustrated in Figure 2.7.

The models that concentrate on individual firms do not allow an overall view of the set of activities leading to the creation of value. Furthermore, they involve obvious difficulties when it comes to

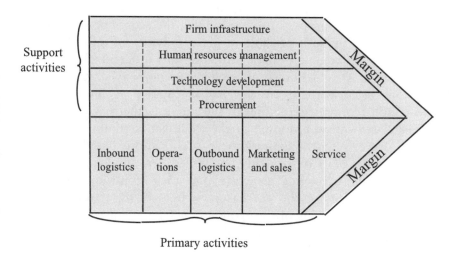

Figure 2.7 Subdivision of value chain activities. Taken from Porter (1985)

representing cases in which the economic player analysed does not entirely undertake a sequential block of activities. This situation exists, for example, when a company is directly involved with only some non-consecutive phases of production and so materials enter and exit many times. In the same way, traditional models do not make it possible to create an adequate representation of the originality of companies which, like Illycaffè, not only perform activities that are specific to their own part of their own value system (coffee roasting), but also selected activities in other phases of the same system (coffee growing and distribution) and in other value systems converging on the final customer (*espresso* machines and coffee cups).

Focusing on companies also leads to the classification of activities on the basis of their position in the value chain of individual companies, rather than on the basis of their economic structure and their contribution towards the creation of value for the final user. Let us take the example of sales force training activities. If these are carried out inside the company that is interested in training its own sales force, they are classified as support activities (as activities related to human resource management) but if exactly the same activities are carried out by a company specialised in training, they are considered to be the primary activities of the latter (operational activities). We feel that the habit of classifying the same activities differently on the basis of a company's make or buy choices is misleading in the context of economic analysis. A classification that is useful for the purpose of understanding the economic structure of a VCS should make it possible to place activities of different kinds and with a different economic structure into different classes. This classification should not be affected by a company's make or buy decisions because these are not *per se* capable of modifying the nature and economic structures of the activities themselves.

The classification proposed by the value net methodology has the aim of overcoming the limitations of classifications based on individual enterprises. Consequently, activities are subdivided on the basis of their economic structure and their contribution to the creation of value for the purchaser, without being affected by the make or buy decisions of the economic players involved (see Figure 2.8).

The activities carried out in VCSs can be divided into three broad groups:

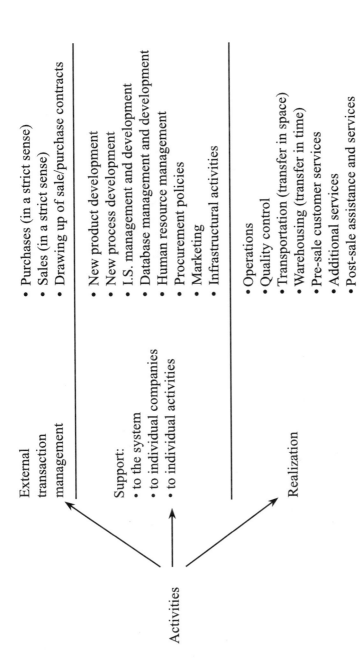

Activities

External
transaction
management
- Purchases (in a strict sense)
- Sales (in a strict sense)
- Drawing up of sale/purchase contracts

Support:
- to the system
- to individual companies
- to individual activities
- New product development
- New process development
- I.S. management and development
- Database management and development
- Human resource management
- Procurement policies
- Marketing
- Infrastructural activities

Realization
- Operations
- Quality control
- Transportation (transfer in space)
- Warehousing (transfer in time)
- Pre-sale customer services
- Additional services
- Post-sale assistance and services

Figure 2.8   The classification of value net activities

• realization (i.e. the activities aimed at the physical creation of a good and its transfer in time and space);

• support (the activities aimed at maintaining or improving the effectiveness and efficiency of other activities and which do not intervene in the physical production of individual products or services);

• external transactions management (the activities aimed at managing and controlling the transactions arising in the presence of exchanges between distinct economic players).

The differences between these classes can be illustrated by making reference to the evolution of economic systems. As we have seen in Chapter 1, economic progress can be interpreted as a result of the affirmation of two types of phenomena: the growing specialization of economic players (leading to the need for increasingly sophisticated activities aimed at managing transactions) and the shifting of resources from realization to support activities, with the significant effects that this has had on the productivity of resources in evolved economic systems.

2.4.1 Realization Activities

These are all the activities aimed at the creation of goods or services and their transfer in time and space. They include physical/technical transformation, the transport of goods (transfer in space), warehouse management (transfer in time), pre-sales customer services (e.g. the study of a furnishing system by an architect who works for a furniture shop), and the supply of principal and accessory or post-sales services.

The Nature of Realization Activities

Realization activities contribute physically to the supply of a good (a product or service), with a given configuration, in a certain place and at a specific time. They also include quality control activities because these influence the quality and the number of defective products put on the market, and thus have a direct impact on the average physical characteristics of the goods delivered to consumers.

As they contribute physically to the supply of a good, realization activities must be carried out every time an additional unit is produced or, as in the case of sample quality control, are proportional to the produced volumes.

Flows Connecting Realization Activities

Realization activities can be tied to each other by a physical flow of goods. In particular, such a flow is present in the case of the production of goods, whereas it may be partially or totally absent in the case of the supply of services. The nodes representing realization activities may therefore be connected by arcs representing not only information flows or influence relationships, but also an actual flow of goods.

The Costs Arising from Realization Activities

Looking at the costs of realization activities in terms of traditional cost classifications, they may be either direct (material buying, direct manpower) or indirect (indirect manpower, depreciation). Realization activities account for most of the variable costs sustained by companies (materials, outworking, the transport of purchase and sales), and also involve fixed costs (manpower and depreciation). If we divide fixed costs into structural costs, development costs and depreciation, realization activities affect structural costs and depreciation, but not fixed development costs*.

2.4.2 Support Activities

Support activities aim at improving the effectiveness and efficiency of other activities, but do not intervene in the physical production

---

*Reference is made here to the classification of fixed costs proposed by Brunetti, Coda and Favotto (1984). In particular, fixed structural costs can be defined as costs related to the production capacity of a company, such as labour costs, maintenance, rents, tax consultancy and so on. Fixed development costs are those related to activities aimed at encouraging the qualitative and quantitative development of a company, such as advertising, research and development, and training.

of individual products or services. They include research and development, design (of both products and processes), human resource management (the search for, and the selection, organization, training and control of personnel), the development of information systems, the definition of procurement policies, marketing, and infrastructural activities (internal administration, finance, legal affairs, the management of relationships with public bodies, planning, etc.). Infrastructural activities do not include the administrative management of relationships with customers or suppliers or the legal definition of contracts because, as we shall see, these should be considered activities aimed at transaction management.

The Nature of Support Activities

As we have seen in Chapter 1, support activities play an increasingly important role in advanced economies because the competition between economic players is increasingly based on their capacity to establish effective and efficient systems of realization, whereas the carrying out of realization activities is becoming less and less resource-consuming. One example of this is the current evolution of grocery retail distribution. In the past, this was characterized by the presence of small and generally family-run salespoints with hardly any product or process innovation, and the personnel almost exclusively carried out activities relating to service realization (the display of goods and customer service) and the management of transactions (order making, delivery checking, management of payments and cash collection). The competition between the different shops was mainly based on their location and the ability of the personnel to render an efficient service and establish good personal relationships with customers. Large-scale distribution has changed the rules of the game in this sector by shifting the stress to support activities. A significant proportion of the resources is now involved in carrying out activities such as marketing, the definition of procurement policies, and the development of information systems aimed at improving the effectiveness and efficiency of the resources used in the realization of the service and the management of transactions. These activities have made it possible to reduce significantly the resources used in the activities of realization and transaction management.

If there has been a decided shift from realization to support activities in a relatively low technology sector such as grocery distribution, in some hi-tech industries or industries with a high information content, support activities represent almost all the activities carried out. In this regard, we can think of the production of software, pharmaceutical or biotechnological products, television and cinema productions, and so on. In some industries, there is an almost total absence of realization activities. For example, in the case of software distributed via the Internet all the costs can be attributed to activities such as design, marketing and the preparation of manuals, whereas there are no costs for the reproduction or physical distribution of the product.

However, what is the mechanism that makes it possible for support activities to improve the effectiveness and efficiency of the other activities? As explained in section 1.2.1, support activities are directly aimed at increasing the stock of intangible resources (especially information and knowledge), which greatly influences the effectiveness and productivity of a company or a VCS. Realization activities also generate a certain amount of information/knowledge as a by-product, but this is necessarily incremental and unlikely to cause any significant change in the way these activities are carried out. By favouring the more rapid accumulation of knowledge, support activities can originate virtuous circles in which increased productivity leads to an increase in the resources available for support activities, and therefore a further increase in knowledge and productivity.

One fundamental difference between support and realization activities is that the latter have to be performed every time an additional unit of the good or service is supplied, whereas the former are carried out in a way that is relatively independent of the volumes actually produced.

The relationship between the amount of resources used and the volumes produced is therefore much less direct than in the case of realization activities. In this regard, it is worth distinguishing two fundamental components of support activities. The first is structural and associated with the complexity of the realization and transaction management activities that need to be supported; for example, current administrative activities, or activities related to the current management of personnel or information systems. The second and sometimes very substantial component is related to the predisposition and development of resources intended to improve the effectiveness and efficiency of the realization and transaction management activities themselves. These include product and process research and development, interventions aimed at modifying the configuration of a company's information system, the preparation of new advertising campaigns, market research studies and personnel training. The resources used in this second area of activities are not so much proportional to the production capacity of the system, but more to its development and the will to modify it. Returning to the example of the large-scale retail distribution of grocery products, the personnel dedicated to shelf restocking (a realization activity) must be proportional to the amount of business done by the salespoint, whereas the resources dedicated to the development and management of the information system vary over time and markedly increase whenever changes or innovations are introduced.

Although not directly participating in the realization of a product or service, support activities may be fundamental to their physical production (e.g. the development of changes in product design that improve its function for the user) and also provide it with an immaterial value (e.g. an advertising campaign that raises its status).

In other cases, support activities do not lead to variations in the offer that are perceptible to purchasers, but which nevertheless serve as a basis for containing costs and improving the way in which the company works. These include the activities aimed at favouring the good functioning of other nodes in the system, such as process design (innovations in production processes as well as the re-engineering of other types of processes), the management of human resources (in terms of selection, training, motivation and co-ordination), the development of information systems (which may be activity-specific or integrated and related to the company as a whole), the preparation and updating of activity-specific or company-wide databases, and infrastructural activities.

There are also cases in which a particular support activity can have an impact on both the offer perceived by the purchaser and the functioning and costs of the organization; e.g. the re-engineering of a business process aimed at shortening delivery times to final customers and simultaneously eliminating sub-activities made superfluous by technological evolutions and process restructuring. These kinds of support activity often include the definition of procurement policies, which can have an effect on the value perceived by the customer, as well as on the costs sustained by an individual economic player and by the VCS as a whole. As far as this last point is concerned, procurement policies should not be confused with the purchasing activities carried out within the framework of specific procurement policies, just as marketing activities should not be confused with sales activities. In the strict sense, purchasing and sales fall within the category of transaction management activities, which will be dealt with later. This situation occurs in all the cases in which a customer can appreciate the quality of the components incorporated into the finished product and, in some cases (such as Loro Piana fabrics for outerwear, Shimano gears for mountain bikes or Intel microprocessors for personal computers), also judge the final product on the basis of these.

Flows Connecting Support Activities

Arcs can be drawn between the nodes representing support activities and the other nodes making up a VCS in order to illustrate influence relationships and/or information, but obviously these activities cannot be involved with physical flows destined for the final customer. In this regard, it is worth mentioning that support activities can sometimes produce physical goods but, as these are not destined for final customers, they must be considered as informational supports rather than goods in the true sense of the word. Examples of these are the models produced by the model workshop of a shoe manufacturer or the prototypes created by the R&D department of a car producer. These are objects that are not intended for sale and so, rather than goods, they can be considered as informational supports that could be totally or partially replaced by others: e.g. the physical prototype of the bodywork of a car could be replaced by a three-dimensional computerized image.

When a support activity more or less directly influences many of the nodes within a system, it is possible to avoid illustrating influence relationships in order to avoid making the model over-complicated. Here we can take marketing activities as an example because these have an impact not only on the creation of value, but also on the ability of the economic players involved to take advantage of this value. However, in the majority of cases, the fact that marketing activities are more or less directly involved with a large number of nodes means that the explicit representation of their influence relationships would excessively complicate the picture without offering any specific elements that may be useful for analysing and understanding the system itself.

A Classification of Support Activities

Not all support activities have the same type of impact on realization and transaction management activities. In relation to this, it is possible to identify three sub-categories:

- the activities that support individual activities;

- the activities that support individual companies;

- the activities that support the system as a whole.

Support for individual activities has a limited range of action and is highly specific; one example of this is the production of metal die-casting moulds or the shoe lasts (metal profiles specifically made for every model and every size of shoe) used for cutting leather. It is worth underlining the fact that the direct relationship between node support activities and the supported activity does not necessarily mean that both need to be carried out by the same economic player. In the production of shoes, for example, shoe manufacturers often outsource leather cutting but retain the activity of last production. It is often the case that the control of node-supporting activities allows indirect control over outsourced activities.

The majority of support activities are not aimed at a particular node, but sustain a number of activities of different kinds. This is the case of marketing, which is aimed at defining the configuration of the product system offered and influencing the perception that purchasers have of it. Marketing is also becoming increasingly involved in the activity of market creation by providing informative inputs and influencing a large number of VCS activities. Another essentially transversal activity is the management and development of information systems, particularly in the case of integrated

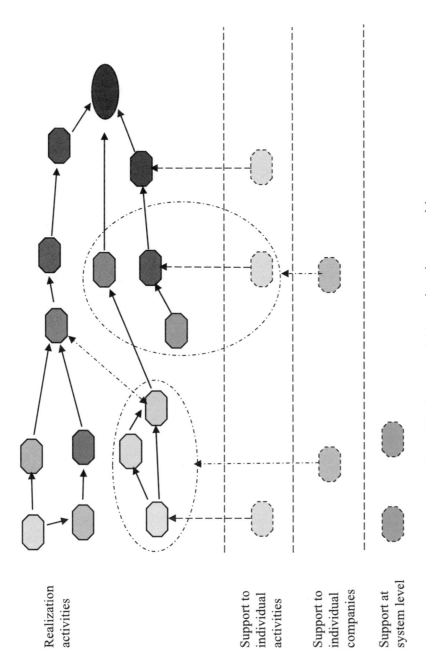

Realization
activities

Support to
individual
activities

Support to
individual
companies

Support at
system level

Figure 2.9 Support activities in the value net model

company or inter-organizational systems. Similar considerations can also be made in relation to the development of new products or processes, which have a great impact on both realization and marketing activities.

The support activities that have relationships with a multiplicity of nodes can be managed at the level of an individual company or at the level of the VCS (or a substantial part of it). The level at which it is actually managed depends not only on the type of activity, but also and above all on the strategies pursued within the analysed system.

Many of the activities that we have called infrastructural (such as, administration, financial management, legal affairs and general management) are typically carried out at company level.

Other activities, such as research and development, the design and control of processes, marketing, the management and development of information systems, the definition of procurement policies and the development of human resources, can be managed at either level, depending on the case. In the past, most support activities were carried out at company level, with each company concentrating on supporting its own activities by developing new products, modifying its production processes, establishing marketing strategies aimed at improving the acceptance of its products by its own direct customers, and by developing its own human resources. However, as was pointed out in the first chapter, this model does not provide a very good description of many of the more innovative and dynamic strategic projects that characterize the current economic context. An increasing number of companies are now orienting themselves towards carrying out support activities at the system level rather than at the level of the nodes they control directly. One of the companies that has been in the forefront of this development is Benetton, and it is no accident that it is a frequently cited example in many management studies. The fundamental difference between Benetton and the traditional producers of wool outerwear is that its strategy has been developed at VCS level by decentralizing many of its realization activities and controlling the entire system by means of support activities designed at system level: the management of advertising campaigns, the development of collections, and the management and development of the Benetton information system. The destiny of the entire VCS that has been formed around Benetton depends on the good functioning of these activities.

Unlike its firm-based counterparts, the VCS-based perspective makes it possible to distinguish clearly those activities designed to provide a company with internal support, and those that are also aimed at other nodes that are not managed by the economic player under consideration, and thus provides instruments that make it easier to describe emerging economic phenomena, such as virtual or lean companies. Virtual (or highly decentralized) companies are specifically characterized by the fact that they internally carry out support activities designed to operate at system level and their realization activities are highly decentralized. Many company cases suggest that the control of support activities positively correlates with the capacity of an economic player to gain a significant share of the revenues received by the system as a whole.

The Costs Arising from Support Activities

Carrying out support activities mainly involves bearing fixed structural costs (for those activities that are carried out continuously and are necessary for the functioning of the company structure) and fixed development costs (for those activities oriented towards the development and/or modification of one or more elements in the system, such as research and development, process re-engineering, the training of human resources, and the management of advertising campaigns). When a support activity is outsourced, it is possible that the contract with the supplier includes a variable payment, as happens in the case of stylists who design collections for clothing manufacturers and normally receive a royalty on sales. However, the presence of a variable cost takes nothing away from what has been said above concerning the absence of a direct relationship between volume sales and support activities. The activities are still not proportional to the number of products sold even if the supplier accepts sharing the risk with the purchasing company and is paid in proportion to sold volumes.

2.4.3 External Transaction Management Activities

External transaction management activities exist when realization and support activities are managed by legally distinct economic players. They essentially consist of purchasing and selling activities in the strict sense of the terms, and therefore exclude support activities such as marketing or the definition of procurement policies (which define the framework within which buying and selling activities are carried out).

These purchasing and selling activities include the solicitation of customer orders, contractual negotiations with individual purchasers or sellers within the ambit of the predefined marketing or procurement policies, the placing and management of orders, the chasing up of deliveries, the drawing up of supply contracts, verification that the terms of the purchasing or sales contracts are being adhered to (e.g. that the quantities indicated in the delivery note correspond to those actually ordered and delivered, or that the prices and terms of payment correspond to those agreed), the handling of protests concerning the respect of the contracts, the management of credit collection and payments, and solicitations for payment.

We have frequently stressed that the value net is intended to provide an instrument for describing VCSs regardless (at least initially) of the way in which the economic players have divided the activities to be carried out. This approach implies that, at least in the first phase of analysis, it is not possible to place transaction management activities because the borders between the different players involved are still not clear. It is therefore possible to limit the representation of VCSs to the nodes representing realization and support activities, with the implicit understanding that transaction management nodes will arise every time there is an exchange between legally distinct players.

On the other hand, when passing from the analysis of a VCS to the analysis of an individual economic player (and therefore defining its borders), it is necessary to include purchasing and sales activities. This is shown in Figure 2.10, which highlights the transaction management activities arising from the exchanges made between a hypothetical company, ABC Corp., and others.

The Nature of Transaction Management Activities

Transaction management activities arise only insofar as economic specialization leads to the exchange of goods between distinct economic players (companies, families, public bodies, non-profit making organizations).

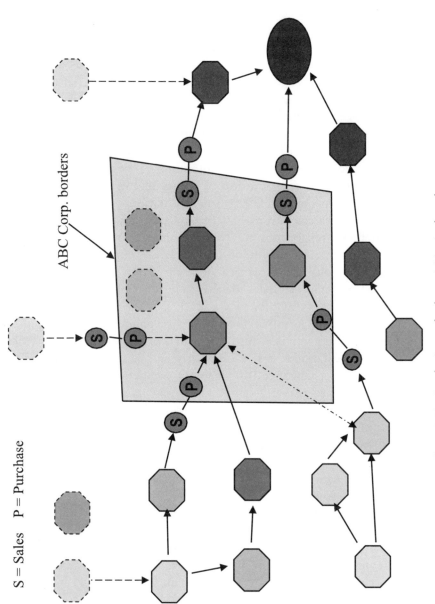

S = Sales P = Purchase

ABC Corp. borders

Figure 2.10 Purchasing and sales activities in the value net

It is therefore possible to have VCSs in which these activities are not carried out, such as in the case of self-consumption. The specialization of advanced economic systems means that certain activities (such as food production, clothes making, entertainment, the education of children, etc.) are carried out by specialized economic players. This system necessarily gives rise to purchase and sales activities between families and companies, as well as between the different companies involved in the various phases of production. Nevertheless, the production of many goods and services for families does not necessarily involve purchase and sales activities; it is possible that the creation of goods takes place entirely within the context of the family, which thus internally carries out the activities of the creation and consumption of value. In a system of this type, there would be no purchasing or sales activities.

To say that transaction management activities (and the specialization that they presuppose) may not be present in a VCS is not the same as saying that this type of activity is not important. Economic specialization and the activities deriving from it can in fact be considered essential elements for the good functioning and efficiency of the system as a whole. Within a VCS, it is the presence of specialized economic players (whether these are connected by long-term or simply market relationships) that makes it possible to identify 'badly managed' nodes easily, thus driving the players involved to improve their performance (by means of competitive pressure or the demands of other players) or, in the worst cases, leading to their expulsion from the system and their replacement with other players. Furthermore, it is the subdivision of tasks that allows individual players to achieve economies of scale and specialization, thus improving their productivity and reducing their costs.

It can therefore be said that economic specialization creates value insofar as it represents an important presupposition for the effectiveness and efficiency of VCSs, and that purchase and sales activities (with their related costs) represent the price we have to pay for the benefits of specialization. In other words, it is the specialization that creates value, and not so much the activities of buying and selling. The value created by a system can be maximized by having appropriate recourse to specialization and reducing the costs of the related purchase and sales activities to a minimum.

In relation to transaction management activities, it is finally worth stressing that:

- it is necessary to avoid confusing sales and purchase activities with the complex of activities carried out by salesmen or the people in a buying office;

- transaction management activities play an important role in distributing the value created by a system.

In addition to sales activities in the strict sense, a company's salesforce can carry out important realization activities (e.g. informing customers how to use the product, studying the most appropriate and economic solution for customers, and/or physically transporting the goods), as well as support activities perceivable by customers (e.g. contributing to the definition of marketing policies, carrying out activities aimed at spreading knowledge of the brand) and those favouring the good functioning of the company (e.g. by updating a data base on customers' purchasing habits).

The people in a purchasing department are likewise not only involved in activities of purchasing in the strict sense, but may also be involved in the selection of suppliers, the definition of purchasing procedures, and so on.

The problem for many companies is that a good part of the time and energy of their buyers and salesmen is spent on the activities of purchasing and selling in the strict sense, which means that they have less opportunity to carry out activities that are more significant in terms of the creation of value. In other words, the time that salesmen spend on bureaucratic activities, such as completing complex order forms, transmitting orders, responding to customer complaints concerning deliveries, etc., leaves less time for them to do things that are much more important in creating value, such as communicating the characteristics of sold goods, understanding customer needs, collaborating with other parts of the company (or system) in order to improve the goods sold or introduce new products.

With reference to the second point, it is important to realize that sales and purchase activities can make a significant contribution to the profitability of a company insofar as they have an impact on the capacity of a given economic player to appropriate a satisfactory share of the value created by the system. A salesman who is well-trained in sales techniques and very able in concluding contracts with purchasers can be of fundamental importance to the company in terms of market share and profitability. In other words, with the same positioning, the same competitive strategy and the same overall value created by the system, one player can increase its profitability (and therefore the share of the value that it manages to appropriate) by being particularly effective in carrying out purchasing and sales activities in the strict sense.

The Costs Arising From Transaction Management Activities

At the level of an individual economic player, the carrying out of activities aimed at external transaction management is a presupposition for increasing revenues (sales activities) and fixed and variable costs (purchasing activities). However, these revenues and costs cannot be attributed to the transaction management activities themselves. The revenues represent the remuneration of all of the activities carried out by the analysed player, and the purchasing costs must be attributed to the different activities in which they are used. Only the costs relating to the carrying out of transaction management activities can be imputed to them, and can be divided into fixed structural costs (administrative personnel and depreciation, the people responsible for sales, etc.) and variable costs (sales commissions, commissions on payments made or received, etc.).

2.4.4 Consumption Activities

In addition to the value-creating activities that we have considered so far, a description of a VCS also requires the representation of nodes reflecting consumption activities. As we shall see in Chapter 4, the definition of consumption activities is a fundamental step in the construction of a value net because VCSs are defined on the basis of how consumption activities are carried out. Market segmentation is therefore a critical phase in the analysis, and must be designed to identify those segments (and their related consumption activities) that lead to (or could lead to) the establishment of differentiated systems.

The figures printed in this chapter represent consumption activities by using just one node. However, in some cases, they can also be broken down into distinct groups. There are cases in which the activities of purchasing and consumption are carried out by different people (e.g. when a mother buys clothes for all of the family), or cases in which consumption involves more than person at the same time (e.g. a newspaper divided into different sections aimed at different members of the family), or cases in which consumption activities pass through different phases (e.g. when you buy a new software package, it is first necessary to learn how to use it and only later is it possible to actually do so).

It is also worth pointing out that consumption activities may not be the only activities carried out by the consumers of the goods produced by the system. It is possible that they are also responsible for some of the activities involved in the creation of the product and its transfer in space and time. Here, we can think of the activities carried out by the customers of the whole range of self-service stores, or the transport, final assembly and installation of goods such as furniture, computers, and so on.

2.4.5   Representing the Activities

In conclusion, we make reference to Figure 2.11, which shows the ways in which the different types of activities will be used throughout the rest of the book. The use and respect of certain

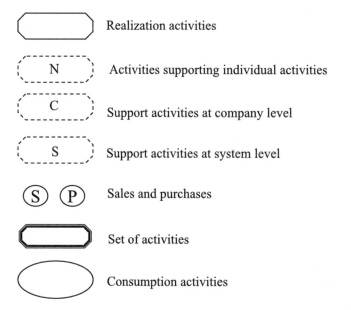

Figure 2.11   The representation of different types of value net activities

conventions can make the representations much clearer and immediately legible; and this effort is particularly worthwhile when it comes to representing such a wide variety of elements as those we have seen in this chapter.

3

The meanings of value

In order to analyse value-creating systems, we have to define exactly what we mean by value, the different meanings the word may have and, in particular, what customer value means. Given that value is a concept that is often interpreted differently by different authors, we shall try to illustrate the specific characteristics of the meaning proposed here and how it differs from the other meanings to be found in the strategic management literature.

Once we have clarified what we mean by the 'net value created by the value-creating system', 'net value for the customer' and the 'net value acquired by the value-creating players', we shall go on to describe the large number of elements that come together to determine value for final customers, as well as the many facets of the concept of value itself.

3.1 THE MEANING OF 'VALUE' IN VALUE NET METHODOLOGY

What exactly do we mean when we talk about value creation in the context of value net methodology? We can say that the net value created by a value-creating system corresponds to the difference between the value a customer attributes to a good or service and the cost borne by the system in supplying it. For the purposes of strategic analysis, it is useful to distinguish the net value created by the system, the net value received by final customers, and the net value acquired by value-creating players.

The net value created by the system: this can be defined as the difference between the gross value that a customer assigns to a product or service (regardless of its purchase price) and the overall costs sustained by the VCS in producing it. The value attributed to a product is directly related to the benefits that consumers expect from it and inversely related to the costs associated with its use (accessory or complementary goods, maintenance and other post-purchase costs).

The total net value created by the system is divided between the final customers and the economic players participating in its creation on the basis of their relative bargaining power.

The net value received by final customers: this can be defined as the difference between the value that customers attribute to a product and the price actually paid for it. The total price paid corresponds to the total revenues received by the players involved in value-creating activities.

The net value acquired by the value-creating players: this can be defined as the difference between the total price that the purchasers have paid to the players carrying out value-creating activities and the total costs that the latter have had to bear.

These different meanings of value are illustrated in Figure 3.1 which shows that the net value created by the system is obtained in part by the purchasers (the difference between gross value and the

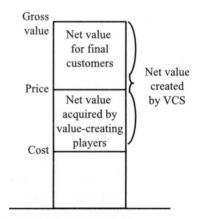

Figure 3.1   The net value created by the system and its components

price paid) and in part by the players participating in the creation of the value (the difference between the price paid by purchasers and the costs sustained by value-creating players). These definitions can be applied at the level of each individual unit of the good and at the level of the complex of goods created by the VCS.

The net value created by the system is divided between the purchasers and the value-creating players on the basis of their relative bargaining power. Sometimes, it is the players involved in value creation who manage to obtain the greater part of the total value created; e.g. when the offer of the VCS has some unique characteristics in comparison with alternative offers, when competitive pressure is not high, or when final customers find it difficult to gain access to other VCSs. In other cases, it is the final customers who manage to obtain the greater part of the created value; e.g. when the offer of the system is standardized and easily comparable with others, when supply exceeds demand, when competitive pressure is high, or when one or more of the players in the VCS adopt aggressive policies aimed at increasing their market share.

In some extreme cases, a VCS can even destroy value. This happens when the value that customers attribute to a product is less than the costs borne in order to produce it. In such cases, the price of the product tends to become less than the costs sustained, thus leading to losses on the part of the players participating in the VCS. However, it is necessary to point out that an overall loss on the part of the value-creating players does not necessarily imply the destruction of value. It can happen that, although a VCS has created value, the market situation is such that the system offer does not generate sufficient revenues to cover its costs. In this case, the purchasers acquire a greater value than that created by the system, and the players creating it suffer losses. Situations of this kind may occur when a VCS has to compete with others that are much more efficient and effective in creating value, or which are very aggressive and determined in their bid to acquire market share.

The net value obtained by the value-creating players corresponds to the profits made by the VCS as a whole. These profits are distributed among the activities (and consequently the players) of the system on the basis of their relative bargaining power within the system itself. If all other conditions are equal, the individual players operating within the VCS will manage to obtain a relatively greater

proportion of the profits the more they manage to control activities:
- that are more critical in relation to the final result;

- whose output has some unique elements in comparison with other goods;

- whose contribution can be perceived by purchasers;

- whose performance requires skills and resources that cannot be easily imitated;

- which correspond to system bottlenecks;

- whose control makes it possible to influence the behaviour of the entire VCS.

The above list illustrates only some of the most important factors that contribute towards determining the attractiveness of a given activity, a subject that we will return to in Chapter 4 when we look at the techniques for analysing the structural attractiveness of value net nodes.

3.1.1 The Meaning of Value in Microeconomics

In order to clarify the meaning of value that we have adopted here, it might be interesting to place the above definitions in the context of some key microeconomic concepts. In microeconomics, the question of customer value is mainly considered by determining the demand curve of a good i.e. the quantity of a good absorbed by the market in relation to its price. On the basis of the demand curve and the price adopted at any given moment, it is possible to identify the gross benefit received by consumers as well as what is known as the consumer surplus. This latter expression refers to the difference between the utility of a product for consumers (that is, the gross benefit received as measured by the price they would be prepared to pay for it) and the reduction in the sum that these have available to spend on the consumption of other products (that is, the price that they have to pay in order to be able to make use of the product). Consumer surplus is a measure of the net benefit

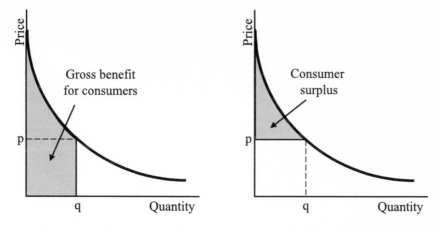

Figure 3.2   The microeconomic concepts of gross benefit and net surplus

received by consumers. Figure 3.2 illustrates the concepts of gross benefit and net surplus, given a certain price (p) and the corresponding quantity of the product sold (q).

3.1.2 The Meaning of Value in the Value Net Approach

The meanings of value proposed at the beginning of this section are consistent with and complementary to the microeconomic concepts described above. In particular, what we have called 'net value for customers' corresponds to the microeconomic concept of consumer surplus, as can be seen in Figure 3.2.

In order to include the value created by the VCS and the net value obtained by value-creating players, it is necessary to add to the classical graph illustrating the consumer surplus the cost (c) that a given VCS must bear in order to supply consumers with a given quantity of goods. For the sake of simplicity, it is hypothesized that the VCS in question is capable of supplying all the quantity demanded by the market in relation to the established price. If this is not the case, the vertical line corresponding to the quantity sold would need to be moved to the left. It is also necessary to bear in mind that the unit cost sustained by the system in order to supply the good may vary in relation to the quantity demanded and supplied (as a result of economies of scale, experience, etc.). As can be seen in Figure 3.3, the value created by the VCS corresponds to

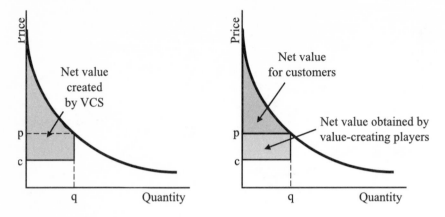

Figure 3.3   The concepts of value in value net methodology

the difference between the utility of a good for customers and the costs (per unit and multiplied by the quantity q) that the system has had to bear in supplying customers the quantity of goods demanded. This value is partially acquired by the customers and partially by the value-creating players in the system. This last component of the value corresponds to revenues (p × q) minus costs (c × q), that is the global economic result of the VCS.

3.1.3   The Meaning of Value in Strategic Management Studies

In addition to those used in microeconomic studies, it is also interesting to compare the meanings of value adopted above with those proposed in strategic management studies. It is likely that the most well-known definition of value among company operators and researchers working in the field of strategy is that proposed by Porter (1985), which states that '... value is the amount buyers are willing to pay for what a firm provides them. Value is measured by total revenue, a reflection of the price a firm's product commands and the units it can sell. A firm is profitable if the value it commands exceeds the costs involved in creating the product. Creating value for buyers that exceeds the cost of doing so is the goal of any generic strategy'.

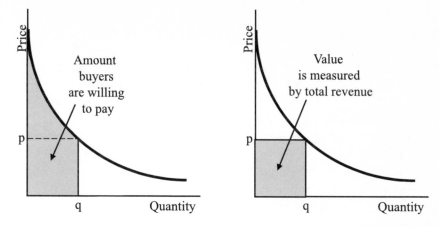

Figure 3.4   The concept of value proposed by Porter (1985)

This definition can be interpreted in a number of conflicting ways. When Porter speaks of 'the amount buyers are willing to pay', he at first seems to be referring to what microeconomists call the gross benefit for consumers. However, when he suggests that value is measured by total revenue, he is concentrating on the value (gross of sustained costs) acquired by a particular company and excluding the net value acquired by purchasers (or the net surplus for consumers). Figure 3.4 illustrates Porter's definition within the context of the microeconomic analytical schema.

The suggestion that value should be measured in terms of the revenue obtained by a company paradoxically makes it difficult to appreciate some of the most interesting messages contained in Porter's work. In particular, he frequently underlines the fact that the profitability of a given company essentially depends on the following factors:

- the benefits that the company manages to create for the purchaser (and therefore the consistency of the advantage of differentiation);

- the costs that the company bears in supplying its offer (and therefore the consistency of the advantage of cost);

- the competitive position and bargaining power of the player inside its own competitive system. Assuming that the benefits guaranteed to customers are equal, the 'price a firm's product commands' will be influenced by the action of competitive forces.

By measuring value on the basis of revenues, Porter immediately highlights the value created by the activities aimed at differentiating the produced good (which have a direct impact on the company's revenues), but leaves in the shade the contribution towards the creation of value made by the activities aimed at containing costs. It is no accident that, in his book *Competitive Advantage*, Porter discusses value for purchasers in the chapter dedicated to the advantage of differentiation and not in that dedicated to the advantage of cost. Porter only considers costs when he passes from the value to the margin of a company, which is defined as the difference between revenues (which he calls value) and costs. Although the use of a gross definition of value does not represent a real limitation (it is enough to specify that gross rather than net value is being referred to), we think that it is simpler and more immediate to adopt a net definition of value, because this allows the activities aimed at increasing the benefits and differentiation of a good, as well as those aimed at containing the costs of the system, to be defined as value-creating activities.

However, the major limitation of Porter's definition is that it identifies value only with the value that the company has managed to obtain for itself, almost as if the net value for customers were not a value in itself. This more restricted definition of value obscures the fact that the value a company manages to appropriate for itself depends on the benefits that it has managed to create for its customers and also on its relative bargaining power (as Porter himself points out in other parts of his book).

An extreme example may help to clarify this point. Let us imagine that, as a result of his reckless lifestyle, a great artist finds himself in serious financial difficulties, and that this induces him to sell off cheaply one of his works to an art dealer, who can subsequently resell it at a very high price. According to Porter, the artist has produced a very limited value because of the low price he was able to command, whereas the art dealer has been capable of producing a very high value.

In our opinion, this is a distortion of the reality. It would be more correct to say that the artist has created a very high global value but has only been able to keep a very small part of it for himself because of his lack of bargaining power; whereas the art dealer, despite the very limited value actually created by him, has been able to keep a large part of the total created value for himself because of his competitive position.

The fact that our definition includes the net value for customers means that it is possible to distinguish the overall value created by the value-creating players (or an individual player) from the value that they (or the individual player) have managed to obtain as a result of their bargaining power. It therefore follows that both the VCSs themselves and the individual players within them can appropriate a greater amount of value for themselves by creating greater value and/or by trying to improve their position in such a way as to acquire a greater share of the total value created.

What we have said above makes it possible to clarify the difference and the relationship between the creation of value as we see it and the creation of value for shareholders, something that many authors have considered in studies essentially aimed at developing methods for creating and measuring shareholders' value and not specifically aimed at the value for final customers. (Rappaport (1986), Guatri (1991) and Copeland et al. (1994)).

When value-creating players create value and manage to acquire a substantial share of the value itself, the prerequisites exist for the creation of value for the holders of the resources used in the system. The value net does not directly deal with the creation of value for shareholders (or for the holders of other resources), but concentrates on the way in which such value is created and the factors influencing its distribution. The capacity of a system to create value, and the capacity of a player to take this value for itself, implicitly represent the necessary requirements for the adequate remuneration of the holders of resources (including shareholders).

3.2 POSSIBLE MEANINGS OF NET VALUE FOR CUSTOMERS

In explaining the definitions of created net value, net value for customers and net value obtained by value-creating players we have simplified the question by speaking of net value for customers in purely generic terms. However, it is important to stress the fact that the concept of net value for customers may be interpreted in different ways and, as it represents a fundamental element in the analysis of VCSs, it is worth considering in more detail.

We only have to think about our own experiences as purchasers to make the substantial nature of the problem immediately obvious. What is the value we give to being able to possess and use a car? The value that we attribute to it depends on a large number of factors: our individual characteristics, environmental factors, the cost of complementary and substitute goods, the characteristics of our own car and the characteristics of the other cars available on the market. Table 3.1 summarizes the factors that can influence the value perceived by customers.

The elements described in Table 3.1 highlight the importance of distinguishing the absolute and differential value of a product.

The absolute net value for a specific purchaser can be defined as the algebraic sum of the value attributed to the absolute benefits connected with the product (or rather the value given to these benefits by the purchaser regardless of the performances and characteristics of alternative products) and the costs sustained by the customer in using the product itself.

The differential net value for a specific customer is the difference between the absolute net value that he can receive from a given VCS and the absolute net value of a similar product offered by a competing system or even the absolute value of a substitute product.

Absolute and differential values must not be confused with what is generally called the exchange value, which can be defined as the price paid for a given good at a given time and in a given place.

If the concept of absolute net value can be useful when analysing the needs of final customers, the concept of differential value is crucial when the competitive position of one VCS has to be compared with that of another, or when it is a question of considering what price should be charged for a product in relation to the alternative offers available.

The next two sections will be dedicated to analysing the elements making up absolute and differential net value; section 3.5 will concentrate on the difference between the value supplied and the value perceived by purchasers.

Table 3.1 Factors influencing the value perceived by customers: the example of cars

Individual factors	Income level, social class, cultural level, number of cars owned, use made of the car (individual use or for a large family, frequent or occasional use, short or long trips, and so on).
Environmental factors	Environmental (hot, cold or damp climate, the distance between inhabited centres, the morphology of the territory) and infrastructural characteristics (the quality of the roads, the presence of motorways, the availability of alternative means of public transport, the availability of complementary services such as, for example, sea connections for the inhabitants of an island).
Cost of complementary goods and competitiveness of substitute goods	The purchase costs of complementary (fuel and lubricants, road tax, motorway tolls) and substitute products/services (motorcycles, scooters, public transport, taxis).
Configuration of the received offer system	Consistency between the above factors and the configuration of the received offer system as a whole. In the case of cars: aesthetic aspects, robustness, the need for maintenance, purchase price, warranties, servicing network, fuel consumption, speed, acceleration, the size of the interior, taxes, ease of driving, internal and external noise, the ability to travel over rough ground, the ability to withstand low climatic temperatures, and so on.
Configuration of alternative offer systems	The configuration of alternative offer systems can affect purchasers' relative degree of satisfaction. For example, a customer who is satisfied with the ease of driving his car may change his mind if he tries a car that is even easier to drive.

3.3 ABSOLUTE NET VALUE RECEIVED BY CUSTOMERS

As mentioned above, absolute net value is the difference between the absolute benefits that a given customer attributes to a given product and the global costs that he has to bear in order to be able to use it.

The absolute net value of a product is difficult to measure and may not have a close and direct relationship with its exchange value. Among other things, the latter depends on the scarcity of the product, competitive pressures and the price policy of the supplier, whereas the former depends above all on the utility of the product for the customer. For example, the net value for PC consumers has considerably increased over recent years insofar as the benefits have increased (in terms of power, speed and ease of use) at the same time as the costs of purchase and learning have diminished; on the other hand, the exchange value has considerably decreased as a result of the reduction in production costs and the effects of competitive pressures.

Even though the absolute net value is difficult to measure, it can still be useful to analyse the elements making it up. Figure 3.5 summarizes the main elements of the net value of a good or service. Before analysing and classifying the elements listed in Figure 3.5, it is worth underlining some of their main connotations:

- some of them can be quantified in monetary terms (e.g. the cost of purchase), others in non-monetary terms (e.g. the length of validity of the warranty), and still others are very difficult to quantify in any terms (e.g. the quality of the product);

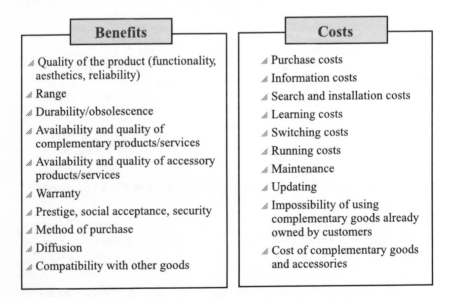

Benefits

- Quality of the product (functionality, aesthetics, reliability)
- Range
- Durability/obsolescence
- Availability and quality of complementary products/services
- Availability and quality of accessory products/services
- Warranty
- Prestige, social acceptance, security
- Method of purchase
- Diffusion
- Compatibility with other goods

Costs

- Purchase costs
- Information costs
- Search and installation costs
- Learning costs
- Switching costs
- Running costs
- Maintenance
- Updating
- Impossibility of using complementary goods already owned by customers
- Cost of complementary goods and accessories

Figure 3.5   The main elements of absolute net value

- not only the initial, but also the life-cycle costs of the good are considered;

- the elements of absolute net value and their relative importance depend not only on the type of product, but also on the market segment at which it is aimed: for example, the value of a home delivery service for automotive spare parts is very different in a densely inhabited country with a large number of service centres (such as Italy) and in a small village in the Australian outback;

- the elements listed in the table do not refer to the product system of a particular company but, in line with the principles described in Chapter 2, to the overall offer system of a VCS.

3.3.1 The Elements of Absolute Net Value: Classification by Nature

As shown in Figure 3.5, the net absolute value for customers derives from the combination of a number of different elements. One way of classifying these elements is on the basis of their nature:

- tangible elements;

- intangible elements;

- services;

- economic elements.

Tangible Elements

These include elements such as the intrinsic quality of the principal product (which can be evaluated in terms of the quality of materials used, its durability, functional characteristics, technological content, ease of use, reliability, compatibility with other goods), its aesthetic appearance, the possibility of receiving gifts or gadgets of various types.

One element that often proves to be particularly important is the availability of complementary products and/or accessories. In the case of cellular telephones, for example, batteries and battery chargers/dischargers are complementary products whereas *viva voce* car kits and protective cases can be considered accessory products. One of the advantages of the value net perspective is the fact that it is based on the point of view of the final customer, which means extending the analysis beyond the boundaries of individual companies. As a result, all the activities that participate in making a particular offer system available to customers are taken into consideration. Among other things, this means incorporating all of the activities that contribute towards the creation of value for customers, including the production of complementary goods or accessories even if these are beyond the control of the company making the analysis.

Intangible Elements

These include elements such as the prestige associated with the use of the product, the degree of security attributed to the product, and whether or not the product bears the signature of a famous designer or stylist.

The presence of a strong trademark is often related to the relevance of intangible elements, although it would be a mistake to consider the trademark an intangible element in itself. It is not the presence of a well-known trademark that constitutes an element of value for the purchaser, but the prestige or sense of security that consumers tend to associate with the trademark and, therefore, the product.

An example may help to clarify this point. Up until the end of the 1980s, IBM's competitive success on the PC market could be ascribed not only to its products, but also and above all to a trademark that was synonymous with security and reliability. The average purchaser was still relatively inexpert and willing to pay a premium price for an IBM product rather than the cheaper price of the technologically similar products available on the market. The average PC purchasers of today have more expertise than those of the past and, in addition to the trademark (which now has less relevance), make their choices on the basis of other factors such as the quality of critical components (e.g. microprocessors and memories) or the after-sales service guaranteed by the distributors. Despite the fact that it is still strong and very well known, the IBM trademark no longer has the same power to sway consumer choices or allow it to apply premium prices in comparison with those of its competitors.

Services

The progressive enrichment and articulation of the offer of goods in advanced economies is making it increasingly difficult to distinguish manufacturing from service companies, because of the growing scarcity of offer systems in which services do not play a significant role. It is enough to think of a product such as a car: automotive manufacturers (and their related concessionaires) compete not only by trying to offer cars whose tangible and intangible elements are capable of convincing potential purchasers, but also by offering a series of collateral services. These include the possibility of test driving the car before buying, a commitment to resell the old car of the purchaser, the provision of financing (often through associated companies), the offer of a capillary maintenance and repair service, the possibility of using a replacement car if the purchased car needs to be repaired, the home delivery of spare parts if the user lives in a remote area, the collection of a car needing repair and its redelivery, and so on. This type of evolution is beginning to affect a large number of industries, including those offering commodities, because the offer of collateral or accessory services may be the only way in which this type of competitive system can distinguish itself from the others.

If we move from companies to value-creating systems, it becomes practically impossible to distinguish those that offer goods from those that offer services because VCSs by definition include activities involved in the physical transformation and production of material goods, as well as service activities responsible for their distribution, installation and maintenance.

Services can be divided into basic, complementary and accessory services.

Basic services define how the product is offered to purchasers and are therefore present in all offer systems regardless of the level of purchaser satisfaction. They include elements such as the breadth of the product range, the means of transport, delivery times, the possibility of receiving the product or service without making an advance order, and the possibility or otherwise of home delivery. In the case of service companies, they include the main service(s) offered; for example, the basic service of air transport can be described in terms of the number of connected cities, the number of flights on a given route, the extent to which the timetable is respected, the comfort of the seats, the reservation system, and so on.

The difference between complementary and accessory services is similar to that between complementary and accessory tangibles. Complementary services are those necessary to ensure that the product can be used in a continuous manner, whereas accessory services are optional. In the case of air transport, for example, baggage handling is a complementary service, whereas on-board restaurant services are accessories.

Another possible classification is to distinguish pre-sales, transaction and post-sales services.

Pre-sales services have the aim of giving purchasers the information and assistance necessary to support them during the decision-making process, and they therefore include product information, the offer of technical product presentations, the checking of customer stock levels, periodic information concerning market and price trends, the supply of free or paid consultancy services designed to help customers in making their product choices.

Transaction services are strictly related to the exchange between the supplier and the purchaser. Transaction services include many of the services that we have previously described as basic services, such as the times and means of delivery, immediate availability or otherwise, the possibility of making or the need to make an advance order. They also include supplying intermediate customers with display shelves or cases, or the possibility of establishing an electronic connection between customer and supplier in order to accelerate the information exchange related to the transaction.

Of particular importance are the services aimed at reducing the effort and time that a customer needs to put into a transaction. An interesting example of this is provided by National, an American car-hire company that has created a club (the Emerald Club) for its regular customers, who are asked to provide detailed information concerning themselves and the means of invoicing at the time they join the club, and then receive a smart credit card that they can use for all subsequent transactions. When they need to hire a car at an airport, Emerald Club members simply go to the National car park, choose the car they prefer and then present their smart card to the guardian at the exit who inserts the card in a reader and checks their driving licence. The same procedure is followed when the car is returned, and this is sufficient to allow the automatic issue of the invoice.

Finally, after-sales services include product education and training courses, assistance, maintenance and repair activities, and telephone hot-line or computer online services.

Economic Elements

Economic elements can be divided into two groups: the purchase price of the product, and all the other economic elements. These include the times and methods of payment, the coverage and duration of any warranties, the cost of complementary and accessory products and services, the possibility of obtaining discounts or other advantages in relation to the acquisition of other units of the good itself or other goods.

It is important to underline the fact that not all the costs listed in the right-hand column of Figure 3.5 should be considered economic elements. For example, information and training costs require the purchaser to invest non-financial resources (time and commitment). We can take the costs sustained by a customer to install and learn how to use a word-processor. This is not an economic cost, but a consequence of the tangible characteristics of the product (ease of use, compatibility, the quality of the instruction manual, the presence of self-installable software) and the services associated with it (for example, the availability of a free telephone support service, demonstrations at the time of purchase, the installation services provided by the reseller).

The price of a product must be clearly separated from all other economic elements because it reflects a synthesis of all of the factors affecting the process involved in a given exchange, and purchasers tend to judge the fairness of a price by comparing it with all other elements of absolute value (see Figure 3.6).

The horizontal axis of Figure 3.6 indicates the value attributed to

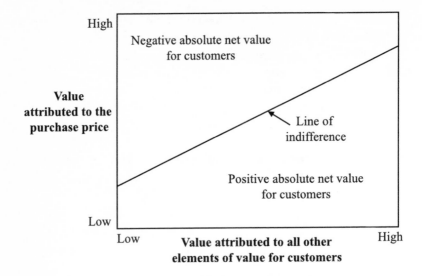

Figure 3.6   Price and the other elements of absolute value for customers

the purchase price and not the purchase price itself. The reason for this is that, even if they attribute the same value to the other elements of absolute value, two purchasers may make different decisions concerning an exchange because they may well attribute a different value to the availability of monetary means. This value will therefore be influenced by factors such as the income of the purchaser and his expectations concerning future income, his attitude towards saving, the need or wish to sustain other expenses, the possibility of relying on other economies in the case of need, and so on.

The real price of a product tends to lie below the line of indifference shown in Figure 3.6 because this guarantees the customer a positive absolute net value; if it were otherwise, the customer would not make the exchange.

3.3.2   The Elements of Absolute Net Value: Other Classifications

Besides being classified by their nature, the elements of absolute net value for purchasers can be grouped in various ways on the basis of other criteria:

- whether they improve the performance of the customer or reduce his costs;

- whether they are 'hygienic' (that is taken for granted) or 'motivating';

- whether or not they are under the control of whoever is making the analysis;

- whether the costs are borne before, during or after the time of purchase.

Increased Performance or Reduced Costs

A VCS can increase the net value given to its customers by adjusting the different elements of its offer in such a way as to increase the level of performance allowed by the product or by reducing the level of total costs that purchasers have to bear. As Porter (1985) suggests, different considerations should be made depending on whether the purchaser is the final customer or a company.

If the purchaser is a company, improving its performance means proposing an offer system that allows the purchaser to increase its differentiation in relation to its own customers. For example, in the case of a manufacturer of men's outerwear, the use of a select cloth whose trademark is also known to the final user increases the differentiation of the garment itself. Similarly, the use of quality flooring materials and fixtures and fittings allows a builder to increase the degree of differentiation of his buildings.

In relation to cost reduction, a company or VCS can influence the level and structure of the costs of their corporate customers in various ways:

- by offering better economic conditions;

- by increasing the productivity of the purchaser;

- by carrying out some of the activities connected with a product on behalf of the purchaser (e.g. a supplier who offers to manage the shelves of a supermarket);

- by supplying complementary goods that help the purchaser to carry out its own activities (e.g. a publishing house could supply bookshops with an easy-to-consult electronic catalogue containing all of its published works);

- by making a purchaser's cost structure more flexible (as can be done, for example, by a company offering temporary employees);

- by reducing the energy consumption of a product or the costs related to its management;

- by offering guarantees that reduce to zero the risk of having to make a monetary payment for repairs over a certain period of time;

- by reducing the risk of breakage or breakdown, and thus reducing maintenance costs;

- by reducing the space required to carry out a particular activity (as in the case of vertically developed automated warehouses), or by increasing the ways in which a space can be used (e.g. by offering a product that guarantees a high rate of stock rotation on supermarket shelves);

- by influencing the way in which the purchaser carries out its own activities (e.g. a manufacturer of packaging machines that allow the purchaser to reduce the number of operations required to package its own products);

- by offering rapid deliveries and thus reducing the stocks held on the premises of the purchaser.

It is interesting to note that many of the connotations that would be perceived by end-users as improvements in performance are evaluated by companies on the basis of their effects on costs. Take the processing speed of a computer, for example. This may have value for an end-user insofar as it allows the better and more rapid visualization of a graphically advanced videogame, whereas a company may assess the advantages of faster processing in terms of greater productivity and, therefore, reduced personnel costs.

Analysis of the net value received by the final customer reveals some differences from what has been said in relation to companies.

For the final customer, improving performance means increasing the overall satisfaction that a purchaser receives from a good. The ways of doing this may vary widely from one type of product to another, but they can nevertheless be summarized as follows:

- improving the principal performance of a product;

- increasing the pleasure to be gained from its use (e.g. a more comfortable car);

- offering products with a greater aesthetic content (e.g. a car with a more attractive line);

- making available a wide range of complementary and accessory products and services;

- offering collateral benefits that are not directly connected with the product (e.g. a magazine with a gift of a perfume sample);

- increasing the possibility of using the product (e.g. a very light portable PC that can be taken everywhere);

- making a product easier to use (e.g. an easy-to-use remote control device for a videorecorder) and install (e.g. self-installed software);

- increasing the prestige, social acceptance and security associated with a product (a prestigious wristwatch, a brand of jeans that is highly fashionable among teenagers, or a car with airbags and lateral bars);

- increasing the ease of purchase (the possibility of receiving a catalogue at home or seeing it on the Internet, the possibility of buying by phone, mail, fax or via the Internet, the presence of a capillary distribution network);

- increasing the pleasure of the purchasing process (large and elegant salespoints with a large number of sales assistants, shopping centres that offer a wide range of services and entertainment facilities for the entire family) and adopting systems for reducing possible tensions among waiting customers (fast checkout points in supermarkets, automated numbering systems for handling queues, comfortable waiting rooms, accepting reservations).

There is also a substantial difference between companies and final customers in terms of those elements of an offer system that lead to a reduction in costs. Almost all the costs of a company can be expressed in monetary terms. The elements that lead to a greater productivity on the part of employees can be interpreted as savings in personnel costs, just as a reduction in the amount of space necessary can be considered in terms of lower rents or property depreciation costs. However, it is usually difficult to express the savings of final customers in monetary terms. If companies tend to interpret as cost reductions those elements which would at first sight appear to be improvements in performance, final customers tend to do the exact opposite. The efficiency of an iron that makes it possible to reduce the time needed to do the ironing is perceived in terms of performance (insofar as it reduces the fatigue associated with the chore) rather than as a saving of time (and money).

Above all in relation to final customers it is therefore important to distinguish monetary and non-monetary costs (those connected with the space and time of the purchaser). This distinction can be rich in interesting hints for a company that is wondering how to increase the absolute net value given to its customers.

The central point is the degree of asymmetry between the way in which final customers and companies evaluate the cost of time. A company sees time as money insofar as it remunerates the time of its employees, whereas final customers very rarely consider time as a cost. Individuals usually think of the use of time as an irritant (if the task that is being carried out is not much liked) or an entertainment (they are prepared to pay in order to pass the time by watching a film or spend a day at a seaside resort). The installation of hi-fi equipment, for example, is considered by a hi-fi shop in terms of the cost of the time of its installation, as an irritant task by a music lover who has purchased the equipment without the service of installation, or as something enjoyable by an electronics buff who sees the equipment less as a music player and more as a set of technological novelties.

This asymmetry means that it is possible to increase considerably both the global value created and the value received by the purchaser by transferring value-creating activities from companies to the final customer in such a way as to make them a pleasure (or at least a limited irritant) for the purchaser. One interesting example in this regard is the offer system developed by Ikea, which makes the final customer responsible for designing the furnishing system, and transporting and installing the purchased furniture. In this way, the costs of Ikea have considerably decreased and it is therefore in a position to practise retail prices that are about 20–30% less than those of its competitors. On its part, Ikea has done what it can to make the activities transferred to final customers less onerous by publishing catalogues that make it easier to prepare furnishing designs, supplying cost-price roof racks to facilitate transport, designing the furniture in such a way that it is easy to transport and assemble, providing clear and comprehensible booklets of assembly instructions, and by making a visit to an Ikea salespoint and the choosing of furniture a pleasant and entertaining occasion for all of the family. With a system of this type, the total amount of time spent on producing, transporting and installing furniture at home may well have increased (we have no data on this point), but the perceived cost has certainly gone down.

Hygienic and Motivating Elements

This distinction is inspired by the model proposed by Herzbeg et al. (1959) who, when studying the determinants of the level of satisfaction of workers, identified the existence of motivating factors that tend to generate satisfaction and hygienic factors that tend to produce a state of non-satisfaction. As sustained by Herberg in the case of workers, it is also possible to distinguish those elements of the offer system that contribute towards the satisfaction of purchasers from those that contribute towards non-satisfaction.

Although it is not possible to generalize, purchasers usually tend to take for granted the attributes associated with the principal element of the offer system (and therefore to consider them as hygienic factors), and to consider the attributes associated with collateral elements as motivating factors. For example, if the users of an airline company are asked which factors have made them dissatisfied with the service received, they tend to mention elements such as the delay or cancellation of the flight, the lack of frequent direct connections with certain cities, the fact that the trip was too expensive. Factors such as the courtesy of in-flight personnel, the quality of in-flight refreshment services, and the provision or otherwise of a daily newspaper are generally described as elements that have contributed towards increasing satisfaction.

The data relating to the hygienic and motivating factors of a given offer system can be graphically presented as shown in Figure 3.7, which describes the possible hygienic and motivating factors in the case of a family car. (The hygienic and motivating factors shown in Figure 3.7 are not the result of a statistical investigation but derive from the perception of the author.)

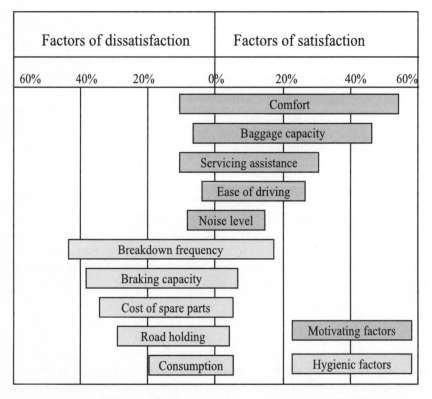

Figure 3.7   Hygienic and motivating factors in the case of a family car

Control of the Element on the Part of an Economic Player

From the point of view of an individual player in a VCS, it is very important to evaluate the degree to which it controls the various elements that determine value for customers. In this regard, three possible situations may occur:

- the element is under the direct control of the economic player;

- the element is not under direct control, but can be influenced by the player in question;

- the element is influenced by external factors beyond the control of the player.

With reference to this point, see Chapter 2 for a description of the breadth of VCSs, the difficulty for an individual player to control all of the determinants of value, and the possibility for a player to influence activities that are not directly controlled.

When Costs are Sustained

The monetary and non-monetary costs borne by a purchaser can be distinguished on the basis of when they are sustained: pre-purchase costs (the collection of information and selection); the costs paid at the time of purchase (price, costs of installation and initial learning, conversion costs); and post-purchase costs (energy consumption, maintenance and service costs, costs of personalization and adaptation during the life of the product).

Once again it is possible to identify considerable differences in the behaviour of company purchasers and final customers. The latter generally consider pre-purchase costs virtually irrelevant, and pay more attention to the costs sustained at the time of purchase than to those arising subsequently. Some companies play on this type of financial irrationality in order to obtain greater overall remuneration; for example, the producers of laser printers who keep the prices of the printers very low but charge high prices for replacement cartridges. A classic example of this approach is Gillette which, at the beginning of its life, overcame the competition of alternative safety razor producers at least partially because of its decision to keep the price of its razors low while selling Gillette-patented razor blades at a relatively high price.

In general, companies can be expected to evaluate the relative importance of the various cost categories in a more rational manner, and therefore to consider post-purchase costs more carefully. However, it is necessary to point out that particular operational mechanisms can falsify the theoretically rational behaviour of companies. For example, if an office manager can autonomously spend up to (say) three thousand Euros, but has to request authorization from top management for purchases that cost more than this sum, he may be led to prefer a computer supplier that offers the machine for three thousand plus a servicing and maintenance contract of 500 Euros per year, rather than another who offers the machine for 3500 Euros + 250 per year for post-sales assistance.

As we shall see more clearly in section 3.5, the considerations made above can be very useful when it comes to analysing the problem of the value perceived by a customer in relation to the value actually supplied.

3.4 DIFFERENTIAL NET VALUE RECEIVED BY CUSTOMERS

However significant the absolute value offered to purchasers may be, it is necessary to bear in mind that their expectations are based on the alternatives available on the market (in terms of similar or substitute goods), and that the value they attribute to a given offer also depends on the configuration of alternative offer systems. It is of little help to a company to survey what its customers think about its products or services unless it evaluates the results with reference to the products of its competitors.

What really counts is knowing what purchasers (the customers of a given company as well as the customers of its competitors) think of one offer in comparison with others. A company (or a VCS) can constantly improve the quality of its goods and services but, despite this, still lose ground in terms of the differential value offered to its customers because its competitors are progressing more rapidly. Furthermore, the company itself may not even realize the fact if it continues to measure only the degree of satisfaction of its own customers, without trying to analyse why other purchasers have chosen alternative offers.

Similarly, a company could consider itself satisfied if a survey of the degree of satisfaction of its customers highlights generally positive judgements that may even show an improvement in relation to previous surveys, but not appreciate the fact that a positive judgement is not enough to keep a customer from evaluating alternative offers and, if these are considered better, from changing supplier.

An interesting case in this regard is that of the General Business Systems Division (GBS) of AT&T, the U.S. market leader in small-business telephone switching systems (Gale, 1994). In this type of market, in addition to the quality of the hardware, customer satisfaction is also related to the quality of post-sales assistance and promotional policies which, in the case of GBS, are under the control of regional managers. Like all other Divisions of AT&T, GBS regularly carried out telephone surveys in which it asked its customers to judge (excellent, good, acceptable, insufficient) the quality of the service received in both specific terms (the quality of the equipment, the sales service, the installation service, repairs, training and invoicing) as well as globally. The results of these surveys were used to control the quality of the services rendered by the branches and formed the basis of the system used to assess the performance of the regional managers.

However, towards the end of the 1980s, the top management of GBS began to perceive that there was some problem with this system of quality evaluation. In particular, two areas of unease emerged. In the first place, the doubt began to spread that customer satisfaction was not sufficient to keep the competition at bay. Throughout AT&T, customer satisfaction was measured on the basis of the percentage of 'excellent' and 'good' responses in relation to the total. In the case of GBS, almost all branches had levels of customer satisfaction approaching 90%, and many exceeded this limit. Despite this, GBS was losing market share in many regions, and a survey revealed that only 90% of the interviewees who had judged the service of GBS to be excellent certainly intended to remain customers, and this went down to 60% in the case of those customers who judged that the service they received was good.

Secondly, it emerged that there was only a poor correlation between the levels of customer satisfaction and the ability of the branches to defeat the competition. The New York branch, for example, enjoyed an optimum competitive position even though the level of customer satisfaction was lower than that recorded by other branches which were less competitively successful.

This apparent inconsistency was explained only after the method of measuring the level of customer satisfaction was changed. GBS began to investigate not only the absolute level of satisfaction of its own customers, but also their judgements on the service received in relation to alternative offers. Furthermore, similar surveys were made of the customers of competitors and potential customers in order to clarify the point of view of those who chose the services of the competition or who were still in the phase of selecting a supplier.

By doing this, GBS realized that the real determinant in the acquisition of market share was not so much the satisfaction of existing customers, but more the perception that the market as a whole had of the differential value of the various alternative offers available. What they found was that changes in the offered net value were followed within 2–3 months by a change in the perception that the market had of the differential value received and, after approximately a further four months, by a change in the related market share. Among other things, this change in approach made it possible to understand that the reason underlying the relatively low level of customer satisfaction in New York was because the customers in this region were particularly demanding. In reality, the average evaluations of all of the competitors were low, but those of GBS were above average and this explained its competitive success.

The case of GBS clearly shows how a company can make the switch from absolute net value to differential net value for customers by modifying its systems for investigating purchasers' perceptions of the value they receive. As said above, the differential net value of a good for a given customer can be defined as the difference between the absolute net value that can be received from a given VCS and that which can be received from a similar good offered by a competing system, or even the absolute net value of a substitute good.

3.4.1 The Evaluation of Differential Net Value: A Simplified Approach

As we have seen in the previous section, although it is very difficult to measure the absolute value of a product for a purchaser, it is possible to think of measuring differential net value by trying to quantify the difference between the offer of one company (or VCS) and alternative offers. These alternatives may be represented by similar product or service systems, or substitute goods even if they are based on completely different technologies from those used in the good being analysed.

An attempt in this sense was made by Forbis and Mehta (1981), who proposed the concept of 'economic value for the customer', which was defined as the maximum amount a customer should be willing to pay, assuming that he is fully informed about the product and the offerings of competitors. Figure 3.8 gives a simple numerical example that may help to clarify the concepts proposed by these two authors.

The concepts presented in Figure 3.8 can be summarized as follows:

• economic value for the customer (EVC) can be defined only in relation to an alternative product of reference;

• in addition to the purchase price of the good, the analysis of EVC requires that consideration is also given to the start-up costs for its use (e.g. training and installation costs) and post-purchase costs;

• let us assume that the alternative product of reference has a total cost of $1000, that the better performance of the analysed product is worth $100, and that the purchaser may consequently be prepared to spend a total of $1100;

• if the start-up and post-purchase costs together amount to $500, the purchaser should be prepared to pay a purchase price of up to $600 ($1100 − $500), the amount that represents the economic value for the customer;

• if the costs sustained by the company to make the product amount

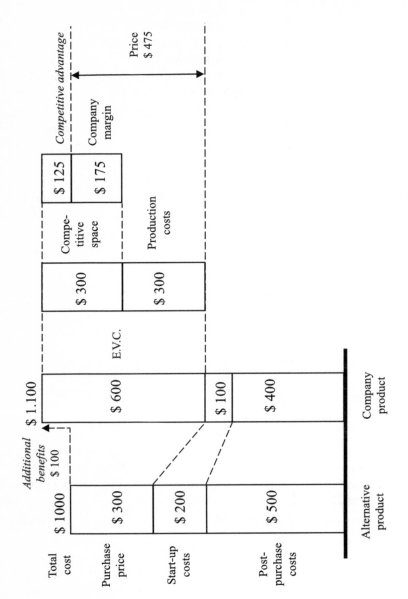

Figure 3.8 Economic value for the customer. Adapted from Forbis and Mehta (1981)

to $300, the space available for acquiring a competitive advantage (the competitive space) can be quantified as $300;

• if the analysed company decides to sell the product at a price of $475, it will have a margin of $175 and a competitive advantage over the alternative product can be quantified as $125.

Despite their simplification of reality, the concepts of Forbis and Mehta have the merit of distinguishing the concept of price from that of the net value received by the purchaser. Using the terminology proposed in this chapter, it can be said that the company illustrated in Figure 3.8 has managed to create more value for each of its customers than the alternative competitor of reference, and that this greater value has been transformed partially into profits for the company under investigation and partially into a greater differential net value received by the customers. This greater value represents a competitive advantage that could improve the company's market position.

3.4.2 The Evaluation of Differential Net Value: A Complex Approach

The concept of differential net value for customers has also been explored by Buzzel and Gale (1987) and Gale (1994), who underline the fact that the value that purchasers attribute to an offer system, and the price that they consider reasonable to pay for it, greatly depend on the performance and cost of alternative offers.

In order to measure differential value, they propose a methodology for evaluating value for customers that essentially consists of the following instruments (Gale 1994):

• the market-perceived quality profile;

• the market-perceived price profile;

• the customer value map.

Although inspired by the instruments proposed by Gale (1994), the methodology described in the following pages is different in a number of respects from Gale's methodology. In order to help the readers who already know the contribution of Gale to make a comparison, the main modifications will be identified in footnotes. The three instruments will be illustrated by comparing the offers of three hypothetical automotive manufacturers operating in the station wagon segment of the market, in an attempt to highlight their strong points, limitations and the aspects that deserve further investigation. In order to help readers to follow the example more readily, it needs to be pointed out that model 1 is now a little old but was once highly prestigious and innovative; model 2 is new, but not as innovative as model 1 was at the time it was introduced; and model 3 is powerful and has high-performance characteristics.

The Market-perceived Quality Profile

The qualitative profile represents the heart of the analysis of value for the customer because it makes it possible to identify the quality attributes that contribute towards creating this value, as well as their relative weight in determining the judgement of the same. The construction of a market-perceived quality profile involves the following steps.

It is first necessary to ask a selected sample of customers (those of the company being analysed, those of the competitors and potential customers) to express their judgement of the value to be attributed to the elements of the offer system, excluding only the economic elements (column 1 of Table 3.2).

The weights of the various attributes must then be evaluated by asking the interviewees to express their perception of the relative importance of each* (column 2 of Table 3.2).

Finally, the interviewees should be asked to give a score (for example, from 1 to 10) to the offer of the company and the offer of some selected competitors or groups of competitors. On the basis of these values, it is possible to calculate the relative performances of the competitors in relation to the various attributes under consideration (columns 3–7 of Table 3.2).

---

*This can be done by asking each interviewee to distribute a total of 100 points among the selected attributes or by asking them to give a score of 1–10 for each attribute and then calculating their relative weights.

Table 3.2 Station wagon: market-perceived quality profile (in columns (3), (4) and (6): 1 = extremely dissatisfied; 10 = highly satisfied)

Quality attributes (1)	Relative importance (2)	Analysed company, Model 1 (3)	Competitor A Model 2 (4)	(3)/(4)	Competitor B, Model 3 (6)	(3)/(6)
Aesthetic appearance	20%	9.0	7.0	129%	8.5	106%
Safety	18%	7.0	7.5	93%	8.0	88%
Seating space	15%	8.0	7.0	114%	7.5	107%
Baggage space	14%	9.0	7.0	129%	8.0	113%
Air-conditioning	10%	7.0	9.0	78%	9.5	74%
Comfort	8%	7.0	8.0	88%	9.0	78%
Service network	5%	6.0	7.5	80%	8.5	71%
Ease of driving	5%	5.0	8.4	60%	8.0	63%
Prestige	4%	8.0	7.0	114%	7.0	114%
Acceleration	1%	6.0	6.5	92%	6.0	100%
Total/weighted average	100%	7.7	7.5	103%	8.2	94%

The attributes selected to describe the quality profile can be ordered in terms of their relative importance or in terms of the life cycle of the attribute. In relation to this, it is possible to distinguish various stages: latency (the attribute has not yet been perceived by the purchasers), desire (the need is perceived but no product is capable of satisfying it), unique (only one competitor is capable of offering the attribute), in development, key (the attribute is at the centre of attention), in decline, and basic (the attribute is taken for granted).

It is worth underlining the fact that the latent, desired and basic elements cannot affect the purchasing decision either because they do not exist in any offer system or because they are present in all of them. Despite this, it may nevertheless be interesting to include them in the list of attributes as a sort of reminder, leaving aside their relative weights.

On the basis of the collected values, it is also possible to construct a graph such as that shown in Figure 3.9 in order to illustrate a direct comparison between the analysed company and one or more competitors, or groups of competitors.

The Market-perceived Price Profile

This can be constructed in the same way as the quality profile, but in this case it is necessary to ask the purchasers to identify the significant economic attributes and their relative importance. The interviewees should therefore be asked to give a score of 1–10 to each attribute (1 = extremely attractive from an economic point of view; 10 = an extremely expensive offer)*. This judgement must be made in relation to the category of goods under investigation (station wagons in our example). Table 3.3 shows the values that could be obtained in relation to the three analysed models.

It has to be pointed out that, unlike in the case of the table

---

*Gale suggests that interviewees should be asked to assess economic attributes in terms of satisfaction rather than in terms of cost. However, this approach may encourage interviewees to make a relative judgement that also takes into account the perceived quality of the product. Purchasers may declare that they are satisfied with a product's economic attributes, not because they judge the overall cost to be low, but because they think that the price is a fair reflection of its quality.

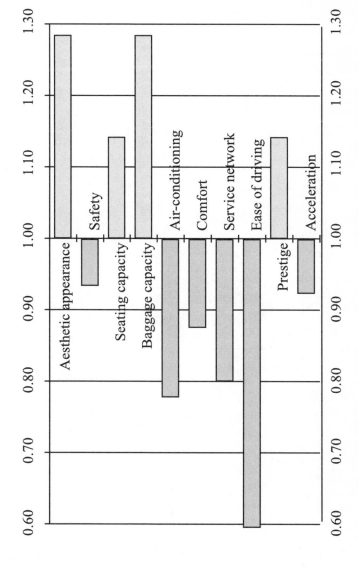

Figure 3.9   Station wagon: comparison of the analysed company with competitor A

Table 3.3 Station wagon: market-perceived price profile (in columns (3), (4) and (6)): 1 = minimally expensive; 10 = extremely expensive)

Price attributes (1)	Relative importance (2)	Analysed company, Model 1 (3)	Competitor A, Model 2 (4)	(3)/(4)	Competitor B, Model 3 (6)	(3)/(6)
Purchase price of basic model	55%	2.0	5.0	40%	8.8	23%
Consumption	20%	9.5	6.3	152%	7.5	127%
Probable resale price	7%	9.0	5.0	180%	2.5	360%
Exchange value	5%	5.0	7.5	67%	9.5	53%
Cost of optional accessories	4%	9.0	2.5	360%	3.8	240%
Cost of spare parts	2%	7.5	5.0	150%	7.5	100%
Financing conditions	2%	5.0	5.0	100%	6.3	80%
Warranty	2%	9.0	3.8	240%	2.5	360%
Servicing costs	2%	6.3	5.0	125%	7.5	83%
Taxes (road tax, etc.)	1%	5.0	5.0	100%	2.5	200%
Total/weighted averages	100%	4.8	5.3	91%	7.6	63%

analysing quality attributes, a lower score indicates a competitive advantage.

As far as the price profile perceived by the market is concerned, it is very important to underline the fact that the difference in the perceived purchase price is not necessarily the same as the percentage difference in the price actually practised by the companies under consideration because the perception of the market may well be different from reality. This type of discrepancy may become even greater when the other economic elements are considered because customers tend to be less attentive to differences in the less important elements of alternative offers (which is one of the reasons why many car manufacturers tend to exclude many accessories from the basic price), and often have only a vague and frequently false perception of post-purchase monetary costs, such as fuel consumption, the cost of spare parts or the cost of servicing.

If we move on to consider the evaluation of the economic offer as a whole, another reason leading to the distortion of customer perceptions is the fact that purchasers do not always assign a weight to the various attributes that is proportional to their relative cost. For example, we can imagine that an average user of a certain model of station wagon spends 22 500 Euros to buy the car, subsequently pays 3000 Euros a year (for fuel, insurance, road taxes, maintenance, etc.) for the next five years, and then resells the car for 7500 Euros. In this case, the fact that a monetary value can be given to all the considered attributes makes it possible to calculate the real incidence of the various costs. If we assume a discounting rate of 10%, the individual costs and their real incidence in relation to the total can be calculated as shown in Table 3.4.

However, it is unlikely that a purchaser (particularly if this is an individual rather than a company) will make this type of calculation, and it is therefore probable that the weight given to the various attributes will be more or less significantly different from their real weight. Table 3.4 shows the perceived weight of the elements indicated in Table 3.3 grouped together in three macrocategories, and highlights the differences that may exist between the perceived and actual price profile.

After having constructed the quality and price profiles of a product, it can be useful to summarize the results in a table such as Table 3.5, which shows the average evaluations made of the three

Table 3.4　Station wagon: real and perceived incidence of economic attributes

Economic attributes	Costs	Discounted total costs	Real incidence	Perceived incidence
Purchase price	22 500	22 500	56%	66%
Annual running costs	3000	12 510	31%	27%
Probable resale price	7500	5122	13%	7%
Total/weighted averages		40 132	100%	100%

models (column 3) and the position of the competitors in relation to these averages (columns 5, 7 and 8).

The Customer Value Map

This makes it possible to summarize the results obtained using the two instruments described above, and visualize the relative positions of the competitors involved. Figure 3.10 illustrates the results summarized in Table 3.5.

The value map clearly shows that model 1 is capable of providing customers with the greatest differential value, whereas model 3 would appear to have a quality/price ratio that is unfavourable for purchasers.

As can be seen in Figure 3.10, in order to be able to affirm that a given offer system provides more or less differential value, it is necessary to draw a curve* on the value map in order to represent the quality and price combinations that the purchasers consider to be fair. Although the considerations to bear in mind may well vary from one type of good to another, it is likely that the curve will be similar to that shown in Figure 3.10. The shape of the proposed

---

*Gale proposes using the diagonal of the map as the line of fair value, on the assumption that purchasers would consider it fair to pay 15% less than the average in order to receive 15% less in terms of qualitative attributes, or 20% more to receive 20% greater quality. However, this approach does not take into account the possible asymmetry between economic and qualitative evaluations, or the probably different behaviour of purchasers at different points of the value map.

Table 3.5 Station wagon: quality and price attributes (both rated on a scale of one to ten)

Attributes (1)	Average evaluations (2)	Analysed company, Model 1 (3)	Model 2 (3)/(2)	Competitor B, (5)	Competitor C, Model 3 (5)/(2)	(7)	(7)/(2)
Quality attributes	7.8	7.7	99%	7.5	96%	8.2	105%
Price attributes	5.9	4.8	81%	5.3	90%	7.6	129%

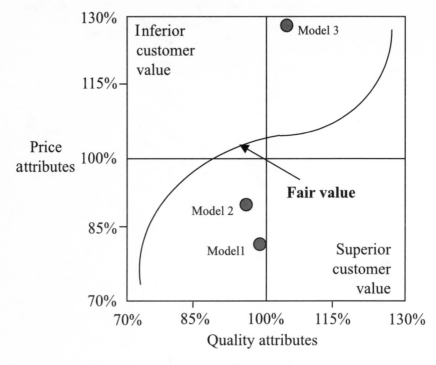

Figure 3.10   Station wagon: the customer value map

curve can be explained as follows:

- the line is always ascendent because greater quality levels always correspond to a greater average willingness on the part of the market to pay a higher price;

- it is likely that purchasers are not willing to accept quality levels that are much less than the average, and so it is probable that the price they are prepared to pay decreases rapidly as the level of quality becomes very low;

- purchasers are aware that it can be very expensive to obtain a level of performance that is much higher than the average, and so it is likely that very high quality levels can command significantly higher prices.

It is worth underlining the fact that the considerations above may vary depending on the product itself, the market segments considered and the levels reached by the various attributes. In reality, the fair value curve can be drawn in such a way as to show above it the companies losing market share, and below it the companies who are acquiring better competitive positions.

3.5 VALUE PROVIDED AND MARKET-PERCEIVED VALUE

One of the factors that helps value-creating players to obtain a major share of the created value is their capacity to make customers perceive the value in a positive manner. It may be that, at the time of making a purchasing decision, a buyer may not be in a position to make a complete and rational assessment of the value connected to a given offer system.

This may be of particular importance in the case that purchasers are incapable of objectively evaluating the intrinsic quality of the product in question because they do not have the necessary technical skills, or because a significant part of the attributes of the product consists of intangible elements or services.

In some cases, purchasers cannot foresee all the benefits that they can obtain from using a product because they do not have any previous direct experience. One example of this could be the difficulty that someone who has never used an electronic spreadsheet to make numerical analyses may find in imagining the advantages associated with its use. A limited knowledge of a product may also induce purchasers to expect more benefits than the product is capable of providing; for example, a customer at a centre specializing in hair loss may expect miraculous results and only subsequently realize the uselessness of the intervention.

Customers may also have a false perception because they do not understand the inconveniences that using the product may involve. For example, a customer who buys a colour printer that guarantees an optimum print quality may only later become aware of its high consumption of toner, or it may happen that customers cannot or do not want to translate some of the available information concerning the use of a product into benefits or monetary costs (as in the case of a customer who buys a dishwasher without having any idea of its energy consumption or annual running costs). As we have frequently mentioned above, purchasers tend to limit their monetary considerations to immediate costs and high unit prices, and pay less attention to post-purchase costs or lower unit prices, or fail to evaluate them rationally, despite the fact that these may have a considerable impact on their own economic systems.

From the point of view of purchasers, perception difficulties may be particularly inconvenient when it comes to buying goods with a high unit price that are bought only infrequently. In the case of frequently purchased goods, any errors in perception can be more easily corrected because a purchaser has the possibility of buying alternative goods over time and can thus refine his judgement capacities.

The examples described above underline the fact that a false perception of the real value of a good is more likely in the presence of:

- intangible elements and services;

- systemic and complex goods;

- benefits that are not immediate;

- post-purchase costs and the costs of consumables;

- products and services that are new to the purchaser and even to the market;

- infrequently purchased goods.

Whatever the reasons leading to customer perception errors, it is very important that companies are aware of their existence and nature, in order to be able to correct them or, in some cases, exploit them to their own advantage. If they want to maintain prices that purchasers are prepared to pay (and consequently their own profitability), companies must try to increase the value perceived by their customers. However great the real value may be, if it is not perceived by customers, it will only help alternative offers.

A company has three fundamental ways of intervening on the perception that purchasers have of their offer: improving or modifying the offer system, or acting on the signals of value.

Improving the Offer System

As we have shown above, it is possible to improve an offer system by increasing the benefits connected to the product, reducing its price and/or consumption costs, favouring the availability of complementary and accessory goods, or promoting an improvement in the contextual conditions that would provide the product with added value (e.g. a major vehicle manufacturer could put pressure on a government to ensure that the development of a country's road and motorway network is favoured over the development of the railway system).

Modifying the Offer System

Purchasers do not necessarily perceive the offer system that is most advantageous to them. If, for example, a purchaser irrationally pays more attention to immediate than post-purchase costs, it is possible that he will favour an offer involving a lower purchase price even if this choice will lead to higher subsequent costs than an alternative offer. In a situation of this type, a company that sells both the principal good and the related consumption materials could find it more profitable to sell the first even at a lower than cost price and raise the prices of the second. In this case, it is possible that although the customer may actually receive less value, he perceives exactly the contrary.

Using the Signals of Value

The signals of value are the indicators used by purchasers to evaluate goods about which they do not have exhaustive knowledge. These include factors such as advertising, the image and reputation that a company has acquired over time, its customer portfolio and market share, the appearance of the premises in which purchasers come into contact with the company, the attitude and appearance of the people representing the company, the name of the product or the type of packaging. For example, after being disappointed by the results obtained after the launch of a new brand of coffee with pastel yellow packaging, a coffee manufacturer decided to offer exactly the same coffee in red packaging. Sales immediately picked up, thus confirming the importance that colour may have in terms of customer perception. What surprised the sales managers more than any thing else was the fact that a survey of purchasers who had bought the coffee in both forms of packaging showed that they considered the coffee in the red packaging to be stronger and with a better aroma.

It is important to stress the fact that companies can act on value signals by sustaining specific costs or by intelligently exploiting the opportunities offered by their everyday activities. The former occurs, for example, when recourse is made to advertising or public relations campaigns, when a product is given free of charge to prestigious customers, in the case of the sponsorship of sporting or cultural events, when special training courses are organized for salesmen in order to improve their interactions with their customers, or when the premises open to the public are restructured or redecorated.

However, in many cases, it is possible to act on value signals at little or even no cost. One very important element in this regard is the signals that may come from existing customers of the company who, if satisfied, can contribute towards spreading a positive image of the good or service.

4

Using the value net

The preceding chapters introduced the terminology and fundamental concepts of the value net model; the aim of this chapter is to show how these concepts can be used in practice to analyse competitive systems, value-creating systems and the strategic profile of individual companies.

The first two sections will illustrate the limitations of traditional models in the analysis of the structural features of industries (particularly if characterized by fuzzy borders) and how the value net can be used to analyse the structural attractiveness of activities. Subsequently, a five-phase method for using the value net will be described, using the example of the publishing industry.

4.1 INDUSTRY ANALYSIS: OVERCOMING THE LIMITATIONS OF TRADITIONAL MODELS

Traditional industry analyses are based on two main pivots: the analysis of attractiveness, and techniques of industry definition and segmentation.

4.1.1 The Traditional Analysis of Industry Attractiveness

The most well known model of industry analysis is undoubtedly that of the five competitive forces proposed by Porter (1980). This model evaluates the structural features of industries by taking into account competitors, potential new entrants, the producers of substitute goods, suppliers and customers. Figure 4.1 shows this model and the elements to consider for each of the five forces as proposed by Porter (1985).

According to Porter, the profitability of a company is determined by the structural features of the industry in which it competes, its positioning choices within the industry, and the consistency between the two.

Porter's model owes its success to the fact that it provided a unitary analytical framework in which to insert, in addition to some original concepts, many of the partial theories of industry analysis developed by studies of industrial economics, such as economies of scale, the degree of concentration and entry barriers.

Although it is beautifully clear from a theoretical point of view, this model is becoming increasingly difficult to apply. As pointed out in Chapter 1, a growing number of industries are difficult to define and delimit, and it is consequently difficult to understand what their boundaries are, which industries should be considered customers and which suppliers, and what is their cost structure. Where are the boundaries in the telecommunications industry? Who are the competitors in the publishing industry? What are the competitive dynamics in the information technology industry?

It can be objected that these are not individual competitive systems but aggregates of competitive systems, and that the analysis of the competitive environment should be made at a more disaggregated level. However, this would lead to the risk of losing a vision of the whole and, furthermore, often does not solve the problem of boundary identification. This is the case, for example, of electronic publishing, one segment of the broader publishing sector. A study of the Italian market (Draebye and Dubini, 1996) has shown that the three main competitors in this sector are defined differently: one directly controls part of retail sales, the others do not; one does its own technical product development, the others do not; one also operates on line, the others only deal with CD ROMs. What are the characteristic activities carried out by the competitors in the electronic publishing sector? There is no answer to this question because each of them has a different configuration. In such a case, it becomes practically impossible to apply the traditional tools of industry analysis. How can you evaluate the bargaining power of customers and suppliers if every

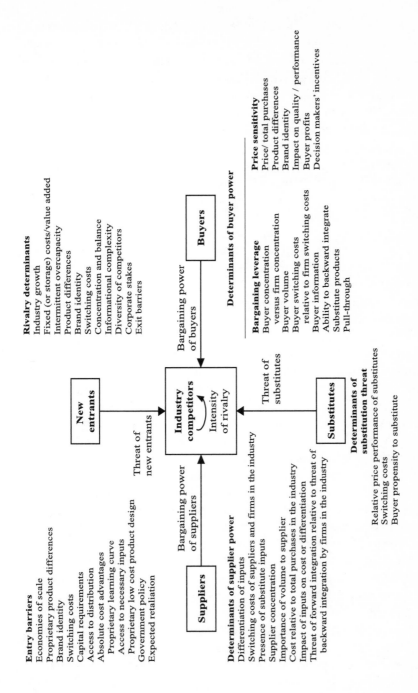

Entry barriers
Economies of scale
Proprietary product differences
Brand identity
Switching costs
Capital requirements
Access to distribution
Absolute cost advantages
  Proprietary learning curve
  Access to necessary inputs
  Proprietary low cost product design
Government policy
Expected retaliation

Rivalry determinants
Industry growth
Fixed (or storage) costs/value added
Intermittent overcapacity
Product differences
Brand identity
Switching costs
Concentration and balance
Informational complexity
Diversity of competitors
Corporate stakes
Exit barriers

Price sensitivity
Price/ total purchases
Product differences
Brand identity
Impact on quality / performance
Buyer profits
Decision makers' incentives

Determinants of buyer power

Bargaining leverage
Buyer concentration
  versus firm concentration
Buyer volume
Buyer switching costs
  relative to firm switching costs
Buyer information
Ability to backward integrate
Substitute products
Pull-through

Determinants of supplier power
Differentiation of inputs
Switching costs of suppliers and firms in the industry
Presence of substitute inputs
Supplier concentration
Importance of volume to supplier
Cost relative to total purchases in the industry
Impact of inputs on cost or differentiation
Threat of forward integration relative to threat of
  backward integration by firms in the industry

Determinants of substitution threat
Relative price performance of substitutes
Switching costs
Buyer propensity to substitute

New entrants

Threat of new entrants

Suppliers

Bargaining power of suppliers

Industry competitors

Intensity of rivalry

Bargaining power of buyers

Buyers

Threat of substitutes

Substitutes

Figure 4.1 Elements of industry structure. Taken from Porter (1985)

competitor purchases different inputs and has a different degree of downstream integration? What can you say about the cost structure of an industry when the activities performed by competitors are different? In other words, how is it possible to make a structural analysis of a competitive system when its boundaries are anything but clear?

The fundamental problem of traditional industry analysis is not that the competitive forces identified by Porter no longer exist, nor that structural analysis of the competitive environment is no longer valid; it lies in the fact that, like the majority of models of strategic analysis, the model of the five forces is applied to what we have called typical bundles of activities. In the case of bundled thinking, the elementary unit of analysis is not the activities that create value, but typical sets of activities. In a perspective of this type, the footwear sector (for example) consists of a set of companies that buy leather hides and other raw materials, design and carry out the working processes necessary for the production of shoes and, finally, sell their products to the distribution channels. As long as the majority of the competitors operate traditionally and have similar value chains, there is no particular difficulty in applying Porter's model, but problems arise when the competition becomes more varied; some companies almost completely outsource the working phases of production, others move them to countries with low labour costs, and yet others continue to do them internally; some concentrate on the research and development of new materials, whereas others concentrate on distribution and the creation of directly controlled salespoints ... and so on. Bundled thinking shows all its limitations when a growing number of companies in a given competitive context stop taking for granted 'who does what' and begin to define their own boundaries in an original manner by choosing to control directly or indirectly sets of not necessarily sequential activities on the basis of their know-how, the attractiveness of the activities themselves, and any inadequacies in the VCS. The more the original definition of bundles of activities becomes the rule rather than the exception, the more difficult it is to apply the model of the five forces. However, the real problem is not the method (i.e. the structural analysis of competitive forces), but the object to which the analysis refers: the industry.

4.1.2 The Traditional Techniques for Defining and Segmenting Industries

According to Porter (1980), an industry can be defined as a 'group of firms producing products that are close substitutes for each other'. According to Airoldi *et al.* (1994), an industry can be defined as 'a homogeneous set of interdependent companies that produce similar goods'. Whatever the definition used, an industry is typically characterized by one product or a set of similar or related products: the pharmaceutical industry, the soft drinks industry, the automobile industry, and so on.

However, such broad definitions make it difficult to make an industry analysis insofar as they represent too broad and heterogeneous sets of competitors. The theory of strategic management therefore always tried to find methods of identifying competitive environments that are sufficiently homogeneous to be analysed. As far as this point is concerned, two popular techniques are the identification of strategic groups and industry segmentation.

The Map of Strategic Groups

Alongside the concept of extended rivalry, Porter attempted to propose techniques for segmenting the industry in such a way as to identify more homogeneous sub-systems to which the five-forces model could be more easily applied. He first indicated a possible solution in his map of strategic groups (see Figure 4.2), with the help of which it is possible to identify sub-groups of competitors within the framework of an industry that follow the same or a similar strategy and, therefore, for which the configuration of the five competitive forces is similar.

Industry Segmentation

In his book *Competitive Advantage* (1985), Porter proposed a technique for segmenting industrial sectors (see Figure 4.3), stressing the fact that 'Industries are not homogeneous. Segments of industry have a structure just as industries do, and the strength of the five

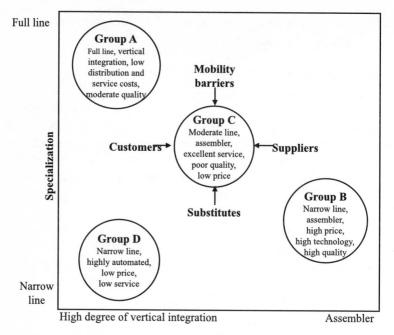

Vertical integration

Figure 4.2   A map of strategic groups in a hypothetical sector. Adapted from Porter (1980)

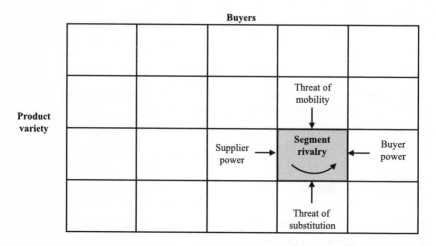

Figure 4.3   Differences in the Five Forces Among Segments. Taken from Porter (1985)

competitive forces often differs from one part of an industry to another. Segments also frequently involve different buyer value chains and/or the value chain a firm requires to serve them well. Segments of an industry thus frequently differ widely in their structural attractiveness and in the requirements for competitive advantage in them.'

Finally, in *The Competitive Advantage of Nations* (1989), Porter repeats the fact that 'many discussions of competition and international trade employ overly broad industry definitions such as banking, chemicals, or machinery. These are not strategically meaningful industries because both the nature of competition and the sources of competitive advantage vary a great deal within them. Machinery, for example, is not one industry, but dozens of strategically distinct industries such as weaving machinery, rubber processing equipment, and printing machinery..., each with its own unique requirements for competitive success.'

4.1.3 The Basic Limitations of Traditional Industry Analysis

Although strategic groups and techniques of segmentation contribute towards solving some of the problems that arise in relation to the application of the model of the five competitive forces, we are still a long way from finding a definitive solution. In fact, the merging of previously distinct competitive contexts (e.g. the transition from office equipment such as typewriters, mechanical calculators, invoicing machines to office automation), the increase in the inter-relationships of once clearly separated industries (e.g. telecommunications products, telecommunications services, software, hardware, the production of multimedia content, the management of television networks), the emergence of atypical competitive strategies and unique value-creating systems (e.g. the originality of the strategy of Disney in the entertainment industry), the variety of the definition of the activities controlled by competitors (of which the textile and clothing, footwear and furniture sectors offer an infinity of examples), has increased the number of cases to which the application of the classical model of extended rivalry is difficult and unconvincing.

The problems associated with the concepts of industry, strategic group and industry segmentation in relation to structural analysis are essentially due to:

- the product-based definition of the competitive system;

- the hypothesis of substantial homogeneity in the configuration of competitors;

- the hypothesis that the boundaries of a competitive system can be defined.

The Product-based Definition of the Competitive System

The definitions of an industry (together with the strategic groups it includes) and its segments are essentially based on products. The industries refer to broad categories (such as the pharmaceutical or television industries), whereas the segments refer to narrower product categories (LCD mini-televisions, portable televisions, table-top televisions, etc.). In the case of industry segments, the definition based on product classes is accompanied by a definition based on customer groups (see Figure 4.3), but this does nothing to change the primacy of the first.

The main hypothesis underlying the product-based definition of competitive systems is that different products imply different value chains, whereas two companies offering the same product have comparable value chains. However, this hypothesis is frequently untrue, as can be seen in the case of the sale and replacement of vehicle spare parts. This type of activity is traditionally sub-divided into segments that represent product sub-categories of the wider category of 'vehicle spare parts'; automotive electricians deal with electrical spare parts, mechanics with mechanical spare parts, tyre dealers with tyres, and coachworkers with the bodywork. However, the most recent developments in the distribution of vehicle spare parts have shown that products belonging to the same product category do not necessarily have to be managed in the same way, whereas products belonging to different categories can be handled in the same manner. The distribution of automotive spare parts is influenced more by factors such as the ease of installation, the frequency of replacement and the breadth of assortment. Those that are easily and frequently replaced, and for which the assortment is limited (such as spark plugs, windscreen wipers and batteries) can be economically distributed via supermarkets or petrol stations, and sometimes mounted by the final customers themselves. The ideal distribution of frequently replaced products with a wide range of items that are not so easy to install (such as silencers, tyres, brake drums or windscreens) is through centres that are well stocked with the complete range of items and guarantee immediate replacement, usually without the need for booking or for keeping the car off the road. The spare parts that are less frequently replaced and more difficult to install (regardless of whether they are electrical, mechanical or of any other type) can only be economically distributed by specialized or multifunctional workshops manned by highly specialized personnel, which maintain low stock levels, order the spare parts after having diagnosed the problem, and require advance bookings and that the car remains with them for a certain period of time.

It is true that different types of product require different production activities, but these generally represent only a small part of the sum of the activities carried out by a company, and an even smaller part of the sum of activities carried out in a value-creating system. For example, the activities involved in the production of a designer-styled suit and a designer-styled pair of shoes (the definition of a style, design, brand consolidation, logistics, the planning and management of sales outlets) may have more in common than those involved in the production of a designer-styled suit and one aimed at the low end of the market.

The Hypothesis of Substantial Homogeneity in the Configuration of Competitors

Although Porter has always stressed the fact that a competitive advantage can be obtained by adopting original competitive strategies, and therefore also through the use of activity configurations that are different from those of competitors, the structural analysis of competitive systems (however they are defined) is actually based on the assumption that, although with different emphases, all the competitors in a system have essentially the same cost structures, economies of scale, entry or mobility barriers, substitute products, and bargaining power in relation to customers and suppliers. If it were not for this underlying hypothesis, there would be no sense in talking of industry (or strategic grouping) cost structure, of the bargaining power of an industry's suppliers and customers, and so on.

However, in the absence of such a situation (i.e. in a competitive context that includes a high degree of variability and differentiation among competitors, and a large number of companies with an original configuration) it becomes difficult to identify the group of competitors upon which to base a structural analysis.

This hypothesis of homogeneity in the configurations of competitors (or at least a group of competitors) raises a growing number of problems when it comes to applying the theory to increasingly complex competitive contexts in which the most interesting competitors have unique configurations and inter-relationships, and therefore a company structure that cannot be compared with that of other companies even if they do operate on the same markets. Furthermore, although such situations occur more frequently in high-technology sectors, not even the most traditional sectors are entirely immune.

The traditional theory admits the possibility of original and unique bundles of company activities. Porter himself allows that strategic groupings may consist of individual companies and that, in such cases, structural analyses need to be made at company level. However, the adoption of this approach leads to the partial loss of one of the most important contributions offered by structural analysis: the possibility of distinguishing the average profitability of a given competitive system (which is related to its structural attractiveness) and the greater or lesser profitability that a company achieves by virtue of its strategic positioning.

The Hypothesis that the Boundaries of a Competitive System can be Defined

This is related to the preceding point insofar as the classical analysis of the five competitive forces assumes that it is possible to identify a sufficiently homogeneous group of competitors that buy

from a definable set of suppliers and sell to a definable set of customers via a definable set of distribution channels, and which are
faced by similar threats from potential entrants and substitute
products. Once again, an increasingly significant role is being
played by competitive contexts in which such a situation is very far
from the truth. This is particularly so in the case of those contexts
that are characterized by profound technological changes, the
presence of technologies common to different industries, the convergence of previously relatively distinct competitive systems, significant changes in the relationships between production and
distribution, and the emergence of alternative distribution channels
and new consumption models.

A particularly good example of the difficulties encountered when
trying to apply classical industry structural analysis to complex
competitive systems that are difficult to circumscribe, and also characterized by very different types of competitors, is provided by the
electronic publishing industry, which is based on the confluence of
skills and technologies originating from such highly diverse worlds
as traditional publishing, software production, telecommunications,
information networks and entertainment. Figure 4.4 illustrates the
main nodes and flows that can be found in the principal types of
value-creating systems in this environment: CD ROM production,
the provision of online services (via the Internet or the pay-as-you-
use information networks managed by value-added network
suppliers), and the supply of audiotext services. In 1995 these three
systems accounted for 80% of the sales of electronic publishing
products in the home market.

As can be seen, the activities leading to electronic publishing
products and services can be divided into four main categories:
those essentially related to the production of content; the technical
support activities for content production; CD ROM production;
and the distribution of the goods to the final users. The first
category includes activities such as authoring, information gathering
and editing (which are common to all value-creating systems), as
well as other activities (such as drawing, animation and story-
boarding) that are specific to particular systems; for example,
animation involves mainly the production of CD ROMs insofar as
animated products are still difficult to distribute on line. Content
production also includes what we have called integration activities:
these are specific insofar as they depend on the support used and,

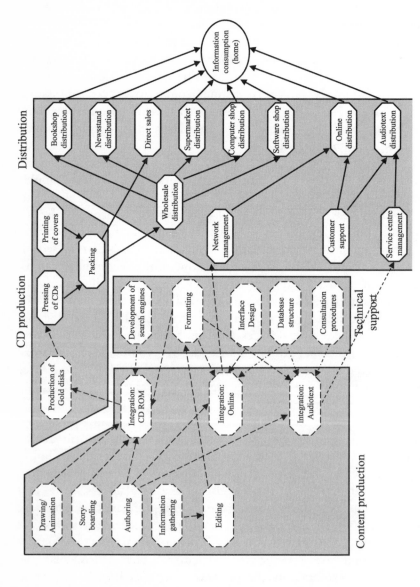

Figure 4.4   The principal value-creating systems in the electronic publishing industry

to a certain extent, can be assimilated to those of the director of a cinematographic product because they are aimed at integrating the contributions of the nodes whose output can be considered more specifically 'artistic'.

Once the content of an electronic publishing product has been assembled, it is necessary to distribute it. If it is distributed by means of a CD ROM, it is necessary to undertake all of the activities involved in its physical production (particularly the pressing of the CD itself); if it is intended to offer it in the form of a service, it is necessary to set up and manage an adequate transmission structure, which means carrying out the activities involved in managing audiotext or online service centres. The goods therefore reach the final customer by means of a series of alternative methods (summarized in the last column of Figure 4.4). In terms of wholesale and retail distribution, it is above all necessary to underline the fact that although only one node has been indicated for the sake of simplicity, the activities of wholesale distribution require distinct networks that depend on the type of retail distribution. Secondly, it is worth remembering that the most important retail distribution channels are newsstands (for low-range products), software shops (for high-range products) and computer shops; furthermore, it is also worth stressing the fact that, although the sales made through any one computer shop are rather limited, this last channel is still important because of the large number of computer shops present on the market.

Having outlined the principal activities carried out in the electronic publishing industry, we can ask ourselves some questions that are fundamental to any analysis of structural attractiveness. Where are its boundaries? Is it possible to consider the three types of support (CD ROM, online services and audiotext) as distinct segments? Do technical support activities form part of the sector? What about the activities involved in CD production?

Although the configuration of this value-creating system is rather complex, we can perhaps nevertheless still apply the classical analysis of the five competitive forces if we can identify a group of competitors who have made similar choices in terms of their configuration and can therefore be considered as representing a significant strategic group. Figures 4.5, 4.6 and 4.7 illustrate the configurations of the three principal Italian competitors: Mondadori Informatica (the Mondadori Group), Opera Multimedia (the

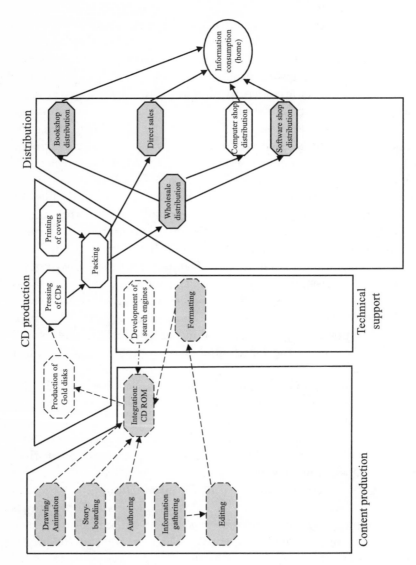

Figure 4.5   The configuration of the activities of Mondadori Informatica

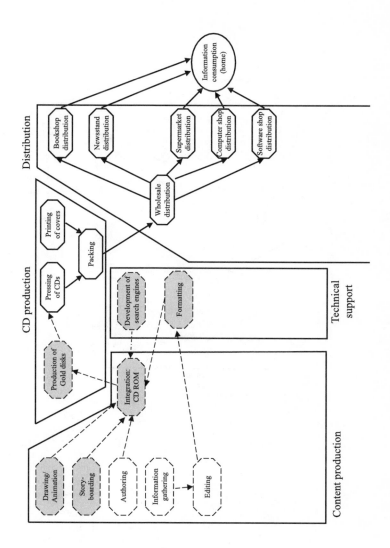

Figure 4.6   The configuration of the activities of Opera Multimedia

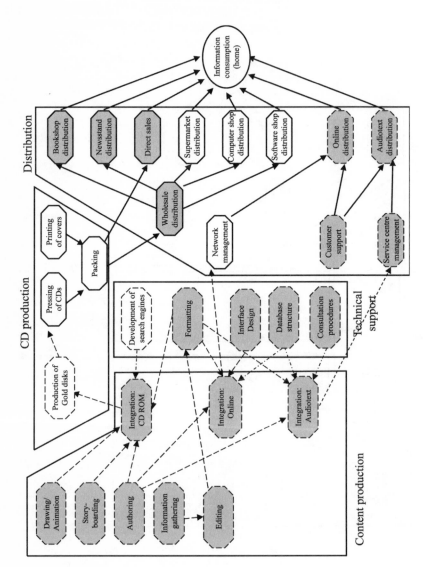

Figure 4.7 The configuration of the activities of RCS New Media

Olivetti Group) and the Rizzoli New Media division of the RCS group*.

In these three figures, the nodes that are directly controlled by the analysed economic player are grey, whereas the activities involved in the creation of value but not controlled by the companies concerned are white; those related to goods not offered by the individual companies have been omitted. For the sake of simplicity, if a given node is managed partially internally and partially externally, we have considered which of the two is prevalent without indicating the extent to which the node is controlled.

As can be seen, not even the configurations of the economic players involved in the electronic publishing industry are of great use in defining which activities have to be considered for structural analysis. The different sectors of origin of the competitors (book publishing, periodical and magazine publishing, daily newspaper publishing, information technology), together with their different strategic objectives and management styles, have led to very different choices not only in terms of competitive strategies but also and above all in terms of the configuration of their activities. The identification of the nodes controlled by the different players reveals such a wide range of configurations that it becomes seriously questionable as to whether any type of unitary structural analysis is possible. The different competitors have different suppliers (in particular, Opera Multimedia tends to concentrate on controlling the technical support nodes and outsources many content production activities, whereas Mondadori Informatica tends to concentrate on content production and looks for outside technical support), different direct customers (Rizzoli and Mondadori directly control some wholesale distribution channels, whereas Opera Multimedia makes use of independent wholesalers), and are differently involved in retail distribution (Mondadori directly manages a number of software shops).

If we set aside the activities related to the integration of multimedia products, the three competitors do not have any significant set of activities in common. Furthermore, Rizzoli New Media also operates in audiotext and online value-creating systems, and thus

---

*The research on which the example of the electronic publishing industry is based was carried out in 1996. Given the turbulence of the industry, some of the information we give may be outdated. Nevertheless, as our aim is not to describe an industry but a technique for industry analysis, this is not a real limitation.

obtains significant synergies at the level of the content production nodes that must be taken into account. As a consequence, the different players have different cost structures, different critical know-hows, and different degrees of bargaining power in relation to customers and suppliers.

In a case such as this, it is obvious that each of the competitors can be considered as a distinct strategic group and therefore, according to the methodology proposed by Porter, we should analyse attractiveness at the level of the individual economic player. However, this solution seems to be unsatisfactory to us because it is does not make it possible to distinguish the profitability determined by the structural features of the competitive context and that determined by the strategic positioning of the company within that context.

One possible solution to this problem could be to carry out the structural analysis of an object that is not the industry or the strategic group, but the individual activities making them up; i.e. the nodes of the value net.

4.2 STRUCTURAL ANALYSIS OF THE NODES IN A VALUE-CREATING SYSTEM

In the perspective of the value net, the natural object of structural analysis is represented by the nodes making it up; i.e. sets of relatively homogeneous activities which, for the purposes of strategic analysis, are worth considering as a whole.

The use of the nodes of the value net as the object of structural analysis makes it possible to recover the methodology of the analysis of structural attractiveness in all those situations in which the classical approach is difficult to apply because of the different configurations of the competitors and the difficulty of defining the boundaries of the competitive system. Even in the most complex competitive environments, nodes are sufficiently homogeneous internally to allow a meaningful structural analysis. This solution means lowering the level of structural analysis by considering elementary units (the nodes indicating sets of economically inseparable activities) rather than their macro-aggregates (the sectors or strategic groups that represent sets of economic players who, in their turn, represent dishomogeneous sets of activities).

This approach can be seen as particularly useful when it is borne in mind that, as was shown in Chapter 1, the emerging economic paradigm is characterized by an increasing variety of company configurations, different attitudes to outsourcing of the players competing in the same arena, and the advent of 'virtual' companies that bring together complementary skills in a flexible manner in order to develop common projects. The inadequacies of the application of classical methods of analysis to these increasingly frequent realities are now more than evident.

4.2.1 Recovering Structural Analysis at Node Level

Each node (or group of nodes) in a VCS presents a set of structural features that determine the structural attractiveness of the node itself. These features can be grouped in the following classes:

- the relationships established with the nodes providing the inputs;

- the relationships established with the nodes receiving the specific outputs of the considered node;

- the competition relating to the specific output of the node;

- entry barriers and potential competitors on the specific node;

- competition from substitute activities.

For each one of these groups of features, it is possible to make a structural analysis that is in many ways similar to that proposed by Porter (1980) for industry analysis. Figure 4.8 summarizes the main features that need to be considered within each group, by adapting Porter's five competitive forces model.

As the majority of the elements indicated in Figure 4.8 are very similar to those involved in classical industry analysis, we shall here limit our comments to the main differences from the model of the five competitive forces. The most complete description of the meaning of these elements in relation to the analysis of extended competitive systems is that provided by Porter (1980).

The fundamental difference between the structural analysis of nodes and that of extended rivalry is that the former describes the

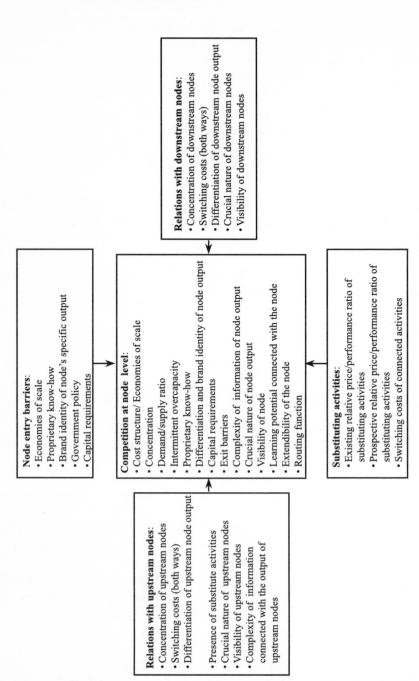

Node entry barriers:
- Economies of scale
- Proprietary know-how
- Brand identity of node's specific output
- Government policy
- Capital requirements

Competition at node level:
- Cost structure/ Economies of scale
- Concentration
- Demand/supply ratio
- Intermittent overcapacity
- Proprietary know-how
- Differentiation and brand identity of node output
- Capital requirements
- Exit barriers
- Complexity of information of node output
- Crucial nature of node output
- Visibility of node
- Learning potential connected with the node
- Extendibility of the node
- Routing function

Relations with downstream nodes:
- Concentration of downstream nodes
- Switching costs (both ways)
- Differentiation of downstream node output
- Crucial nature of downstream nodes
- Visibility of downstream nodes

Substituting activities:
- Existing relative price/performance ratio of substituting activities
- Prospective relative price/performance ratio of substituting activities
- Switching costs of connected activities

Relations with upstream nodes:
- Concentration of upstream nodes
- Switching costs (both ways)
- Differentiation of upstream node output
- Presence of substitute activities
- Crucial nature of upstream nodes
- Visibility of upstream nodes
- Complexity of information connected with the output of upstream nodes

Figure 4.8   Analysis of the structural attractiveness of the nodes

structure and relationships of the nodes of a VCS, whereas the latter describes the structure and relationships of groups of economic players. Nevertheless, despite this significant difference, it is not necessary to make any major changes in relation to the 'vertical' elements of the original model; i.e. the factors that determine the degree and type of competition at node level, the threat of new competitors, and that coming from substitute activities.

Although few changes have been made in relation to direct, indirect and potential competition, it has been necessary to adjust the 'horizontal' elements, as these relationships are no longer considered in terms of economic players but in terms of nodes. This means that bargaining power needs to be replaced by more generic relationships. Nevertheless, it has been possible to make use of many of the elements involved in the classical analysis (particularly the switching of costs to other upstream or downstream nodes, the degree of differentiation, the relative concentration). What has been eliminated from the traditional analysis are the threats of upstream and downstream integration, which have no meaning when we talk in terms of nodes.

4.2.2 New Determinants of Structural Attractiveness

Besides recovering many of the classical elements of industry analysis, the structural analysis of nodes highlights some relevant determinants of attractiveness that are not considered when working at industry level. These elements can be summarized as follows:

- the critical nature of the node for the creation of value;

- the extent to which the node is perceived by final customers;

- the learning potential connected with the node;

- the extendibility of the know-how and resources associated with the node;

- the routing function of the node.

Whereas the first two elements listed above partially overlap those included in the traditional analysis (particularly differentiation and brand identity), the remaining three are not considered at all despite the fact that they represent key factors in the determination of structural attractiveness, especially when this is considered from a dynamic point of view. What follows are some specific comments relating to the five elements listed above.

The Critical Nature of the Node

This depends on the importance that the specific output of the node has in terms of creating value for the final purchaser of a good; for example, the most critical nodes in the value-creating system of CD ROMs are those relating to the activities of integration and story-boarding.

The extent to which the individual nodes of a value-creating system may be critical depends not only on the type of product, but also on the market segment at which it is aimed. The quality of printing is critical only for some segments of the publishing sector (catalogues, art books, collection items), and has little importance for others, such as the paperback market. In the sector of earth-moving machinery, the rapid delivery of spare parts may be fundamental for customers who use the machines in scarcely populated and non-industrialized areas (e.g. for road building in Amazonia), but it is less important for those working in large industrialized cities in which specialized customer service centres can be easily found. The relationship between the critical nature of a node and market segments strictly depends on the relationship between the market segment and the relative importance of the different elements of the value received by the final customer (see Chapter 3).

Furthermore, the critical nature of individual nodes can change over time as a result of the changes in the competitive strategies adopted by the different economic players or the changes provoked by technological developments. For example, in the computer industry, the growing use of microprocessors to integrate functions previously performed by different electronic components has increased the critical nature of the activities of microprocessor design and production, and reduced that of the activities relating to the design and assembly of PCs. Over the last few years, this development has made the integration of separate electronic components considerably less critical and thus threatened the profitability of the companies controlling this activity (such as IBM).

Finally, critical nodes are those corresponding to weak points or bottlenecks in value-creating systems. A study of the PC industry carried out in 1990 highlighted the presence of a gap between the availability of very powerful hardware and that of appropriate software. One of the interviewees explained the problem in the following terms: 'The application programmes currently used on IBM-compatible personal computers (which are ten times more powerful than they were three years ago), have not changed. There has not been the development [in Italy] of new applications that make it possible to take advantage of the greater power made available by hardware technology, and this means that hardware producers find it difficult to obtain adequate remuneration for the greater power supplied.' In 1990 the bottleneck in the development of applications software prevented the full use of the potential offered by the hardware. However, just two years after this interview, the distribution of Windows 2.1 and other software applications involving complex graphic interfaces more than bridged this gap and shifted the emphasis back towards the hardware sector, thus stimulating the upgrading of the latter and therefore significantly contributing towards improving the profitability of the sector as a whole, and mainly that of its most critical nodes (particularly those involved in the design and production of microprocessors).

Visibility of the Node

There is generally a strict relationship between the critical nature of a node and its visibility. However, this is not to say that a highly critical node is necessarily perceived as fundamental by the final customer. We have already pointed out the essential and growing importance of microprocessors to the personal computer VCS because they represent the main factor responsible for the functioning, speed and processing capacity of PCs. Nevertheless, up to a few years ago, the average user paid more attention to the brand of computer (IBM, HP, etc.) than to the brand of microprocessor. It was precisely in order to change this state of affairs that in 1993 Intel began a highly successful promotional campaign as part of which computer manufacturers were asked to place an 'Intel inside' label on their PCs. The campaign was officially promoted as a means of combatting the sale of clones using the microprocessors produced by competitors, such as Advanced Micro Devices; but the actual result was to increase users' perception of the importance of microprocessors and encourage them to think that, all in all, the brand of PC was of relatively little importance in comparison with the brand of microprocessor.

Learning Potential of the Node

One structural element that the classical analysis of attractiveness fails to highlight is the learning potential associated with the management of a given node within a VCS. In some cases, the learning potential can be an even more interesting source of structural attractiveness than concentration, cost structure or entry barriers. For example, the operators in the electronic publishing industry consider that one of their greatest problems is a lack of knowledge of the worldwide offer, the market and the real needs of customers. This problem is partially related to the fact that electronic publishing products are still in the initial phase of being introduced to the market, and partially to the continuing technological turmoil that makes it difficult to monitor the evolution of an industry that sees the almost daily entry of new products and new companies. Many of the players already operating in this competitive context, as well as those that would like to do so, have responded by undertaking or commissioning market research studies aimed at clarifying (as far as possible) the type of offer present on the market, the needs expressed by customers, and the areas of the market that are still uncovered. However, this is not the only way of collecting this type of information. In Italy, for example, Mondadori Informatica entered the electronic publishing industry (see Figure 4.5 above), not only by publishing new titles in the form of CD ROMs, but also by opening software shops in the five largest Italian cities and thus entering the most important retail distribution channel for this type of product. Its management of these sales points provides Mondadori Informatica a cheap means of gathering such vital information as the extent of the existing offer (the shops sell the titles of all manufacturers), sell-out data, the demands and purchasing habits of customers, and the methods of selling products that are in many ways very different from the traditional publishing products to which they are often erroneously assimilated.

Another interesting example is provided by Microsoft which, among other things, uses its local branches to manage training courses relating to Microsoft products. The use of special software programmes designed to monitor the behaviour of the participants while they are doing the practical exercises allows Microsoft to identify the critical steps in application programmes, the points at which the majority of users make mistakes, and the displayed messages that prove to be unclear. This information is then used to improve the products offered by the company.

These examples make it possible to underline two important points. In the first place, managing a node does not automatically lead to learning opportunities; it is necessary to seek and develop the means that allow the carrying out of activities to be transformed into knowledge. If it were not for the programme designed to reveal errors on a statistical basis, Microsoft would not be able to take advantage of all the potential benefits offered by the fact that it organizes such courses.

Secondly, the learning potential of an activity may be greater for one player than another; for example, the management of a software shop provides information that is more significant for CD ROM publishers than for the companies responsible for physically pressing the CDs themselves. If a node offering a high degree of learning potential is not managed by a player who is interested in the information that it can generate, the information is generally lost. However, this does not mean that the node has lost its potential, but rather that the learning opportunities it offers have simply been ignored: for example, even an independent software shop could exploit its potential by systematically gathering information and selling it to whoever can make use of it.

Extendibility of the Node and/or its Related Know-how and Resources

In some cases, the management of a given node in a VCS not only makes it possible to acquire critical know-how and skills, but may also allow its specific output (as well as its skills and resources) to be used in other VCSs.

In the publishing sector, activities such as authoring (or the conception of an editorial product) and the gathering of information typically generate resources and skills that can be used in a number of different areas. The articles originally written for a magazine that specializes in offering fiscal advice can be transmitted to readers by means of relatively different VCSs; i.e. printed on paper, collected on a CD ROM or made available through an online database with payment on access. In this case, the specific output (the library of articles) is used within the context of different types of VCS that can be managed by a single enterprise or by other enterprises that acquire rights to the archive or act as go-betweens in its diffusion.

The specific output of a node can sometimes be used in many similar VCSs that lead to the production of the same product. For example, Canon produces laser printers and laser printer engines, which represent their most critical component insofar as they determine print quality and efficiency. Canon internally uses only some of the engines it produces, and sells the rest to a large number of other printer manufacturers as an 'original equipment manufacturer' (OEM). This means that the world market share of Canon in terms of the production of laser printer engines is more than 80%, whereas its share of the market of the finished product (laser printers) is much less.

A third type of extendibility is related to the distinctive skills that the management of a particular node can feed. The technological, organizational or marketing skills developed by carrying out a given activity can be synergistically used to carry out other activities requiring the same type of know-how; for example, Canon's know-how in the field of the production of laser printers and laser printer engines is used in the production of photocopiers or laser fax machines.

With reference to the literature concerning core competencies, what we call extendable nodes often correspond to the activities of research, design and production of core products that Prahalad and Hamel (1990) define as the intermediate goods between the core competencies of a company and its final products or services. However, it is worth pointing out that technological know-how does not necessarily represent the most important core competence, and that organizational and marketing skills (that do not contribute to the production of any core product) are often equally or even more important. Benetton's strategy of extending its product range from external knitwear to other clothing items and accessories was due more to its organizational and marketing skills than to the exploitation of common technologies.

In order to clarify the meaning of node extendibility, we can consider the case of a company that manages a database containing the information relating to all the calls for tenders made in Europe and publishes a fortnightly magazine containing all of the data contained in the database. The most extendable node is that represented by the support activities involved in the management and updating of the database itself. Figure 4.9 illustrates the various types of extendibility related to the node and its related know-how.

Whenever structural analysis highlights the presence of an extended or potentially extendable node, it is worthy of particular attention because its correct management may well lead to significant competitive advantages for both the original and inter-related value-creating systems. However, this does not mean that it is necessary to control such nodes at all costs. It is first necessary to consider that the use of a potentially extendable node in only one value-creating system may lead to competitive disadvantages in relation to other players who fully exploit the extendibility of similar nodes. An example of this can be seen in an interview given in the mid-1980s by a manager of Mandelli (an Italian company that once played a leading role in the factory automation industry and subsequently left the market), who had this to say about the decision of the company to produce its own control units for its machining centres: 'This decision distinguishes Mandelli from the other producers of industrial automation machinery. It is a choice that has involved considerable investments in terms of financial and human resources aimed at acquiring the technological skills necessary for carrying out adequate research activities. However, the choice is strategically justified by the critical nature of this component and the advantages it offers in terms of the quality of the final product and our ability to provide an effective after-sales service'. This justification of the decision to produce control units internally is convincing if we consider its critical contribution to the value-creating system to which Mandelli belonged. However, it is clear that Mandelli's market share for the finished products was not

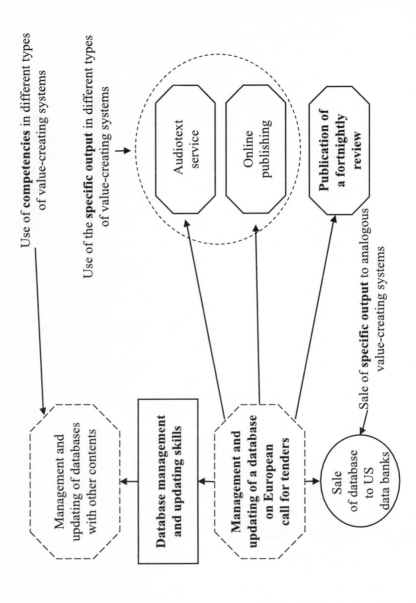

Use of **competencies** in different types of value-creating systems

Use of the **specific output** in different types of value-creating systems

Audiotext service

Online publishing

Publication of a fortnightly review

Sale of **specific output** to analogous value-creating systems

Management and updating of databases with other contents

Database management and updating skills

Management and updating of a database on European call for tenders

Sale of database to US data banks

Figure 4.9   Analysis of the structural attractiveness of nodes: extendability

large enough to justify the investments necessary for carrying out this activity with excellence, and therefore led to an under-use of the know-how and skills related to the node and the absence of synergistic relationships with other value-creating systems. In other words, when a node has a high degree of extendibility, it is necessary to decide whether to take direct advantage of such a possibility (e.g. Mandelli could have tried selling its control units to other producers of factory automation equipment) or leave the management of the node to others who are capable of managing it more effectively and efficiently.

Node Routing Function

One final element that can influence the structural attractiveness of a node is any routing function that it may have; i.e. the capacity of whoever manages it to direct customers towards other economic players. A classic example of routing is represented by the activities of general practitioners, who send their patients to see other medical specialists or prescribe them medicines and thus favour one pharmaceutical company over another. The Internet features many examples of routing because the management of a much visited site provides an opportunity to direct visitors to other sites. The nodes that have a routing function are generally highly profitable for their managers insofar as they make it possible to receive explicit remuneration (or other benefits) not only from the players who are routed (patients or the visitors to an Internet site), but also from those who benefit from the routing (the medical specialists, pharmaceutical companies, or connected Internet sites).

At the end of this section dedicated to the analysis of structural attractiveness, it seems to be important to stress the fact that the use of nodes as the subject of investigation not only makes it possible to recuperate all of the concepts of classical analysis, but also to overcome some of its inherent limitations even when the boundaries of a sector are clearly definable and the competitors have similar configurations.

We can take the example of a strategic group of competitors operating in the industrial biscuit-making segment and characterized by a set of competitors with a good brand image and a wide range of products. Let us also suppose that all these competitors internally carry out all of the activities of new product development, marketing, production and packaging, directly manage their relationships with large-scale distributors, and have stable collaborative relationships with the wholesalers who handle distribution to the other retail outlets. The application of the traditional analysis of attractiveness to this strategic group would lead us to believe that its cost structure is characterized by a prevalence of fixed and variable structural costs over policy costs (let us suppose an average of 10% development costs, 35% variable costs and 55% fixed costs), that economies of scale are quite significant, that the importance of its exclusive know-how is medium-high, and that the entry barriers are medium-low. In reality, these considerations come from the average of the characteristics of the different groups of activities (or nodes) that can be identified within the strategic group. Economies of scale, for example, are very large in relation to marketing activities (which include specific brand support activities), but medium-low when it comes to the physical production of the goods (production and packaging); the development costs stem mainly from support activities (the development of new products and marketing) and have little to do with other activities; and the entry barriers are relatively high in the case of marketing and new product development activities (which depend on specific know-how and capital, particularly in relation to advertising campaigns aimed at brand support), but are medium-low in the case of production activities.

Even in the case of a clearly defined competitive system such as that of the branded industrial biscuit-making sector, basing the analysis of structural attractiveness on individual nodes and not on a typical bundle of activities reveals the characteristics and determinants of the attractiveness of the individual activities, and thus provides a more adequate basis for any choice of strategic positioning.

4.3 THE FUNDAMENTAL STEPS IN VALUE NET ANALYSIS

The aim of this section is to outline the fundamental steps of value net analysis. Although specific cases may well require different approaches, a possible general sequence can be defined as follows:

- preliminary identification of consumption activities;

- description of the most widespread traditional VCS:

  — definition of production and support activities, their aggregation in nodes and the identification of significant flows;

  — identification of the boundaries of the economic players;

  — structural analysis of the nodes;

- market segmentation on the basis of ideal VCS configurations;

- analysis and comparison of alternative value-creating systems;

- identification of opportunities for innovation.

4.3.1 Preliminary Identification of Consumption Activities

VCSs do not constitute an objective reality, but represent a set of activities whose composition may vary in relation to the way in which its consumption activities are defined. It follows that the choice of the consumption activities upon which to base the analysis is a highly delicate but essential step for the correct definition of the VCS itself. We can go back to the example of the use of personal computers; the VCS of stand-alone PCs includes the lines of hardware and software; that of multimedia PCs includes the activities relating to the production of multimedia contents; that of multimedia PCs inserted in a network has to be further extended to include telecommunication products and services, as well as added value online services.

Whenever possible, the analysis should be made from the point of view of the final customer because this encourages a broader vision that makes it possible to question the traditional system, and is more useful for developing an understanding of how to increase created value.

However, although concentrating on the final customer is often enlightening, it may lead to an over-complex representation and, in such cases, it may be worth constructing the net by taking an intermediate customer as the point of reference. For example, in the case of the system leading to the production of a machine for moulding plastic materials, starting from the final customer would mean starting from the end-user of the final product. However, this approach is likely to make things extremely complicated and, more importantly, is unlikely to provide a model that would be useful for someone who has to make strategic decisions concerning the production of moulding machines; it would therefore be better to interrupt the representation of the VCS before it reaches the final customer, and to take the company that uses the machine for its own production as the consumer.

It is important to underline that beginning strategic analysis by defining consumption activities and adopting the point of view of the final customer does not mean basing everything on the needs expressed by the customers themselves.

In proposing core competencies as the starting point for strategic analyses, Hamel and Prahalad (1994) criticize the 'fashion of customer orientation' and state that companies need to be able to go beyond what their customers ask for. In their book *Competing for the Future*, they support their point of view as follows: 'It is much in vogue to be customer-led. From their bully pulpits ... CEOs tell the troops that "everything begins with the customer". Companies claim to be reengineering their processes from the customer backward. Rewards and incentives are tied to measures of customer satisfaction ... We applaud the sentiment ... On the other hand if the goal is to get to the future first, rather than merely preserving market share in existing businesses, a company must be much more than customer-led. Customers are notoriously lacking in foresight.'

A similar concept is expressed by Akio Morita, the President of Sony, who says that: 'Our plan is to lead the public with new products rather than ask them what kind of products they want. The public does not know what is possible, but we do. So instead of doing a lot of market research, we refine our thinking on a product and its use and try to create a market for it by educating and communicating with the public.'

At first sight, the contraposition between core competencies on the one hand and final customers and products on the other, as well as the assumption that strategic innovation should be essentially based on the first, appears to conflict with one of the key assumptions of the value net model; i.e. that VCSs can be defined by beginning with the final activity of consumption and need to be analysed by adopting the point of view of the customer (particularly the final customer).

In reality, the core competence and value net approaches are anything but incompatible, and are in many ways complementary.

Adopting a customer perspective does not necessarily mean basing one's strategy on what customers demand at a given moment and blindly following the indicators of customer satisfaction. Although the indications coming from final customers may be important for refining the offer of the system, adopting a customer perspective essentially means looking at the VCS as a whole from the point of view of the end user in order to identify any inconsistencies, inadequacies and bottlenecks that may be present in the offer and/or the configuration of the system.

Within the framework of a given social and technological context, adopting a customer perspective therefore means:

- asking oneself what constitutes value for the final customer;

- establishing the activities that come together in creating value;

- verifying the presence of any inadequacies in the VCS;

- verifying that the customer manages to take full advantage of the potentially created value.

The perspective of the final customer is therefore something different from customer satisfaction, and it is not necessary to make costly market research studies in order to understand what creates value for customers. For example, one of the elements of the success of Ikea is the containment of final customer costs that is also due to the fact that it is the customers themselves who are responsible for the transport and mounting of the products they buy. It is unlikely that such an innovation could have been triggered by a market research study because, before the arrival of Ikea, it was simply taken for granted that furniture retailers delivered and mounted the products they sold.

From a more long-term point of view (and therefore one that also takes into account the possibility of changes in the social and technological context), the adoption of a customer perspective means that a company has to put itself in its customers' shoes and, on the basis of its own interpretation of future social and technological developments, think of new products, new functions and new value-creating systems that its customers are in no position to imagine.

For example, in the case of a television company, customer orientation does not necessarily mean adjusting its programming schedule on the basis of audience figures because, over the long term, this would lead to the continuation of previously successful formulas and a consequent absence of innovation; it is more a case of trying to understand how to respond to needs that its customers have not yet formulated. One example of this is that, before the advent of CNN, many people thought that it would be impossible to manage an exclusively news-based television network. Ted Turner confounded the sceptics by adopting an original view of the social, economic and technological changes that were modifying the lifestyles of a certain segment of users for whom information was also important at the level of work and whose longer and unpredictable working hours were incompatible with fixed-time news broadcasts. Furthermore, he recognized that there was a demand for in-depth international news that was practically impossible to satisfy by means of a generalist channel aimed at a public with primarily national or local interests, and was also sensitive to the technological developments that would change content production (high-quality cameras and portable satellite-based transmitters that allow an enormous reduction in production costs) and transmission (cable and satellite technologies that make it possible to reach every part of the world), as well as to regulatory changes which, in the USA, favoured the development of cable television. The combination of all of these developments created the basis for the success of an increasingly global network (in terms of both content and delivery) that transmits news around the clock.

However, the ability of CNN to adopt a customer perspective is also clear from the way in which it has defined its business; it is not just a television network, but a company that tries to offer an effective and efficient response to the information needs of a particular market segment also by means of parallel value-creating systems. In addition to the supply of a teletext service (something that is offered by many other television networks), it manages an information-rich Internet site (CNN Interactive) by means of which it is possible to obtain the complete transcription of its transmitted broadcasts, undertake searches by means of key words or subjects and request the texts of broadcasts made even many months before, request information concerning stock exchange quotations and exchange rates, and interact with CNN by means of electronic messages.

The details and examples given above demonstrate that the customer perspective proposed by the value net is perfectly compatible with that of the core competence model. Companies are capable of providing an innovative response to the needs expressed by their customers thanks to the use of their technological, marketing and organizational skills; and it is precisely the adoption of a customer perspective that allows the identification of customer needs and the obstacles preventing their satisfaction.

As we shall see below, a precise analysis of VCSs means a careful segmentation of the market in order to identify those segments that require different types of VCS. However, it is usually better to begin with a general and widely-accepted definition of consumption activities, analyse the traditional VCS based on such activities, and only then move on to a more sophisticated market segmentation and the description of emerging and innovative VCSs.

We shall use the case of book publishing as a means of providing a concrete illustration of the various phases of value net analysis.* In general, this means that we shall concentrate on the consumption activities aimed at satisfying the need for reading and study materials, and non-periodical information: i.e. we shall look at the consumption of books while bearing in mind that the activities of this consumption can also be satisfied by products and services other than books.

4.3.2 Description of Traditional VCSs

Once the needs and the consequent consumption activities in which we are interested have been defined (even in general terms), it is worth analysing the most common and typical VCS that responds to these needs.

---

*The information referring to the publishing industry and the figures relating to this case are taken from a paper currently in the course of publication by Paola Dubini and Cinzia Parolini entitled: 'Redefining segments, boundaries and value-creating systems in the book publishing industry'.

Definition of Production and Support Activities, their Aggregation in Nodes and the Identification of Significant Flows

This phase begins with the identification of all of the activities involved in the manufacture of the final production and the aggregation of these activities in nodes that simultaneously ensure a representation that is both clear and sufficiently detailed. We have already seen that every VCS can be divided into a practically unlimited number of nodes, which is why the activities should be aggregated whenever possible. However, this aggregation should be limited to distinguishing the nodes that:

• lead to the creation of autonomously sellable goods;

• can be managed by different players within the system;

• represent activities that have a different nature (realization, support, transaction management);

• have different structural characteristics.

Figure 4.10 shows the traditional VCS of book publishing. A number of methodological considerations need to be made in relation to Figure 4.10.

• The individual value-creating activities have been grouped into four macro-categories: publishing (i.e. the elaboration of the content and the production of all of the supports necessary for physical production), printing, distribution and the management of returns.

• The activities of purchase and sale in the strict sense between the different players are not included because their positions depend on the effective legal boundaries of the players.

• Wholesale distribution activities are represented in a simplified manner; in reality, the national and regional distributors are different, depending on whether the product is delivered through bookshops or bookstalls. Given the level of the analysis, this simplification should not lead to any significant distortion.

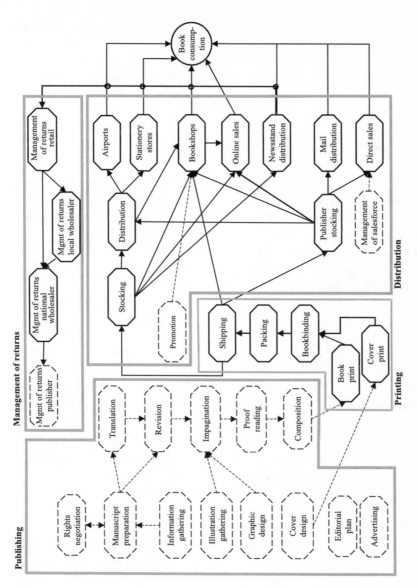

Figure 4.10   Traditional book publishing VCS

- For the same reason, retail distribution activities have been simplified by not distinguishing those carried out by independent bookshops from those carried out by shop chains, although a more thorough analysis should take into account the different configurations of the two types.

- Not all the activities and flows have been represented, but only those considered to be most relevant and interesting.

Identification of the Boundaries of the Economic Players

The principal players operating in the traditional VCS are authors, publishing houses, printers, wholesalers and retailers. In addition, there are some specialized players (translators, graphic artists, editing companies) who are sub-contracted (generally by the publishers) to undertake clearly circumscribed activities. Figure 4.11 illustrates the division of the activities in the traditional VCS between these players.

Obviously, Figure 4.11 shows the most common boundaries of the players operating in book publishing, but it is possible to find other situations. For example, some large-scale publishers also control the activities of intermediate distribution and, in some cases, directly manage retail salespoints. Furthermore, bookshop chains may be large enough to justify upstream integration with intermediate distribution. In some cases, these chains may even undertake publishing activities by launching their own collections. As we have seen in the example of electronic publishing, the value net can be a useful means of comparing players who, although they operate in the same sector, present different definitions of activities.

With the aid of Figures 4.10 and 4.11, we now try to highlight the essential characteristics and, above all, the limitations and problems of the traditional book publishing VCSs.

The first phases of book publishing involve content development up to the preparation of the films from which the book will be printed. This set of activities is carried out on the basis of the sensitivity of the authors and the orientation of the publishers; with the exception of some products (such as encyclopedias and works published in instalments), it is unlikely that a preliminary market analysis is made in order to verify product acceptance. As a sector

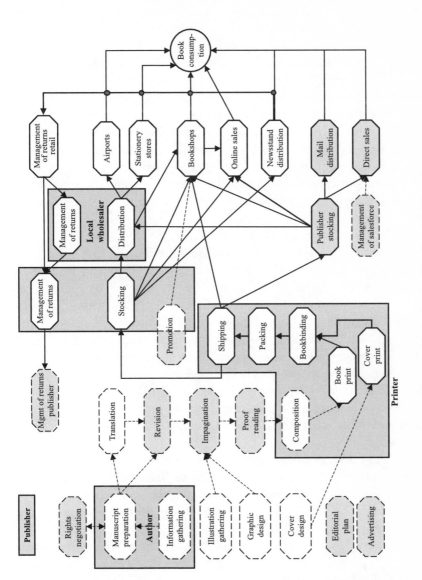

Figure 4.11 Traditional boundaries of book publishing players

saying has it: 'the best market research consists in getting the books on the shelves of the bookshops'. In addition to the authors and publishers, the creation of the product also involves a series of specialized players such as translators, graphic designers and editing companies.

Once the contents have been prepared, the next step is the physical production of the book. The production activities and characteristics of the traditional distribution channels mean that publishers tend to produce a minimum number of copies (about 1500–2000) even in the case of books whose market potential is limited or very uncertain. This is partially due to the requirements of traditional printing technology (which has very high unit costs for limited print runs) and partially to the fact that the fragmentation of the distribution system means that a large number of books have to be printed in order to be able to deliver at least one or two copies to a good number of bookshops.

After printing, the books can be distributed through many different and not mutually exclusive channels. They can be sent to the warehouse of the publisher or directly to that of national or regional intermediate distributors. In some cases, newly printed books may even be sent directly to the bookshops, particularly when they are large and the book is printed in a large number of copies. In other cases, they may follow a longer and more tortuous path from the publisher to an intermediate distributor and wholesaler before arriving at the retailer. Although this way of operating is necessary to guarantee good territorial coverage, the diseconomies and complexity connected with so many intermediate stages are self-evident.

The inefficiencies of the distribution system are aggravated by the presence of a considerable flow of returns. Intermediate distributors and retailers often purchase books whose sales potential they cannot evaluate. For this reason, the sector makes widespread use of the right of return. When a book remains unsold for too long, retailers can decide to return it and thus set underway an extremely costly backwards process. In some cases, returned books are diverted by intermediate distributors or the publishers themselves towards other sales channels; in others, they have to go back along the complete path and are finally pulped. In Italy, about 40% of the books on display in sales points remain unsold and are eventually returned, and the figures in other countries are comparable.

No description of the book publishing VCS would be complete if it did not also include the role and activities of final customers. Figures 4.10 and 4.11 refer simply to a generic activity of consumption, but this can and must be analysed in more detail if we really want to understand the dynamics of the sector.

The role of final customers in the traditional book publishing VCS is articulated and differentiated. In addition to reading, they are also involved in activities of collecting and selecting information, which can be rather onerous because of the inability of the system to supply adequate information beyond that offered by the physical copy of the book. Only in the case of books that have great market potential can publishers and distributors engage in advertising and promotional support activities, providing information by means of daily newspapers, periodicals, organized events and, more rarely, the radio and television. In this context, information is mainly spread by the consumers themselves and word of mouth is by far the most effective method of communication.

Another of the activities carried out by consumers is photocopying. Photocopying (and the consequent lack of remuneration for the activities carried out by the whole publishing chain) is a problem that is taken very seriously by publishers. Little used in some sectors, in others it has taken on worrying proportions: for example, about 50% of the demand in the segments of university and professional publishing is covered by photocopies. Although publishing houses try to oppose the illegal act of photocopying, it cannot be denied that it is often precisely their way of operating that drives consumers to commit it. Books are photocopied not only to save money on purchasing costs, but often also because of difficulties in finding the book itself (it is out of print, cannot be traced or can only be found after a long period of waiting) or because the reader is interested only in a small part of it. In some cases, therefore, photocopying is the only alternative; in others, purchase is possible but too expensive in relation to the real need of the reader.

One final observation that can be made is that the consumer and purchaser of a book are not always the same person, as when a book is bought by a library or as a present for someone else.

As far as consumer analysis is concerned, by generalizing what we have seen in the case of book publishing, we can underline the following points:

- When analyzing any value net, it is important to articulate the activity of consumption, particularly when the final customer does not correspond to the final user. In some cases, the roles surrounding consumption are even more complex than in publishing; an extreme example is that of medicinal products, which are chosen by physicians, paid for by a public body, purchased by an individual and consumed by the same person or a member of his family.

- It is also important to represent the activities of value creation that the final purchaser may carry out (such as the activity of photocopying) because, in some cases, these are highly relevant. The customers of Ikea, for example, design, transport and assemble their furnishing systems, and it is precisely this different way of involving customers that represents one of the company's main advantages over its competitors.

Structural Analysis of the Nodes

Once the nodes of a VCS have been defined, and the boundaries of the main players outlined, it is worth making the structural analysis described in the first part of this chapter. This is a very important phase that makes it possible to determine the attractiveness of individual nodes by providing suggestions for the definition of make, buy or connect choices.

One classical element of structural analysis is the degree of concentration of the offer. The traditional non-periodical publishing VCS is highly fragmented both upstream (content production) and downstream (retail sales), whereas it is relatively concentrated in the phases of intermediate distribution. In some countries, downstream fragmentation has decreased as a result of the market success of chains of bookshops, but this has essentially led to a concentration in the ownership of salespoints, whereas their territorial fragmentation remains. The upstream and downstream fragmentation is, respectively, due to the naturally extreme variety of the content and the geographical dispersion of the market. The activities that have a relatively more concentrated offer are those of intermediate distribution, with benefits in terms of the bargaining power of the players controlling them.

Other interesting structural characteristics of the book publishing VCS include the great learning potential of retail sale activities (often not exploited), the high degree of extendibility of the activities of content production (again often not exploited), and the large variety of situations in terms of the visibility of the different activities. In some cases, the consumer is attracted by the author, in others he may be swayed by the name of the publisher and, in particular, may be attracted by special collections or series. In yet other cases, consumers recognize and are significantly influenced by the retail salespoint.

What is it that has led to this picture? The main factors determining the configuration of a VCS can often be identified by considering the characteristics of the flows of goods and information. In our case, we can make the following observations.

The traditional book publishing VCS essentially developed as a result of the needs and characteristics of goods flows: the concentration during the printing phase and the fragmentation of retail distribution are both due to the characteristics of these flows and the technologies available to manage them. Having to reach a geographically highly dispersed market with a large variety of predefined titles, and given the available technology, the traditional VCS could not take on any other configuration.

The information flows in the traditional VCS are highly limited and mainly one-way: in the traditional system, information is mainly bundled with its physical support (the books) and this makes the information flows as tortuous and inefficient as those of the goods. Furthermore, the flows are mainly from up- to downstream for the same reason. This overlapping of goods and information flows determines the essence of the traditional VCS and has a number of significant consequences.

- Consumers can find the information necessary for their purchasing decisions almost exclusively by physically consulting the book. This not only leads to multiple distribution and the consequent need to have relatively large minimum print runs, but also to the complex and costly management of returns described above.

- The direct communication channels between consumers and publishers are very limited. This means that the authors and publishers do not have the means to present their products in the best way, or to collect timely information from the market that would be useful for the development of editorial plans.

- The bundle of contents cannot be personalized. The lack of two-way communications in the traditional VCS means that the bundle of the contents of a book can only be defined by the authors and publisher, and consumers cannot define personalized contents on the basis of their own needs. This is one of the reasons for the extreme variety of the products on the market. In the case of tourist guides, for example, a traveller who wants to visit Italy and stay in Rome, Milan and one of the minor cities has no possibility of receiving only the information that interests him (e.g. the gastronomy, art, entertainment and cycling itineraries in the places he is going to). He will find tourist guides on Italy in general, guides to individual cities, some gastronomic guides that are very generic and others that are too specific. It is unlikely that he will find anything about cycling itineraries, and he will need to consult the local press for information concerning entertainment. As a result, he will have to purchase a lot of information that does not interest him and will not receive other information that interests him very much. In the traditional VCS, publishers cannot do anything but try to satisfy readers' needs by putting on the market a large variety of pre-packaged products and hoping that one or more of them will succeed, as a whole, in satisfying the majority of the needs of individual consumers. Nevertheless, despite the large variety of proposals, consumers often fail to find what is useful to them and consequently decide to create their own bundle of contents by photocopying what interests them from various sources.

4.3.3 Market Segmentation on the Basis of Ideal VCS Configurations

We have seen that, given the technology available up to a few years ago, the book publishing VCS could not have any other configuration than the one it has. However, recent advances in technology have created interesting opportunities for innovation not only in terms of products (many publishers have already launched multimedia products), but also in terms of processes. In this context, it is important to identify trends and try to understand which activities and market segments will undergo the most significant changes. Should we expect radical changes throughout the system or only in some parts of it (for example, in distribution)? Will the new technologies have a strong impact on all segments of the market or only some of them, and, in this last case, which segments will be most affected?

It is striking to note that the traditional form of market segmentation in the publishing sector (as in many other sectors) does not distinguish market segments for which it might be worthwhile to structure differentiated VCSs. The market is traditionally segmented by genre (thrillers, romance, non-fiction, school texts, narrative, etc.) and channel (bookshop, bookstall, direct mailing, door-to-door, online, etc.). Although functional in terms of communication, segmentation by genre does not take into account the characteristics of the VCSs, but leads to distinguishing genres (e.g. thrillers and romantic novels) whose content may well be different but whose needs in terms of management are exactly the same. In other cases, products requiring differentiated management are grouped together in the same segment (non-fiction includes both popularizing works as well as specialized texts, despite the fact that they need to be handled differently). Segmentation by channel is more suited to distinguishing products with different VCSs but still has a number of limitations insofar as it considers only one part of the system (distribution) and reflects the distribution choices already made by the operators in the sector. In other words, it is a type of segmentation that, by describing the distribution choices of the past, does not provide the best basis for questioning the traditional way of doing business.

In order to evaluate without prejudices the opportunities for innovation created by the new technologies, it is necessary to segment the market by distinguishing different ways of using publishing products. This makes it possible to distinguish segments for which different ways of creating value can be conceived and consequently upon which the impact of the new technologies is likely to be greatest. Figure 4.12 shows a market segmentation based on these criteria.

As can be seen in Figure 4.12, if it is required to identify market segments that have (or could have) different methods for creating value, it is worth segmenting the demand on the basis of the

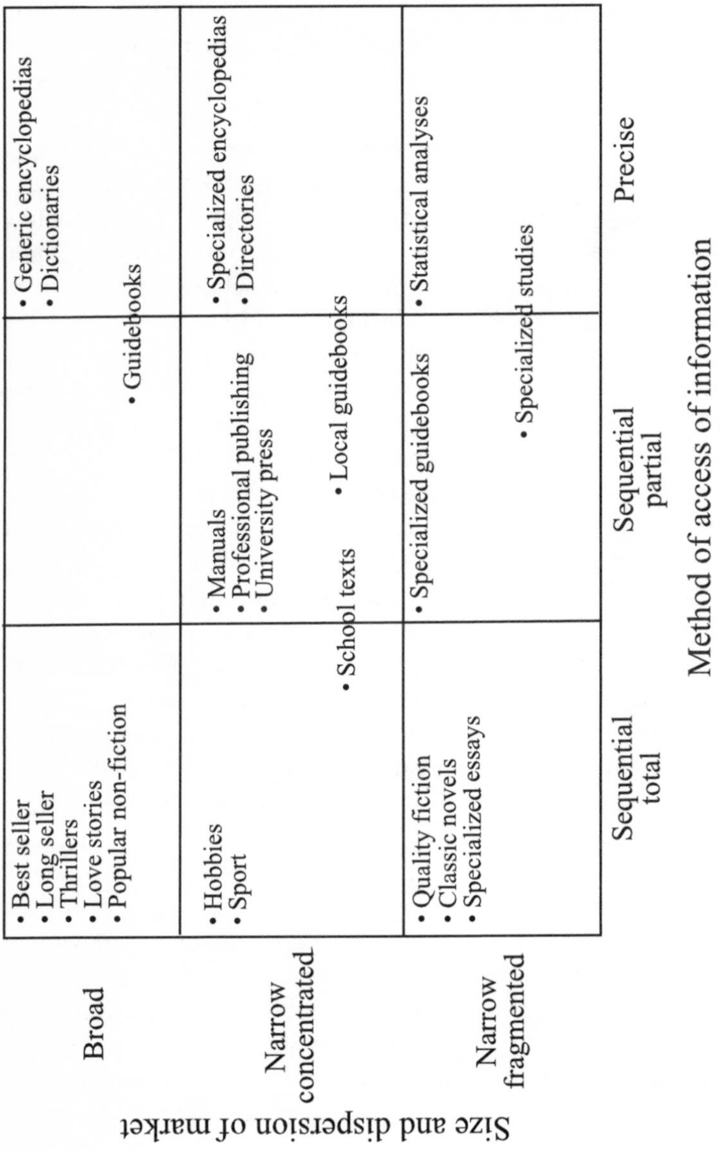

	Sequential total	Sequential partial	Precise
Broad	• Best seller • Long seller • Thrillers • Love stories • Popular non-fiction	• Guidebooks	• Generic encyclopedias • Dictionaries
Narrow concentrated	• Hobbies • Sport • School texts	• Manuals • Professional publishing • University press • Local guidebooks	• Specialized encyclopedias • Directories
Narrow fragmented	• Quality fiction • Classic novels • Specialized essays	• Specialized guidebooks • Specialized studies	• Statistical analyses

Method of access of information

Size and dispersion of market

Figure 4.12   Segmentation of the publishing market

size and dispersion of the market and methods of gaining access to information. It is possible to add a segmentation based on the frequency with which the contents are updated (despite its partial overlapping of the segmentation by method of access); this is not shown in Figure 4.12 in order not to over-complicate the matrix.

As far as size and dispersion of the market are concerned, the market of a publishing product can be broad (e.g. best-sellers and popularist non-fiction), narrow and concentrated on easily localizable customer segments (e.g. professional or university texts), or narrow and fragmented in terms of the distribution of customers (e.g. quality fiction and highly specialized non-fiction works). Although the traditional VCS generally manages to provide an adequate response in terms of the products that have a broad market, its limitations become all too clear when it comes to products that have a narrow market (especially if this is also fragmented). For example, it often happens that a certain book remains unsold on the shelves of one bookshop while a customer is uselessly looking for it in another (one study carried out by McKinsey estimated that about 35% of the people entering a bookshop do not find the book they are looking for). In these cases, it can happen that the book remains unsold and the potential customer gives up his idea of reading it or, if he is very motivated, decides to photocopy it.

With reference to the method of access to information, although important because of its effects on the method of distribution, segmentation by market size does not make it possible to identify the real needs of consumers. For this purpose, it may be useful to segment the market on the basis of the method of access to information by distinguishing total sequential reading (typical of novels), partial sequential reading (typical of manuals and professional or university texts) and precise consultation (typical of dictionaries and encyclopedias). If the reading is sequential and total, the consumer wishes to read all of the work, usually in the sequence established by the author. If the reading is sequential and partial, he tends to read only a part of the book sequentially (e.g. a chapter), and the other parts may not be read at all or be read in a sequence established by the reader. Finally, if the method of access is precise, the consumer does not want to 'read' but simply consults the book in order to identify the information of interest.

It is worth underlining the fact that the method of access depends not only on the product, but also on the type of reader. A classic novel, for example, can be read by one consumer totally and sequentially, whereas an academic may only want to read a chapter or consult some specific parts.

The traditional VCS is reasonably satisfactory if the method of access is total and sequential, but has many limitations in the case of partial or specific reading. In this last case, for example, the consumer is forced to purchase a lot of information he will never use; furthermore, traditional printed dictionaries and encyclopedias are slow to consult and difficult to update. As far as partial sequential reading is concerned, the limitation of the traditional VCS is that it makes available pre-defined bundles of content, only part of which is of interest to the consumer. Once again, the result is that the consumers try to 'disassemble' the bundle by means of photocopying. The classic example of this is that of university students who, only having to work on one chapter of a book, make a photocopy of it in order to avoid purchasing the entire book.

As regards the content update, this may not be necessary (as in the case of a novel), may happen rarely (as in the case of a high school mathematics book), may be quite frequent (encyclopedias) or may even be continuous (as in the case of directories or some statistical information). Once again, the traditional VCS is reasonably functional in some cases (when no or infrequent updating is necessary), but has clear limitations when it comes to the need for frequent or continuous updating. When updating is essential to the usefulness of the information (stock exchange quotations, for example), the traditional VCS cannot provide an acceptable product.

As pointed out above, there is a certain relationship between the method of access to information and the frequency with which it is updated. The products that are normally read in a sequential and total manner do not normally require updating, whereas those intended for specific consultation are generally updated more frequently. However, there are many exceptions to this correlation: e.g. dictionaries are used for specific consultation but do not require frequent updating.

The traditional VCS adequately responds to the upper-left segment in Figure 4.12, but its limitations become increasingly evident

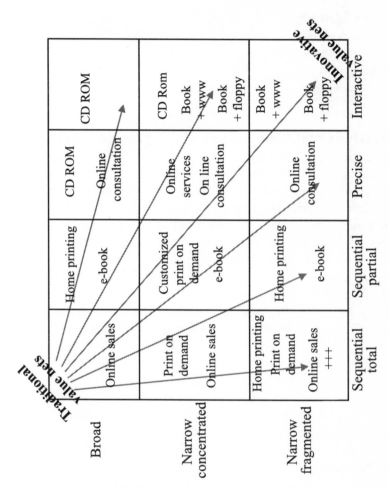

Figure 4.13 Innovations by segment in non-periodical publishing.

moving downwards and towards the right, where it is consequently more seriously threatened by alternative VCSs capable of exploiting the potential of new technologies. Figure 4.13 shows some of the innovative solutions that can provide an adequate response to the needs of the different segments.

As can be seen, Figure 4.13 includes a new form of gaining access to information (the interactive method) that was not considered in Figure 4.12 insofar as it cannot be managed by the traditional VCS. It provides a clear picture of the alternative and innovative VCSs that will be described in the next section.

4.3.4 Analysis and Comparison of Alternative Value-creating Systems

In some sectors it is possible to identify only one type of VCS. In such cases, the various competitors operate within similar VCSs and differ only in terms of the type and number of controlled activities. However, other competitive contexts simultaneously include alternative VCS configurations. In particular, highly innovative strategies lead to configurations that are different from those of the traditional VCS and, in this case, it is very interesting to make a comparison between the new and old configuration in order to identify their differences and evaluate their advantages and disadvantages.

The non-periodical publishing sector provides an excellent example of this insofar as a large number of highly innovative competitive formulae are beginning to emerge which, in some cases, are radically changing the traditional way of doing business. Many of these formulae are still in the experimental phase, and the financial results of most of them have been disappointing, when they have not been completely negative. Nevertheless, this lack of profitability does not make them any the less interesting; in some cases, it can be presumed that the financial problems will be solved once the new formulae have become more established, although it is also possible that some have structural flaws that can only be corrected by means of radical changes. In any case, these configurations are very different from the traditional VCS because they are capable of responding differently to customer needs and therefore worth analysing very carefully.

One of the most significant developments concerns the VCSs oriented towards online sales. Their main difference from the traditional configuration is related to distribution, although their associated structural modifications imply consequences on the whole system. An interesting aspect of online sales is that, as often happens, the operators in the sector initially tried to graft it onto the traditional system, and obtained only disappointing results. The first experiments involved bookshops that decided to put their catalogues online in order to allow remote purchasing. Some publishers also moved in the same direction, considering the system simply as a new direct sales channel. These limited initiatives can be related to the traditional VCS and are represented as one of the possible distribution channels in Figures 4.10 and 4.11. With the exception of some publishers operating in the narrow concentrated segment (e.g. Harvard Business School Publishing), the first attempts at online selling were not very successful, mainly because they reflected the extreme fragmentation of the salespoints and publishers; hundreds of online sales sites were set up on the Internet, but the majority failed to acquire visibility and did not provide an adequate service.

The online sale of books started to emerge from the experimental phase when Amazon.com entered the market with a commitment and level of investment that made all previous attempts look very slight in comparison. Amazon.com was the first company to take into account the structural differences between online and traditional distribution. In particular, it understood the enormous economies of scale and the importance of market share in this type of distribution, and was consequently the first to invest heavily in advertising. Just a few years after the start-up of Amazon.com (founded in 1994), it is already clear that only a very small number of companies can successfully compete on the market of online sales because of the irrelevance of a capillary territorial presence and the fact that the majority of the activities involved are those of support, with the consequent impact on cost structure described in detail in Chapter 1.2. The other major online competitor on the United States market is Barnes & Noble, America's largest bookshop chain which, in 1997, opened its own site for online sales. The most active player on the European market is Bertelsmann, a large and diversified publishing enterprise that has recently announced a collaborative agreement with Barnes &

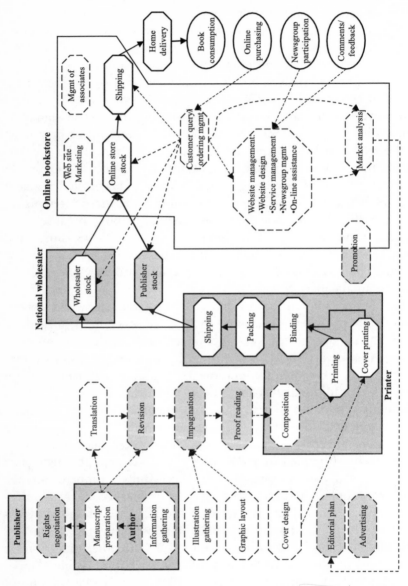

Figure 4.14   The value net of online bookshops

Noble. Figure 4.14 summarizes the value net of a large-scale online bookshop.

In relation to Figure 4.14, it is worth pointing out the following.

- Online sales make it possible to increase the value-creating activities carried out by the final customer, who is directly involved in the data entry relating to his purchase(s) and can significantly contribute to the spread of information by making available his own reviews and participating in newsgroups.

- The management of the site is a highly articulated activity that includes the development of a series of online services (detailed information about the books, communications with some authors, a purchasing and gift suggestion service) and the management of information flows initiated by customers.

- Website management initially appeared to be the key activity in the running of online bookshops, but the weight of order, warehousing and shipping management soon made itself felt. According to Bezos, the founder and CEO of Amazon: 'The logistics of distribution are the iceberg below the waterline of online bookselling'. Eighty percent of the investments made by Amazon for the development of software during its first five years involved the development of logistics and administration software but, despite this, Amazon was capable of satisfying directly only about 5% of the orders received in November 1997. When an online bookshop sells a title that it does not have in stock, the order is passed on to a distributor who generally delivers it within 24 hours. Subsequently, the bookshop has to bear the costs of repackaging and shipping the books to its customers (which have a great impact in a business characterized by very narrow margins).

- The need to optimize the flow of goods makes it critical to be able to satisfy customer requests directly (which means investing heavily in warehousing) and manage complex logistic flows. Serious competition could therefore come from companies such as Barnes & Noble (that besides the chain of bookshops partially controls intermediate distribution), intermediate distributors aiming at downstream integration by beginning their own online sales, or consortia of publishers. From a structural point of view, logistical activities require specific know-how and a lot of investments, to the extent that it may be easier for a distributor to establish a good web site than for an online bookseller to set up an efficient logistics system. On the other hand, the entry of distributors into online sales is held back by the conflict that would arise with their traditional customers. For Amazon.com, this kind of risk became a worrying reality when Barnes & Noble first decided to use online sales and subsequently acquired control of Ingram, the most important wholesaler in the United States.

- Marketing activities to support the site include publicity on other sites, but also costly advertising campaigns through traditional channels.

- In order to increase sales, it is very important for online bookshops to have a large number of associates; i.e. other websites that create links with the original site and receive commissions on the sales generated. Amazon.com was the first to launch an associate programme, immediately followed by Barnes & Noble. In 1997 Amazon had more than 30 000 associates, including AOL, Netscape and Microsoft Explorer; Barnes & Noble could count on about 10 000 associates, including *The New York Times Book Review* and CNN.

- Website management offers considerable learning potential, thus placing whoever controls this activity in an ideal position to collect market information useful for the development of editorial plans. Although it is still little developed, this type of activity would allow an information flow to be opened between the market and publishers, and thus overcome one of the main limitations of the traditional VCS.

Online sales can involve all the market segments identified in Figure 4.13, but are of particular interest to the narrow and fragmented segment. Although best-sellers could also be sold via the Internet, online sales would offer an enormous competitive advantage to titles destined for a narrow (and particularly fragmented market) insofar as they would significantly contribute towards reducing the number of returns. The use of online sales would mean that limited-run titles would not be scattered in hundreds of bookshops because they could remain in the warehouse of the intermediate distributor or publisher, and consumers could receive online the information necessary for a purchasing decision and would not need to see the book itself. Sending the information unbundled from the product makes it possible to optimize both physical and information flows without the need for compromises.

In relation to segmentation by method of access, online sales are particular suited to the 'totally sequential' segment and some of the products in the 'interactive' segment (e.g. classical books consisting of text + a floppy disk or CD ROM, or even stand-alone CD ROMS). On the other hand, online sales alone are not sufficient to respond adequately to the needs of the segments in which access to the information is partially sequential or precise; they may well make distribution more efficient, but have no impact on the contents of a product or its ability to satisfy different methods of access.

Furthermore, online sales do not solve the problems connected with traditional printing. As we have seen above, minimum print runs in the traditional VCS are quite large not only because of distribution needs, but also because traditional printing technology makes it uneconomic to print fewer than a thousand copies. Online selling does not solve the problem of printing many copies 'in the dark' that perhaps will never be sold.

In order to solve the problem of minimum print runs, one very interesting new technology is what is known as print-on-demand. Print-on-demand machines represent the confluence of photo-copying, data handling and telecommunications technologies (it is no accident that the main suppliers are IBM and Rank Xerox). Put very briefly, print-on-demand machines make it possible to store texts in digital form, and therefore to print and bind even single copies of the stored titles. The minimum individual print or reprint run is thus reduced to one copy, and the overall minimum print run for a single text (connected with the initial composition costs) is about 1000 (if the text is on paper and needs to be scanned) or about 200 copies (if it is already in digital format). Given its cost, the total volumes that any individual machine must produce remains high (currently about 500 copies per day), although it can be hypothesized that the spread of this technology will lead to a reduction in purchase costs and the number of copies necessary to amortize them. As things stand today, the variable unit costs of print-on-demand are considerably higher than those of off-set printing, and so the technology is only economic in the case of small print runs.

As we have already seen with online sales, companies are tending to graft print-on-demand on the traditional VCS, using it for small runs but otherwise continuing to use mainstream technology. These operators (usually printers) continue to print in batches, although these have been reduced from a minimum of 1000–1500 to 500–700 copies. Once printed, the copies are distributed in the traditional manner. However, print-on-demand manages to express its full potential only if it is part of a VCS that is significantly different from the traditional system (see Figure 4.15).

The following can be said in relation to Figure 4.15.

• The boundaries of the economic players have not been outlined because printing activities in this type of VCS could be carried out by typographers, but also by distributors, publishers or, in the future, even by retailers. Looking at the most interesting examples so far, it is generally the intermediate distributor who takes on the activity of print-on-demand; for example, Ingram in the United States has set up a print-on-demand service used by about 120 publishing companies.

• The activities remain substantially the same as those of the traditional VCS until the production of proofs, after which composition for printing is replaced by print-on-demand composition. This includes the activities of scanning the text (if it is in the form of a paper copy), formatting, the printing and control of a first copy and, finally, the storage of the file in the print-on-demand machine. Once archived, even single copies of the text can be printed and so there are no limitations concerning minimum print runs.

• One important support activity that does not exist in the traditional VCS is the definition of printing standards. As already said, although there are no minimum limits for individual print runs, print-on-demand machines must print quite large total volumes in order to cover fixed costs. As they are suitable for small print runs, print-on-demand machines are therefore used to print a large number of different texts often ordered by different publishers. In order to reduce costs, it is very important that these texts are

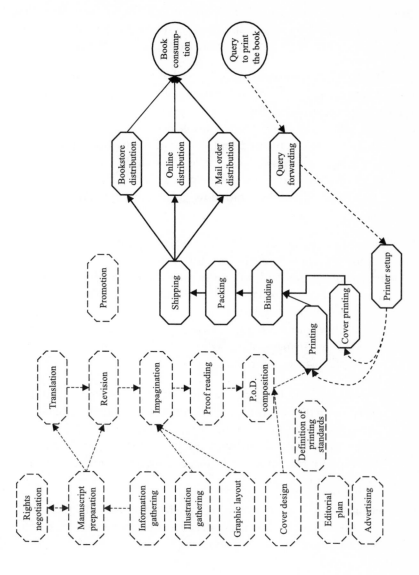

Figure 4.15 The print-on-demand value net

printed in a limited number of formats, have the same type of covers and are printed on the same type of paper. If this were not the case, the passage from the printing of one text to another would become complicated and expensive. This implies a rather complex process of making the texts as homogeneous as possible, particularly when working with many different publishers.

- The fact that print-on-demand allows the printing of single copies revolutionizes material and information flows insofar as it allows a change from printing for stock to printing by commission: the customer orders the book from a bookshop, via the Internet or by mail, and the book is printed and delivered to the bookshop or the customer's home. Online sales make it possible to centralize the storage of finished products; print-on-demand makes it possible to eliminate stocks altogether and thus solve the problem of returns at its root.

- In many cases, print-on-demand is used for reprints but, if the demand for a certain book is very uncertain, it is possible to think of using print-on-demand from the start and not printing even a minimum number of initial copies. However, to make this work, there needs to be the possibility of communicating the existence of the book even without its physical presence. As we have seen, this can be done by using online sales, which can thus be usefully combined with print-on-demand.

- For the concentrated fragmented segment (e.g. university texts), it is conceivable that, in a future when the cost of the machines and their economies of scale have decreased, physical printing will no longer need to be centralized with the publisher or distributor, but could be done by the operator in direct contact with the final user (a retailer or library).

- Print-on-demand is also particularly effective for products that require quite frequent updating because it eliminates the risk of being left with unsold, obsolete copies.

Especially when combined with online sales, print-on-demand permits an optimal response to the needs of the total sequential reading/narrow market segment. However, as described, it does not solve the problem of the bundling of contents; the book is printed on request, but its contents continue to be defined only by the authors and publishers. In order to unbundle the content, it is necessary to combine the new printing technologies with interactive online communication. One interesting example of this is given by McGraw Hill, which has recently launched a new service on its website aimed at university teachers. This service, which has already been mentioned in Chapter 1, allows teachers to gain access to a database of materials (articles, case studies, chapters of books) originally published by different publishers, to select the material they want and even add their own, to define the sequence and obtain the printing of a personalized bundle of contents (see Figure 4.16).

Figure 4.16 is relatively simple and does not require any particular additional comments. However, one aspect that is worth underlining is the importance of having a very large database in order to ensure the success of an initiative of this kind. Teachers preparing the materials for their courses do not want to be restricted to a single publisher but demand a wide choice. This means that this type of business is subject to a high degree of concentration and that one of the most critical activities is that of rights negotiation: obtaining exclusive rights from a very large number of publishers will make it possible to create a very strong entry barrier.

A variant of customized print-on-demand is the home printing of unbundled materials downloaded from the Internet. For example, in addition to its online sale of books and multimedia materials, Harvard Business School Publishing has put a good proportion of the case studies of the Harvard Business School and the articles published in the Harvard Business Review on the Net. This material can be viewed free of charge and purchased on-line in paper or digital form. In this last case, it is the user himself who does the printing.

The VCSs described above are capable of responding effectively to the needs of the segments characterized by total and partial sequential access, and to those of a part of the interactive access segment, but none of them are particularly capable of satisfying the needs of the segment which accesses the information in a very specific and precise way. However, for this kind of access, the new technologies make it possible to configure the VCS in such a way as to eliminate the use of paper supports almost completely, with all the advan-

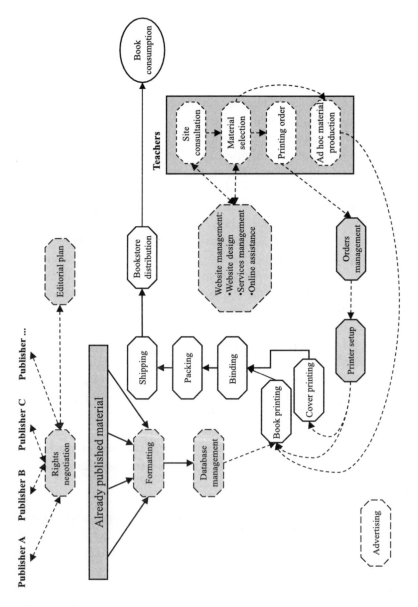

Figure 4.16   The value net of customized university texts

tages that this brings in terms of possible interactions, ease of consultation, updating and personalization.

There are many examples of on-line consultation services (Britannica on-line, Encarta on-line) and multimedia products (encyclopedias and dictionaries on CD ROMs). However, in addition to these widely known examples, it seems to us to be interesting to describe the experience of a small Italian company (Res Cogitans) that has launched a service for the consultation of classical texts. Res Cogitans makes available on line the full texts of a series of university and classical texts that may be of interest to academics and university students. The users can purchase the texts from Res Cogitans in digital form and print them themselves. What distinguishes Res Cogitans from the many other sites that allow the downloading of full text documents is that the downloaded texts are indexed and, by using a free of charge software consultation programme, it is possible to make textual analyses, conduct searches using key words and add other indices. In other words, Res Cogitans offers its users both the texts and the instruments for analysing them. The Res Cogitans net is shown in Figure 4.17.

This list of possible innovative VCSs could be extended even further because technological evolution has opened up an enormously wide range of strategic opportunities in the non-periodical publishing sector. However, we should perhaps stop here because the purpose of this chapter is not to provide a complete description of the developments currently taking place in this specific sector, but to show how the value net can be used to analyse sectors as a whole.

At this point, it may be interesting to generalize and underline some of the key steps to which attention needs to be paid when making a value net analysis:

- VCS-oriented market segmentation: the present section should have clearly demonstrated that VCS-oriented segmentation is a crucial step in value net analysis because it is only in the light of this that it is possible to evaluate the development prospects of alternative VCSs.

- Comparison of alternative offer systems: when a strategic analysis is made at the level of economic players, one of the elements that

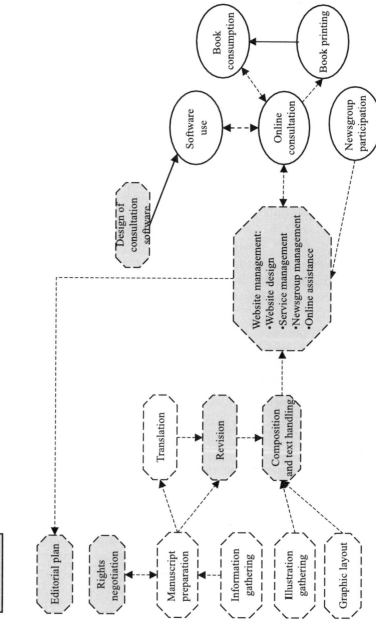

Figure 4.17 The value net of Res Cogitans

needs to be considered is the product system of the analysed company and its competitive advantages. If the analysis is made at the level of the VCS, it is possible to evaluate not so much (and not only) the product system of individual companies, but the overall offer system allowed by a certain net configuration. The characteristics and advantages for final customers implicit in different VCS configurations have always been compared in all the analysed publishing sector cases by considering the offer of the various economic players involved as a whole.

• Performance measures at VCS level: in order to compare the effectiveness and efficiency of alternative VCSs (be they similarly or differently configured), it is necessary to be able to identify the performance measures of the system. These include elements such as the overall costs, financial requirements and profitability of the system (measures that can be analysed at the level of individual companies as well), but also other measures that only have sense at the level of the VCS. For example, even if they can be calculated for each individual company, in the eyes of the final customer, measures such as lead times or times to market only have sense at the system level. Another performance measure at the VCS level is the speed with which information passes from one system node to another. In the case of the publishing sector, no quantitative measures were given, but the albeit approximate description of the different VCSs did reveal differences in stock levels, the presence and rapidity of information flows, the incidence of returns of unsold books and the level of service. It may be interesting to quantify such differences in a more detailed analysis.

4.3.5 Identification of Opportunities for Innovation

The value net methodology not only provides a valid working basis for an in-depth comparison of the strategic configurations of the different players in a given context, but also offers a starting point for identifying the opportunities for innovation existing in a specific system and defining appropriate positioning strategies.

We shall therefore conclude this chapter by presenting some rules and suggestions that may help in the formulation of strategies for changing and innovating the system (i.e. the reconfiguration of system activities), as well as in terms of positioning strategies within the framework of a given system. These can be summarized as follows:

- compare the analysed system with emerging alternatives;

- borrow strategies and solutions from similar systems;

- identify system bottlenecks;

- identify inefficient nodes;

- identify new ways of involving final customers;

- identify compromises in VCS configuration that can be overcome;

- identify the consequences of technological trends;

- redefine the boundaries of system players;

- control support activities;

- exploit the possibilities of extension.

Comparing the Analysed System with Emerging Alternatives

Particularly at the time of changes in the structure of a competitive system, companies need to analyse value nets other than those traditionally associated with their sector of activities. Although it is obviously important to consider the most successful emerging formulae (not least because of the threat they represent), it is also important to analyse the reasons for the lack of success of less fortunate formulae.

In the non-periodical publishing industry, for example, examples such as that of Res Cogitans (described above) or e-books (books that remain in digital form) may now seem to represent only distant threats to traditional competitors. However, it would be a serious mistake to neglect making a thorough analysis of such initiatives regardless of their competitive success or otherwise, because such an analysis could lead to the emergence of important clues for innovation.

Borrowing Strategies and Solutions from Similar VCSs

In some cases, the source of inspiration giving rise to innovation processes in a value-creating system is not related to the analysis of value nets operating in the same sector, but to changes in strategies and solutions that have been successful in systems aimed at the production of different goods but which have some common or similar aspects.

For example, an analysis of the online distribution of editorial products may be extremely useful for indicating possible developments in the music sector.

Identifying System Bottlenecks

System bottlenecks can be defined as flows or nodes that limit the productivity and capacity of the entire value-creating system by inducing an under-use of the potential of other nodes.

A simple example of this could be that of an Internet provider that equips itself to transmit data to its subscribers at a speed of say 115 200 bps. However, this certainly does not mean that the subscribers would necessarily receive the potential value (in terms of speed) supplied by the company because their modems may only be capable of receiving the information at a speed of 14 400 bps. The speed of data transmission could be further slowed by the transmission speed of local telephone lines, which may only be able to transmit at a speed of 9600 bps.

In all probability, a situation such as this would have negative consequences on the profitability of the provider because it is clear that it would find it more difficult to acquire customers (insofar as many may be discouraged by the slowness of the connection) and would be unlikely to be able to charge a price that is proportionate to the potential value supplied because its customers would not be able to receive this value.

Identifying bottlenecks makes it possible to discover which elements to improve in order to ensure a rapid increase in the performance of the system as a whole (and which are therefore worth working on), and which elements are already over-sized (as any improvement in this area would only be minimally perceived by the final users).

A glaring example of a bottleneck in the publishing sector is the particularly poor upward information flow between the market and publishers.

Identifying Inefficient Nodes

This partially overlaps with what has just been said. An inefficient node is one that does not add adequate value in comparison with the costs sustained, or even subtracts value from the system, something that can obviously occur if its current configuration involves very high costs and/or adds too limited benefits.

An example of this is represented by the activity currently carried out by estate agents. These companies act as intermediaries between the sellers and buyers of real estate essentially by means of transaction management, but they do not add any intrinsic value to the properties they handle. In a certain sense, it can even be said that they subtract value by increasing the purchase price (as a result of their commission) without offering any added value. However, if this is the case, why are the majority of transactions conducted through them? It is obviously because the majority of property sellers fail to come into direct contact with potential buyers: the currently available systems that allow direct contact (mainly newspaper advertisements) are not efficient enough to bring together the supply and demand side. However, this situation could change significantly when the spread of the Internet makes it possible to construct very large databases that can be easily accessed and consulted by both buyers and sellers. Such databases could allow searches based on various keys (location, size, price range, the age of the property, necessary renovations, free or rented, etc.) and, particularly in the future, could contain three-dimensional images, films and sounds as well as text. It is not difficult to understand that a value net at least partially based on the management of an online database could significantly reduce the role currently played by estate agents by offering potential buyers an alternative means of acquiring the necessary information and thus greatly reducing the number of direct viewing visits.

If estate agencies provide an example of over-high costs, the problem in other cases may be essentially due to the inability of the node to contribute adequately to the creation of benefits. One can think of the distribution of electronic publishing products by means of the channels used for traditional publications, such as book-shops. These channels are generally not technologically equipped (e.g. with multimedia computers), and do not have staff with the necessary background to explain the characteristics of multimedia products to their customers. As a result, they limit themselves to selling such products as if they were books or magazines (with the exception that they cannot be leafed through by potential purchasers).

A similar example is provided by software and hardware resellers who, partially as a consequence of the continuous appearance of new products, are often insufficiently trained and updated. They may therefore be unable to suggest to their customers the best solutions for their needs or to explain all of the features of the products they sell, thus leading to an under-use of the purchased systems and/or causing a series of problems (sub-optimal configurations, the failure to describe some key functional characteristics) that may actually prevent customers from fully enjoying the potential value of the goods.

An example of a publishing sector node that subtracts value from the system is represented by all of the activities necessary for the management of returns. However, in this case the problem lies less in the inefficiency with which these are carried out and more in the intrinsic inefficiency of a system that generates such a large flow of returns.

As in the case of bottlenecks, the identification of inefficient nodes makes it possible to discover the limitations of a system, and often simultaneously provides clues for possible solutions.

Identifying New Ways of Involving Final Customers

We have more than once seen during the course of this book that the greater involvement of customers has frequently made it possible to increase significantly the competitiveness of a system and the value it creates, for fundamentally three reasons.

Firstly, the involvement of final customers is often an essential prerequisite if it is required to offer relatively personalized mass-produced goods, as is the case of customized publishing.

Secondly, customer involvement makes it possible to separate the supply of a service from company opening hours and the availability of dedicated staff (e.g. automatic telling machines and Internet databases).

Finally, as in the case of self-service outlets, the involvement of customers often makes it possible to reduce the costs sustained by a system while simultaneously increasing the speed and flexibility of the service, and therefore the benefits for consumers. In other cases, actual overall costs may not decrease (or may even increase), but are seen by consumers as being less onerous. The mounting of Ikea furniture could probably be carried out more efficiently by specialists, but the final customers (or more precisely the type of final customer that Ikea is interested in) attributes less value to the free time spent in mounting the furniture than to the additional cost it would be necessary to pay if this were done by the company.

What has been said above shows that there are essentially two ways of involving customers, which may be adopted separately or jointly:

- customers can be involved in defining the specifications and personalizing the goods they are buying, in the development of new products, and in identifying any inadequacies in the system and suggesting improvements;

- or they may be involved in value-creating activities by taking personal responsibility for some of them.

Finally, it is worth stressing that innovative means of involving customers generally require a complete reconfiguration of the entire value-creating system; the Ikea formula described above could never have been developed using traditional furniture salespoints.

Identifying Compromises in VCS Configuration and Opportunities in Process Streamlining

We have seen in the first chapter that many information flows in the past were embedded in physical flows, and that this led to compromises in the configuration of VCSs involving the bundling of activities with different characteristics and different economies of scale. The possibility of unbundling information from goods flows opens up a series of new opportunities for innovation insofar as it eliminates many of these compromises; for example, the introduction of online sales in the publishing sector has led to a distinction between the transmission of product information and the physical delivery of the publications themselves.

Overcoming compromises often accompanies the identification of methods for streamlining the processes carried out in a VCS; one example of this was the innovation in leather cutting introduced by Gucci and described in Chapter 1. A further example of a streamlining opportunity comes from the publishing industry; the books that are not stocked by the online bookseller but purchased from an intermediate distributor could be delivered directly to the end-user without passing through a bookseller, thus making the flow of goods much more efficient.

Identifying the Consequences of Technological Trends

We have previously pointed out that technological developments can:

- change the structural attractiveness of nodes (e.g. the production of microprocessors is becoming increasingly more important than the integration of discrete electronic components and the assembly of PCs);

- lead to the establishment of new value-creating systems (e.g. those associated with the new electronic publishing products);

- lead to the emergence of new economic roles and players (e.g. the recent advances in telecommunications have increased the number of uses to which a PC can be put, and introduced new players such as Internet access providers and online brokers);

- modify one or a group of value-creating activities.

In relation to this last point, it is interesting to return to the example of electronic publishing in order to highlight the evolutions in its value-creating that can be expected over the next few years (see Figure 4.18).

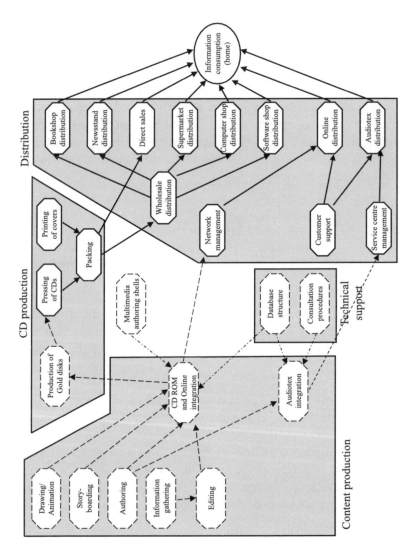

Figure 4.18   Technological trends in electronic publishing

As can be seen from a comparison of Figures 4.18 and 4.4, one of the likely major evolutions in this sector is the merging of the (currently distinct) activities of integrating CD ROM contents and online distribution. The main reason for this expectation is that the growing spread of faster and more powerful telecommunication networks will allow the online distribution of contents (particularly images, films and sounds) that are currently only available on CD ROMS. This evolution will inevitably lead to a certain development in the key success factors of the industry and the emergence of new and greater synergies.

A further significant evolution is the replacement of search engines constructed *ad hoc* for each new product by the use of standard authoring packages (multimedia authoring shells), which could represent an insidious threat for companies such as Opera Multimedia whose strong points are based on their technical competencies.

Redefining the Boundaries of System Players

In some cases, the innovation of a value-creating system can be obtained without modifying its configuration, by adjusting the definition of the boundaries of the players involved; i.e. by switching the activities from one player to another or by entrusting them to specialist companies.

Examples include the outsourcing of information or logistics systems.

Controlling Support Activities

Almost all examples given in this book show that the control of support activities is generally more profitable than the control of production activities for two main reasons.

First of all, support activities are generally more attractive because, even though they are more difficult to manage, they offer greater room for innovation, and imply more exclusive specific know-how and a higher degree of extendibility.

Secondly, they have a particular cost structure insofar as they are upstream activities that do not need to be repeated every time an additional unit is supplied, which is why (if properly managed) they have greater power of leverage because they can be used synergistically on various fronts.

Exploiting the Possibilities of Extension

A final suggestion concerns the strategic importance of being able to exploit the extension of controlled nodes in various VCSs.

Disney is an emblematic example. Ever since the 1930s, it has been famous throughout the world for its ability to create characters and its skill in the production of (particularly full-length) animated cartoons. However, following the death of its founder, it continued to rely on only slightly retouched business plans based on the production of cartoons and full-length films, and the management of Disney amusement parks. The long-term inability of the company to invent new paths of development led first to a considerable decrease in profitability and then, in 1984, to a management revolution that saw the entry of Michael Eisner, a manager from a leading film company.

Eisner revolutionized the composition of Disney's turnover, mainly by concentrating on the widest possible use of the characters created by means of the production of full-length films. This represented a very different approach from that adopted in previous years, during which the company's managers had 'rationed' the use of Disney characters because they feared that their excessive exploitation would tire the public. To recount only one episode, after the introduction of the Disney Channel, they decided to stop granting other television networks the right to transmit Disney cartoons on the grounds that this would reduce the number of subscribers to their own channel. Despite the fact that this strategy proved to be unsuccessful (the public tended to forget who the Disney characters were rather than take out Disney Channel subscriptions), it was maintained until the entry of Eisner.

The advent of Eisner led to a radical change and the beginning of a period of great development and success. The general value-creating system introduced by Eisner (which actually consists of a large number of closely related value systems) is shown in Figure 4.19.

As can be seen, Eisner's strategy can be regarded as a sort of

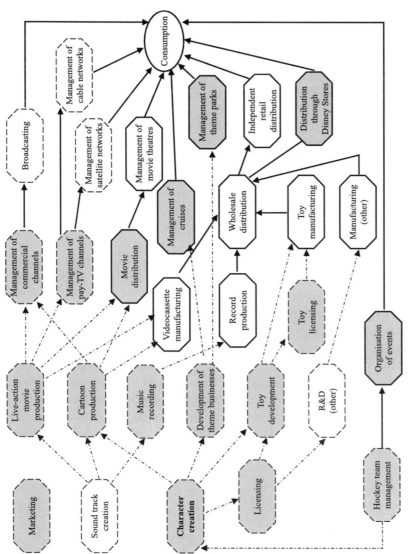

Figure 4.19   The VCSs controlled by Disney

'encircling' of final customers by means of a large number of complementary and synergistic value-creating systems. In particular, Eisner increased the number of new films from one in 4 – 5 years to more than one each year; introduced the sale of videocassettes (by gradually putting all the company's production on the market); encouraged licensing (by granting licences allowing the use of Disney characters in relation to a wide range of products, including clothing, toys, biscuits, chocolates, and so on); launched the Disney Store chain; strengthened the company's presence in the field of amusement parks by means of new openings and its entry into the sector of small virtual parks (DisneyQuest); entered the business of theme cruises; opened a Disney Internet site; acquired ABC and thus entered into the management of commercial television; and even supported the creation of a new ice-hockey team (the Anaheim Mighty Ducks, whose angry duck symbol has already become a new character) that takes part in the senior league on the basis of a highly original formula that includes its games within a broader entertainment framework.

The strategy of Eisner is a perfect example of what it means to exploit the possibilities of extending one or more critical nodes in a value-creating system.

These considerations certainly represent only a partial attempt to offer a systematic methodology for the identification of strategic innovations. However, although there is still a long way to go, the starting point is clear: the formulation of innovative company strategies requires an ability to move away from consolidated approaches and acquire a global vision of the value-creating system in which a company operates. This means adopting the perspective of final consumers, whose choices determine the success or failure of value-creating systems, and justify their very existence.

References

ABEGGLEN, JAMES, and STALK, GEORGE, *Kaisha, The Japanese Corporation*, New York, Basic Books, 1985.

ABELL, Derek F., *Defining the Business: The Starting Point of Strategic Planning*, Englewood Cliffs, Prentice-Hall, 1980.

ABELL, DEREK F., *Managing with Dual Strategies*, New York, The Free Press, 1993.

ABELL, DEREK F., and HAMMOND, JOHN S., *Strategic Market Planning*, Englewood Cliffs, Prentice-Hall, 1979.

AIROLDI, GIUSEPPE, BRUNETTI, GIORGIO, and CODA, VITTORIO, *Economia Aziendale*, Bologna, Il Mulino, 1994.

ALCHIAN, ARMEN A., and DEMSETZ, HAROLD, Production, information costs, and economic organization, *American Economic Review*, No. 62, December 1972.

ANDREWS, KENNETH R., *The Concept of Corporate Strategy*, Homewood, Irwin, 1971.

ANSOFF, H. IGOR, *Implanting Strategic Management*, Englewood Cliffs, Prentice-Hall, 1984.

AROGYASWAMY, BERNARD, and SIMMONS, RON P., *Value-Directed Management*, Westport, Quorum Books, 1993.

BALLÉ, MICHAEL, *Managing with Systems Thinking*, Cambridge, McGraw Hill International, 1994.

BARNEY, J.B., and OUCHI, WILLIAM B., Information costs and organizational governance, *Management Science*, 1984.

BARTLETT, CHRISTOPHER. A., and GHOSHAL, SUMANTRA, The multinational corporation as an interorganizational network, *Academy of Management Review*, 4, 1990.

BETTIS, RICHARD, A., and HITT, MICHAEL A., The new competitive landscape, *Strategic Management Journal*, Volume 16, Special Issue, Summer 1995.

BLACKBURN, JOSEPH D. (Editor), *Time-based Competition. The Next Battle Ground in American Manufacturing*, Homewood, Irwin, 1991.

BRUNETTI, GIORGIO, CODA, VITTORIO, and FAVOTTO, FRANCESCO, *Analisi, previsioni, simulazioni economico–finanziarie d'impresa*, Milano, Etas Libri, 1990.

BUZZEL, ROBERT D., and BRADLEY, T. GALE, *The PIMS Principles: Linking Strategy to Performance*, New York, The Free Press, 1987.

CHANDLER, ALFRED DUPONT JR., *The Visible Hand. The Managerial Revolution in American Business*, Cambridge, The Belknap Press of Harvard University Press, 1977.

COASE, RONALD H., The nature of the firm, *Economica*, 4, 1937.

CODA, VITTORIO, *L'analisi delle relazioni causa–effetto nel governo delle imprese*, Finanza, Marketing e Produzione, No. 2, 1983.

CODA, VITTORIO, *La valutazione della formula imprenditoriale*, Sviluppo & Organizzazione, Marzo–Aprile 1984.

CODA, VITTORIO, *L'orientamento strategico dell'impresa*, Torino, UTET, 1988.

CODA, VITTORIO, *Il problema della valutazione della strategia*, Economia & Management, No. 12, 1990.

COMMONS, JOHN R., *Institutional Economics*, Madison, University of Wisconsin Press, 1934.

COOPER, ROBIN, and KAPLAN, ROBERT S., How cost accounting distorts product costs, *Management Accounting Review*, April 1988.

COPELAND, THOMAS, KOLLER, TIM, and MURRIN, JACK, *Valuation. Measuring and Managing the Value of Companies*, New York, John Wiley & Sons, 1994.

CRANE, DWIGHT B., and BODIE, ZVI, Forms follows function: the transformation of banking, *Harvard Business Review*, March–April 1996.

CROSBY, PHILLIP B., *Quality is Free*, New York, McGraw-Hill, 1979.

DAEMS, HERMAN, *The Determinants of Hierarchical Organization of Industry*. In *Power, Efficiency and Institutions*, Francis, A. et al. (Editors), London, Heinemann, 1983.

D'AVENI, RICHARD A., *Hypercompetition*, New York, The Free Press, 1994.

DAVENPORT, THOMAS H., *Process Innovation. Reengineering Work through Information Technology*, Boston, Harvard Business School Press, 1993.

DAVENPORT, THOMAS H., and SHORT, JAMES, The new industrial engineering: information technology and business process redesign, *Sloan Management Review*, Summer 1990.

DAVIDOW, WILLIAM H., and MALONE, MICHAEL S., *The Virtual Corporation: Structuring and Revitalizing the Corporation for the 21st Century*, New York, Harper Collins Publishers, 1992.

DEMING, W. EDWARDS, *Quality, Productivity and Competitive Position*, Cambridge, MIT Center for Advanced Engineering Study, 1982.

DEMSETZ, HAROLD, *The Theory of the Firm Revisited*. In *The Nature of the Firm*, Williamson, O. E., and Winter, S. G. (Editors), New York, Oxford University Press, 1991.

DRAEBYE, MIKKEL, and DUBINI, PAOLA, *The Electronic Publishing Industry in Italy*, ANEE, 1996.

DRUCKER, PETER F., The new productivity challenge, *Harvard Business Review*, November–December 1991.

DRUCKER, PETER F., *Managing for the Future: The 1990s and Beyond*, New York, Dutton, 1992.

DUYSTER, G., and HAGEDOORN, JOHN, Strategic groups and value networks in international high-tech industries, *Journal of Management Studies*, No. 32:3, 1995.

ECCLES, ROBERT G., The quasi-firm in the construction industry, *Journal of Economic Behavior and Organization*, 2, 1981.

EVANS, P. B., and WURSTER, T. S., Strategy and the economics of information, *Harvard Business Review*, September–October 1997.

FOMBRUN, CHARLES J., Strategies for network research in organizations, *Academy of Management Review*, 7/2, 1982.

FOMBRUN, CHARLES J., amd KUMARASWAMY, ARUN, Strategic Alliances in Corporate Communities: The Evolution of Telecommunications 1980–88, Paper presented at the *International Conference on Innovation and Global Strategy*, Tokyo, 1988.

FORBIS, JOHN, L., and MEHTA, NITIN T., Value-based strategies for industrial products, *Business Horizons*, May–June 1981.

FORRESTER, JAY W., *Principles of Systems*, Cambridge, Mass., Wright Allen, 1968.

FRUHAN, WILLIAM E. JR., *Financial Strategy: Studies in the Creation, Transfer and Destruction of Shareholder Value*, Homewood, Irwin, 1979.

GALE, BRADLEY T., *Managing Customer Value*, New York, The Free Press, 1994.

GARUD, RAGHU, and KUMARASWAMY, ARUN, Technological and organizational designs for realizing economies of substitution, *Strategic Management Journal*, Volume 16, Special Issue, Summer 1995.

GRUNDY, TONY, *Corporate Strategy and Financial Decisions*, London, Kogan Page, 1992.

GUATRI, LUIGI, *La teoria di creazione del valore*, Milano, EGEA, 1991.

HAMEL, GARY, and PRAHALAD, C.K., *Competing for the Future*, Boston, Harvard Business School Press, 1994.

HAMMER, MICHAEL, and CHAMPY, JAMES, *Reengineering the Corporation: A Manifesto for Business Revolution*, London, Nicholas Brealey Publishing, 1993.

HEARD, JULIA A., *JIT for White Collar Work – The Rest of the Story*. In *Strategic Manufacturing: Dynamic New Directions for the 1990s*, Patricia E. Moody (Editor), Homewood, Dow Jones–Irwin, 1990.

HERGERT, MICHAEL, and MORRIS, DEIGAN, Accounting data for value chain analysis, *Strategic Management Journal*, Volume 10, 1989.

HERZBERG, F., MAUSNER, M., and SNYDERMAN, B., *The Motivation to Work*, New York, John Wiley & Sons, 1959.

HOFER, CHARLES W., and SCHENDEL, DAN, *Strategy Formulation: Analytical Concepts*, St. Paul, Minnesota, West Publishing Company, 1978.

IMAI, KENICHI, NONAKA, IKUJIRO, and TAKEUCHI, HIROTAKA, *Managing New Product Development: How Japanese Companies Learn and Unlearn*. In *The Uneasy Alliance*, Clarke, G. B. et al. (Editors), Boston, Harvard Business School Press, 1985.

INVERNIZZI, GIORGIO, La costruzione della mappa strategica di un'impresa, Sviluppo e Organizzazione, Gennaio–Febbraio 1982.

JARRILLO, CARLOS J., On strategic networks, Strategic Management Journal, Volume 9, 1988.

JOHNSON, H. THOMAS, Activity-based information: a blueprint for world-class management accounting, Management Accounting, June 1988.

LAGO, UMBERTO, On inter-firm networks' development and performance: a transaction cost perspective, Paper presented at the conference Rent IX: research in enterpreneurship, Piacenza, 23/24 November 1995.

LEWIS, JORDAN D., The Connected Corporation, New York, The Free Press, 1995.

LIEBERMAN, MARVIN, Inventory Reduction and Productivity Growth, A Study of Japanese Automobile Producers. In Manufacturing Strategy, J. Ettlie et al. (Editors), Boston, Kluwer Academic Publishers, 1990.

LIPPARINI, ANDREA, Imprese, relazioni tra imprese e posizionamento competitivo, Milano, Etas Libri, 1995.

LORENZONI, GIANNI, L'architettura di sviluppo delle imprese minori, Bologna, Il Mulino, 1990.

LORENZONI, GIANNI (Editor), Accordi, reti e vantaggio competitivo, Milano, Etas Libri, 1992.

LØWENDAHL, BENTE, and REVANG, ØIVIND, Changes to Existing Strategy theory in a Post-industrial Society, Strategic Management Journal, Vol. 19, August 1998.

MASINI, CARLO, Lavoro e risparmio, Torino, UTET, 1978.

McHUGH, PATRICK, MERLI, GIORGIO, and WHEELER, WILLIAM A. III, Beyond Business Process Reengineering, Chichester, John Wiley & Sons, 1995.

McKENNA, REGIS, Marketing is everything, Harvard Business Review, January–February 1991.

MERRILS, ROY, How Northern Telecom competes on time, Harvard Business Review, July–August 1989.

MINTZBERG, HENRY, The Rise and Fall of Strategic Planning, Englewood Cliffs, Prentice-Hall, 1994.

NACAMULLI, RAUL, and RUGIADINI, ANDREA (Editors), Organizzazione & Mercato, Bologna, Il Mulino, 1985.

NAUMANN, EARL, Creating Customer Value, Cincinnati, Thomson Executive Press, 1995

NONAKA, IKUJIRO, and TAKEUCHI HIROTAKA, The Knowledge-creating Company, New York, Oxford University Press, 1995.

NORMANN, RICHARD, Management for Growth, Chichester, John Wiley & Sons, 1977.

NORMANN, RICHARD, Service Management. Strategy and Leadership in Service Businesses, Chichester, John Wiley & Sons, 1984.

NORMANN, RICHARD, and RAMÍREZ, RAFAEL, From the value chain to the value constellation: designing interactive strategy, Harvard Business Review, July–August 1993.

NORMANN, RICHARD, and RAMÍREZ, RAFAEL, *Designing Interactive Strategy: From the Value Chain to the Value Constellation*, Chichester, John Wiley & Sons, 1994.

OHMAE, KENICHI, *The Mind of the Strategist: The Art of Japanese Business*, New York, McGraw-Hill, 1982.

OUCHI, WILLIAM G., A conceptual framework for the design of organizational control mechanisms, *Management Science*, September 1979.

OUCHI, WILLIAM G., Markets, Burocracies and Clans, *Administrative Science Quarterly*, 25, March 1980.

PAROLINI, CINZIA, *Nota sul settore dei personal computer*, Copyright SDA-Bocconi 1990.

PAROLINI, CINZIA, *Le imprese ad alta tecnologia. Profili imprenditoriali e manageriali*, Milano, Franco Angeli, 1991.

PAROLINI, CINZIA, *Rete del valore e strategie aziendali*, Milano, Egea, 1996.

PASTORE, ANTONIO, *La funzionalità economica dell'impresa*, Bari, Cacucci, 1984.

PENROSE, EDITH T., *The Theory of the Growth of the Firm*, New York, John Wiley & Sons, 1959, (most recently Oxford, Basil Blackwell, 1995).

PETROZZO, DANIEL P., *Successful Reengineering: An In-depth Guide to Using Information Technology*, Van Nostrand Reinhold, New York, 1994.

PETROZZO, DANIEL P., amd STEPPER, JOHN C., *Successful Reengineering*, New York, Van Nostrand Reinhold, 1994.

PEZZOLI, SANDRO, *Un'analisi delle relazioni fra sistema informativo e organizzazione aziendale*, Padova, CEDAM, 1983.

PORTER, MICHAEL E., *Competitive Strategy: Techniques for Analyzing Industries and Competitors*, New York, The Free Press, 1980.

PORTER, MICHAEL E., *Competitive Advantage: Creating and Sustaining Superior Performance*, New York, The Free Press, 1985.

PORTER, MICHAEL E., *The Competitive Advantage of Nations*, New York, The Free Press, 1989.

PORTER, MICHAEL E., and MILLAR, VICTOR E., How information gives you competitive advantage, *Harvard Business Review*, July–August 1985.

PRAHALAD, C. K., and HAMEL, GARY, The core competence of the corporation, *Harvard Business Review*, May–June, 1990.

QUINN, JAMES BRIAN, *Intelligent Enterprise: A Knowledge and Service Based Paradigm for Industry*, New York, The Free Press, 1992.

RAGHU, GARUD, and KUMARASWAMY, ARUN, Technological and organizational designs for realizing economies of substitution, *Strategic Management Journal*, Volume 16, Special Issue, Summer 1995.

RAPPAPORT, ALFRED, *Creating Shareholder Value: The New Standard for Business Performance*, New York, The Free Press, 1986.

RAPPAPORT, ANDREW S., and HALEVI, SHMUEL, The computerless computer company, *Harvard Business Review*, July–August 1991.

RAYPORT, JEFFREY F., amd SVIOLA, JOHN J., Exploiting the virtual value chain, *Harvard Business Review*, November–December 1995.

RIPARBELLI, ALBERTO, *Correlazioni e interdipendenze fra organismi aziendali*, Pisa, Cursi, 1962.

RUGIADINI, ANDREA, *L'efficienza delle scelte manageriali fra organizzazione e mercato*. In *Organizzazione & Mercato*, Nacamulli, Raul, and Rugiadini, Andrea (Editors), Bologna, Il Mulino, 1979.

RULLANI, ENZO, *Divisione del lavoro e reti di impresa: il governo della complessità*. In *Nuovi modelli d'impresa. Gerarchie organizzative e imprese rete*, Belussi, Fiorenza, and Bianchi, Patrizio (Editors), Milano, Franco Angeli, 1992.

SCHENDEL DAN, Technological transformation and the new competitive landscape (Editor's introduction), *Strategic Management Journal*, Volume 16, Special Issue, Summer 1995.

SENGE, PETER M., *The Fifth Discipline: The Art and Practice of the Learning Organization*, New York, Doubleday/Currency, 1990.

SHANK, JOHN K., and GOVINDARAJAN, VIJAY, *Strategic Cost Management*, New York, The Free Press, 1993.

SIMON, HERBERT A., *The Science of the Artificial*, Cambridge, The MIT Press, 1969 (2nd edition: 1981).

SMITH, GERALD E., and NAGLE, THOMAS T., Frames of reference and buyers' perception of price and value, *California Management Review*, Volume 38, No. 1, 1995.

STALK, GEORGE JR., Time – the next source of competitive advantage, *Harvard Business Review*, July–August 1998.

STALK, GEORGE JR., and HOUT, THOMAS M., *Competing Against Time: How Time-based Competition Is Reshaping Global Markets*, New York, The Free Press, 1990.

STEWART, G. B., *The Quest for Value*, New York, Harper Collins, 1991.

STORPER, MICHAEL, and HARRISON, BENNET, *Flessibilità, gerarchie e sviluppo regionale: la ristrutturazione organizzativa dei sistemi produttivi e le nuove forme di governance*, in *Nuovi modelli d'impresa. Gerarchie organizzative e imprese rete*, Belussi, Fiorenza, and Bianchi, Patrizio (Editors), Milano, Franco Angeli, 1992.

TAPSCOTT, DON, and CASTON, ART, *Paradigm Shift*, New York, McGraw-Hill, 1993.

TEECE, DAVID J., Economies of scope and the scope of the enterprise, *Journal of Economic Behavior and Organization*, Volume 1, 1980.

TOSCANO, GIUSEPPE (Editor), *Il calcolo dei costi per attività lungo la catena del valore*, Milano, Edizioni Unicopli, 1991.

VARALDO, RICCARDO, *Il sistema della imprese calzaturiere*, Torino, Giappichelli, 1988.

WACHER, M., and WILLIAMSON, OLIVER E., Obligational markets and the mechanics of inflation, *Bell Journal of Economics*, 9, 1978.

WATSON, GREGORY H., *Strategic Benchmarking*, New York, John Wiley & Sons, 1993.

WERNERFELT, BIRGER, A resource-based view of the firm, *Strategic Management Journal*, Volume 2, 1984.

WIKSTROM, SOLVEIG, and NORMANN, RICHARD, *Knowledge and Value, A new perspective on corporate transformation*, Routledge, London, 1994.

WILLIAMSON, OLIVER E., *Markets and Hierarchies: Analysis and Antitrust Implications*, New York, The Free Press, 1975.

WILLIAMSON, OLIVER E., Transaction costs economics: the governance of contractual relations, *Journal of Law and Economics*, 22, October 1979.

WILLIAMSON, OLIVER E., *The Economic Institutions of Capitalism*, New York, The Free Press, 1985.

WILLIAMSON, OLIVER E., Comparative economic organization: the analysis of dicrete structural alternatives, *Administrative Science Quarterly*, June 1991.

WILLIAMSON, OLIVER E., and OUCHI, W. G., The markets and hierarchies program of research: origins, implications, prospects. In *Perspectives on Organization Design and Behaviour*, Van de Ven, A. H, and Joyce, W. F. (Editors), New York, John Wiley & Sons, 1981.

WILLIAMSON, OLIVER E., and WINTER, SIDNEY G. (Editors), *The Nature of the Firm*, New York, Oxford University Press, 1991.

ZAN, LUCA, *Strategia d'impresa: problemi di teoria e di metodo*, Padova, CEDAM, 1985.

ZANDA, GIANFRANCO, *Nuovi modelli di organizzazione*, Padova, CEDAM, 1979.

ZAPPA, GINO, *Le produzioni nell'economia delle imprese*, 3 tomi, Milano, Giuffrè, 1957.

Index